The First Book of
PS/1™

The First Book of
PS/1™

Kate Miller Barnes

A Division of Macmillan Computer Publishing
11711 North College, Carmel, Indiana 46032 USA

©1991 by SAMS

FIRST EDITION
FIRST PRINTING—1991

All rights reserved. No part of this book shall be reproduced, stored in a retrieval system, or transmitted by any means, electronic, mechanical, photocopying, recording, or otherwise, without written permission from the publisher. No patent liability is assumed with respect to the use of the information contained herein. Although every precaution has been taken in the preparation of this book, the publisher and authors assume no responsibility for errors or omissions. Neither is any liability assumed for damages resulting from the use of the information contained herein. For information, address SAMS, 11711 N. College Ave., Carmel, IN 46032.

International Standard Book Number: 0-672-27346-2
Library of Congress Catalog Card Number: 90-63945

Product Manager: *Marie Butler-Knight*
Acquisitions Editor: *Stephen R. Poland*
Manuscript Editor: *Charles A. Hutchinson*
Cover Design: *Held & Diedrich Design*
Illustrator: *Don Clemons*
Production Assistance: *Hilary Adams, Jeff Baker, Scott Boucher, Martin Coleman, Joelynn Gifford, Sandy Grieshop, Tami Hughes, Betty Kish, Bob LaRoche, Sara Leatherman, Lisa A. Naddy, Howard Peirce, Cindy L. Phipps, Tad Ringo, Suzanne Tully, Johnna VanHoose, Lisa A. Wilson*
Indexer: *Jill Bomaster*
Technical Reviewer: *David Knispel*

Printed in the United States of America

Contents

Introduction, xi

1 *Hello PS/1, 1*

In This Chapter, 1
Practical Uses for Your PS/1, 1
The Basic PS/1 Package, 3
Capabilities through Add-Ons, 5
What You Have Learned, 8

2 *Get Set, 9*

In This Chapter, 9
Where To Set Up Your PS/1, 9
Setting Up the Hardware, 10
Using the Hardware, 13
Backing Up Your Software, 22
Turning Off the PS/1, 28
Troubleshooting, 28
What Your Have Learned, 30

3 DOS — Using the Main Group, 31

In This Chapter, 31
The What and Why of DOS, 31
DOS and Your PS/1, 32
Setting the Date and Time, 34
Preparing a Diskette for Use by Formatting, 35
Copying a Diskette, 38
Copying a File, 41
Backing Up and Restoring a Fixed Disk, 44
Going to the DOS Command Prompt, 47
Changing Colors on Your Display, 49
Customizing How Your System Starts Up, 49
Changing Your Hardware Configuration, 51
What You Have Learned, 54

4 DOS—File Handling, 55

In This Chapter, 55
Handling Your File System, 55
The Action Bar Selections, 59
Creating a New Directory and
Adding Files, 67
What You Have Learned, 69

5 Changing the DOS Group and Your Software, 71

In This Chapter, 71
Changing the Main Group, 71
Your Software, 82
The DOS Folder in Your Software, 84
DOS Error Messages, 85
What You Have Learned, 87

6 Using Information (Especially Prodigy), 89

In This Chapter, 89
Investigating Information, 89
Free Class: System Tutorial, 90
Free Class: Works Tutorial, 91
Notes on Using On-line Services, 91
Signing On and Off Prodigy, 93
Using Prodigy, 102
What You Have Learned, 113

7 Prodigy Services—Users' Club and Others, 115

In This Chapter, 115
Tutorials, 115
IBM PS/1 Users' Club Services, 116
Mail and Messages, 118
Shopping On-line, 122
Traveling, 123
Money and Banking, 125
Sports and Hobbies, 126
Kids' Stuff, 127
Solving Prodigy Problems, 128
What You Have Learned, 131

8 MS Works—Getting Started, 133

In This Chapter, 133
Microsoft Works Capabilities, 133
Starting Works, 134
Using Menus and Commands, 134
Creating a New File, 135

Saving a File, 136
Opening an Existing File, 138
Closing a File, 139
Exiting Works, 140
Windows and the Mouse, 140
Commonly Used Keys, 142
File Management, 143
Calculator and Alarm Clock, 144
What You Have Learned, 145

9 MS Works—Beginning Word Processing, 147

In This Chapter, 147
Entering and Editing Text, 147
Selecting Text, 149
Copying Text, 151
Moving Text, 152
Undo, 153
Pages, 154
Printing, 155
What You Have Learned, 156

10 MS Works—Advanced Word Processing, 157

In This Chapter, 157
Page Setup and Margins, 157
Indents and Line Spacing, 159
Headers Footers and Page Numbers, 161
Formats, 166
Search and Replace, 170
Spell Checking, 171
What You Have Learned, 172

11 MS Works—Spreadsheet and Charting, 173

In This Chapter, 173
Spreadsheets, 173
Entering and Deleting Labels and Numbers, 175
Entering a Series of Cells, 176
Formatting, 176
Headers Footers and Margins, 179
Copying and Moving, 179
Inserting and Deleting Rows and Columns, 181
Absolute Cell References, 181
Using Formulas, 182
Hiding Cells, 184
Printing the Spreadsheet, 184
Sorting, 185
Protecting Cells, 185
Saving and Closing the Spreadsheet, 186
Charts, 186
What You Have Learned, 189

12 MS Works—Database and Reporting, 191

In This Chapter, 191
Databases, 191
Entering Field Names and Data in Form View, 192
List View, 197
Report View, 199
Query View, 203
Views and Printing, 208
What You Have Learned, 208

13 Communications and Integrating Your Tools, 209

In This Chapter, 209
Communications, 209
Putting a Chart into Word Processing, 215
Form Letters and Mailing Labels, 217
Copying and Moving Between Tools, 220
What You Have Learned, 220

14 Promenade, 221

In This Chapter, 221
Promenade versus Prodigy, 221
In and Out of Promenade, 222
Promenade Screens, 224
Promenade Services, 225
Mail, 227
Members Menu, 228
What You Have Learned, 228

15 Basics of BASIC, 229

In This Chapter, 229
BASIC: Why Bother?, 229
Getting In and Out of BASIC, 230
Getting Down to BASICs, 231
Not To Be BASIC, 235
What You Have Learned, 236

Index, 237

Introduction

Although the appearance of the PS/1 and related documentation is simple and basic, don't let it fool you. The PS/1 packs a powerhouse of computing capacity. Just the variety of manuals from manufacturers of distinct products can be confusing enough! But don't despair. *The First Book of PS/1* brings it all together for you in a step-by-step, integrated approach.

Starting out with the most basic issues—"Where do I put my computer?" and "What do I do with it?"—*The First Book of PS/1* takes you through all you need to know to progress from a novice to a well versed PS/1 user. All this comes in a short, easy-to-follow book. And, if you want to progress to the expert level, this book points you in the right direction.

Conventions Used in This Book

Throughout *The First Book of PS/1*, you will notice various typographical elements used to highlight different aspects of the book. Words or letters that you type appear in **boldface**. New or important terms appear in *italic*. Also, on-screen prompts or messages and items you select on-screen appear in a `special typeface`.

In addition, you will discover boxed tips and cautions to guide you in learning to operate your new IBM Personal System/1.

Acknowledgments

Thanks to Marie Butler-Knight, Steve Poland, Chuck Hutchinson, and all the other hardworking folks at the publisher who helped make this book possible.

Trademark Acknowledgments

All terms mentioned in this book that are known to be trademarks or service marks are listed below. In addition, terms suspected are capitalized. SAMS cannot attest to the accuracy of this information. Use of a term in this book should not be regarded as affecting the validity of any trademark or service mark.

CompuServe is a registered trademark of CompuServe, Inc. and H&R Block, Inc.

Dow Jones News/Retrieval is a registered trademark of Dow Jones & Company, Inc.

EAASY SABRE is a service mark of SABRE Travel Information Network, a division of American Airlines, Inc.

Grolier's Academic American Encyclopedia is a trademark of Grolier Electronic Publishing, Inc.

Hayes is a registered trademark of Hayes Microcomputer Products, Inc.

IBM is a registered trademark of the International Business Machines Corporation.

MasterWord, Quantum, Quantum Space, QuickFind, Phantasy Guild, RockLink, Quiz Quest, Teacher's Information Network, Career Center, Interactive Education Services, Academic Assistance Center, Idea Exchange, Industry Connection, and InterCom are service marks of Quantum Computer Services, Inc.

MS-DOS, Microsoft, and Microsoft Works are registered trademarks of Microsoft Corporation.

Personal System/1 and PS/1 are trademarks of the International Business Machines Corporation.

Prodigy is a registered service mark and trademark of Prodigy Services Company, a partnership of IBM and Sears.

The following are also service marks or trademarks of Prodigy Services Company: ACTION, GUIDE, JUMP, JUMPwindow, JUMPword, LOOK, PATH, PATHlist, VIEWPATH, and ZIP.

Promenade is a service mark of Quantum Computer Services, Inc. The education and entertainment on-line service for IBM Personal System/1 computer owners is a trademark of Quantum Computer Services, Inc.

Other product and service names are trademarks and service marks of their respective owners.

Chapter 1
Hello PS/1

In This Chapter

- *Practical uses for the PS/1*
- *What's included in the basic PS/1 package*
- *What capabilities are available to you with add-ons*

Practical Uses for Your PS/1

Welcome to the world of the IBM Personal System/1. Whether you're mulling over buying a PS/1 or whether your desk already sports one, you'll want to consider how to get the most from this work- and playhorse. Because the PS/1 opens up so many options for you, it will probably be an exercise in setting priorities among many useful alternatives.

Peruse this list to identify the PS/1 functions you may find useful. If you're like most of the 25% and growing households in the United States, you'll want to use your personal computer for more than one activity. So, once you identify useful functions, set priorities based on your needs for what to learn first. Regardless of what functions you choose, go through Chapter 2, "Get Set," in this book.

Then concentrate on the chapters devoted to the functions you most want to perform using the products available through the PS/1 listed here, such as Microsoft Works and Prodigy.

 Note: You also can use your own products on the PS/1.

1. **You want to:** Compose letters, develop reports, write articles or papers, address envelopes, or complete written homework assignments. Wordsmithing is where most PS/1 users start.

   Then use: The PS/1's word processing with Microsoft Works.

2. **You want to**: Be reminded automatically of important times and dates such as birthdays, meetings, or upcoming events, or use your computer as a calculator. (Beware: The computer may replace your dog as your best friend.)

   Then use: The PS/1's alarm clock and calculator with Microsoft Works.

3. **You want to**: Perform mathematical calculations and changing "what if" scenarios. Chart the results if you desire. You can work with a monthly budget, taxes, a financial investment strategy, math homework, your checkbook, sales information, grades, or any problem involving numbers. You don't have to be a math whiz to work through complex problems when you have a spreadsheet for your helper.

   Then use: The PS/1's spreadsheets and charts with Microsoft Works.

4. **You want to**: Get organized once and for all! Develop customer or organization lists; holiday lists; mail lists; phone directories; insurance or house records; recipe files; contents of your book, videotape, or music library; inventories; credit card lists; or organize any collection of notes.

   Then use: The PS/1's database and reports with Microsoft Works.

5. **You want to:** Develop form letters with customized names and other information, complete with mailing labels. This function is commonly called *mail merge*. It is typically a "must have" for anyone running a small business or organization with the PS/1.

   Then use: The PS/1's word processing and database with Microsoft Works.

6. **You want to:** Link into a variety of services you may have never used—or thought possible—from your desk. Send information to others, receive information, access programs in the public domain, see weather reports, check on airline reservations, play games with others, shop, use an encyclopedia, or take classes. Or link into your computer at work or at school. Whew! There's a lot you can do and several alternatives to get you there.

   Then use: The PS/1's communications capabilities with any of the following:

   ▶ Microsoft Works Communications (link to work, school, a friend's computer, bulletin boards, or other services).
   ▶ Information—Prodigy (for news, weather, sports, shopping, stock market, airline reservations, consumer reports, games, and bulletin boards).
   ▶ Information—Users' Club (for words to and from IBM, along with useful PS/1 information).
   ▶ Add-on to your PS/1—Promenade (for classes, an encyclopedia, software, mail, and more).

7. **You want to**: Use the IBM compatible programs that are used at work or school. That way, your labor is not lost. The work you do away from your PS/1 can be continued on your PS/1. Just install your own programs, for example, a tax or financial package, new games, or Promenade, which is one software program that comes with your PS/1.

   Then use: Your own programs installed on the PS/1.

8. **You want to**: Develop your own programs to process information your way. Try this if you can't find what you want in the above list or if you have a technical computer bent. BASIC is easy to learn. This book will get your toes wet. Many other books are available to direct you in the right way.

   Then use: Programs you write using BASIC on the PS/1.

The Basic PS/1 Package

Your PS/1 packs a lot in a small package (see Figure 1.1). The basic PS/1 includes a *system unit* which holds the "brain" of your computer. The processing chips, memory, electronics, diskette drive, and modem are housed in this component.

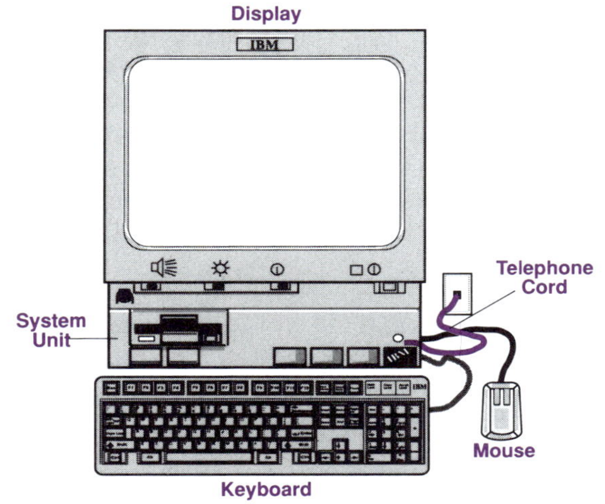

Figure 1.1 The IBM Personal System/1

You'll have a 10MHz 286 chip, to be precise, which means the machine is not the fastest nor the slowest around and is perfect for most users.

You may have one or two *diskette drives*, meaning you'll run your programs off diskettes. Or you may have gone the distance and invested in the 30M hard disk and a diskette drive. The advantage of a hard disk is that you will be able to work faster—with much less "talking" back and forth between diskettes. Active memory is a minimum of 512K. For more memory availability while you work, you may choose the 1M memory model.

The *modem* is used to send and receive information over phone lines. This capability enables you to communicate with other computers to exchange information. You can't see your modem, but you use the telephone cord on the back of the PS/1 to connect your modem into your telephone line.

The basic PS/1 also comes with a *keyboard* and a *mouse*. You may use both to tell the computer what to do. Also, the PS/1 has a color or monochrome *VGA display monitor* which allows you to see sophisticated graphics.

That sums up the hardware, which is the part of the computer you can see and touch. Your PS/1 also comes with software, which are the instructions to the machine to perform its magic. The software you'll get includes the powerful Microsoft Works for word processing, spreadsheet, charting, database, and communications activities. You'll also get two other packages for communications, Prodigy and Promenade. Another critical piece of software is DOS 4.0. This is IBM's Disk Operating System version 4.0 which is the "traffic cop" of your system, making all the hardware and software work together. You also get BASIC, which is a computer language to write your own instructions/programs to the computer. Finally, you have access to the PS/1 Users' Club for questions and answers along with tutorials for your PS/1 system in general and Microsoft Works specifically.

Capabilities through Add-Ons

The most obvious capability missing in the basic PS/1 package is a printer. Without a printer, you cannot make paper copies of your work. If you are simply linking with other computers, you may not need a printer. However, only the rare user doesn't want a paper version of a letter, mail list, budget, report, or picture of a screen on occasion.

When you purchase a printer, consider its use. If you want to print many pages very fast but do not care about high quality of the print, an inexpensive *dot-matrix printer* (where characters are made up of dots) may suit you. On the other hand, if you want the "letter quality" you get with a typewriter, slower, letter-quality *impact printers* are available for a low cost. The best of both worlds is the *laser printer*, which will give you letter quality, excellent charts and graphics, and speed. A laser printer costs more than the other alternatives, but it may be worth the expense depending on your use.

You can augment the capabilities of your PS/1 through the options available from IBM. The options are briefly described here.

▶ The IBM PS/1 Printer is a dot-matrix printer. If you are comparison shopping, the following printer facts will be useful. You may do draft and letter-quality printing on the PS/1 Printer. In draft mode, it prints 192 characters per second in 12 pitch (12 characters per inch) and 160 characters per second in 10 pitch. In letter-quality mode, it prints 64 characters per second in 12 pitch and 53 characters per second in 10 pitch. The printer prints in 10, 12, 15, 17, 20, and 24 pitch. The *fonts* (character styles) include Courier, Prestige, Gothic, and Draft. Graphics may be printed at 180x360 dots per square inch. You may use single sheet paper or continuous forms up to 11 inches wide. You can easily replace the ribbon cartridge. The most interesting feature of this printer is the operator panel (see Figure 1.2). Through it you can easily control *pitches* (size of characters), fonts, and paper movement.

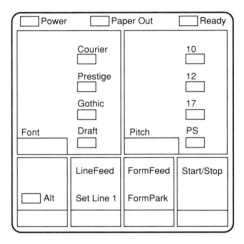

Figure 1.2   *IBM Personal System/1 printer operator panel*

- ▶ You may place a *memory expansion card* in the machine for additional memory to be available while you work. All the software products which make up the PS/1 package work quite well with the memory supplied. However, if you are adding your own software to the machine which will take up significant memory or which simply requires more memory, you'll want to add a memory expansion card.
- ▶ A *fixed disk* (also called a hard disk) is the norm on some PS/1 models. Instead of reading and writing information from and to a diskette, the fixed disk makes processing go faster because access to the fixed disk is quicker than to a diskette. A fixed disk also stores more information than a diskette. This capability leads to less swapping of diskettes as you find the information you need.

▶ Another norm on some models but not all is the color PHOTOGRAPHIC display monitor. Turning a dull, black, white, and grey world into vibrant color is fun and interesting.

▶ If you don't have a fixed disk, you may want a second 3.5" 1.44M diskette drive. This puts more information at your disposal without swapping diskettes in the drives. Having the additional drive also enables you to copy or move information from one diskette to another without swapping the diskettes out of a single drive.

▶ If you don't have a second 3.5" diskette drive, you may want a 5.25" diskette drive. This is a useful option if you carry 5.25" diskettes from work or school to use at home (or vice versa). It is also useful if you already have a lot of software and files on 5.25" diskettes to use.

▶ Though no expansion slots are available in the basic PS/1, you can add an *adapter card unit* to allow up to three additional slots. This way, you can add more power and specialized uses to your computer. With the adapter card unit, you may add two cards up to 280 mm or 11 inches each and one card up to 241 mm or 9.5 inches. The Users' Club (which you reach using your PS/1) identifies a list of adapter cards which will work with the PS/1. Check it before you invest to make sure your plans can be executed successfully.

> ▶ **Note:** If you add a memory card with the adapter card unit, you must also have the memory expansion card in the PS/1 system unit.

▶ If you're a game player, you may purchase an audio card and joystick to provide joystick capabilities, an interface cable, and improved audio sound. Some users like to use a joystick for games. The add-on capability also improves the audio sound. Check out the options that will work with the games you want to play before spending your money here.

▶ If you want to play with a friend, you can do it through communications. But, if you want to see the whites of their eyes as you beat them one on one, you may want to invest in a second joystick.

> **Note:** The PS/1 is modular in its design. Many of these add-ons may be purchased and installed by you, armed with a screwdriver. If you install your own hardware add-ons, carefully follow the directions supplied with the add-ons. Always unplug the system from the electrical source before you start the installation. Finally, don't be intimidated by the cables, chips, and electronics inside your unit. If you follow the directions and don't bend or bump anything else, you'll be okay.

What You Have Learned

In this chapter you've learned

- The general types of functions you may perform with your PS/1 and the importance of setting priorities relative to the functions to learn first.
- The basic features of PS/1s.
- The add-on capabilities you may want to expand into in the future.

Chapter 2

Get Set

In This Chapter

- *Where to set up your PS/1*
- *Setting up your hardware*
- *Using the hardware components*
- *Setting up your software*
- *Using the System menu*
- *Troubleshooting*

Where To Set Up Your PS/1

Before setting up your PS/1, give some thought about where to set it up. Some tips may be obvious. Don't put your PS/1 where there will be extremes in heat or cold, such as next to a furnace or stove or in an unheated room where the temperature will drop significantly. Don't put your machine where it might get wet, have food or drink spilled on it, or risk being bumped off a table. (When you clean the case of the PS/1, use mild cleansers and damp—not wet—cloths.) Make sure there is a properly grounded outlet and that the cords and cables for the machine aren't in a location that will cause accidents.

Also make sure there is plenty of ventilation and that books and other articles do not obstruct the ventilation holes in the PS/1's case. Although the PS/1 can be a wonderful tool for children, you may want to take some care with very little ones to make it easy for them to observe the "rules of the road."

A common concern most PS/1 users overlook is where to put the PS/1 for maximum usability. Make sure an electrical outlet and telephone jack are close by the area. That way you won't need long cords draped across doorways and carpets. Make sure the lighting is adequate. Typically, placing the PS/1 in front of a window is not a good idea. Both the light and the heat behind the monitor will be a problem. Ensure that there is plenty of desk space. You will need space to refer to manuals, to store manuals, to move the mouse, and elbow room for paper versions of your work.

If you are sharing the machine with other members of your household or business, put it in a place accessible to all. Make sure everyone knows to leave the manuals near the computer and how to use the computer safely—to protect them and the computer.

> **Tip:** If several people are using the PS/1, having a procedure for *backing up* (making copies of) work that people create using the computer is usually a good idea. You may decide that every person is responsible for backing up his or her own work or that one person will back up all the files for everyone periodically. How to back up work is covered later in this chapter.

Setting Up the Hardware

Even if you've owned a computer before, getting your PS/1 is like getting a great birthday present. But, in the excitement, taking the proper steps to set up your hardware can mean the difference between immediate success and having to start over to figure out what went wrong.

Follow these hardware set-up steps to set up the basic system. Refer to the set-up information specific to any add-on features you may have purchased. Don't force any connection. The cables should slip in the connectors easily. If in doubt, check the size of the connections to make sure they are correct. Also, check the drawings on the back of the system unit (see Figure 2.1). They will confirm the accuracy of what you are plugging in where.

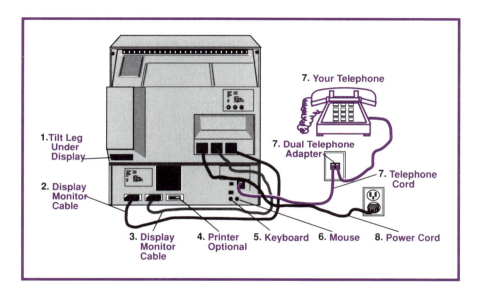

Figure 2.1   Hardware connections

1. Place the system unit in the location where it will be used and set the display monitor on top of the system unit.

   You may tilt the display down for ease of viewing or getting rid of a nasty glare. Just pick up the back of the display monitor and pull down the display tilt leg located in the center of the bottom of the display. Pull the leg until it is totally extended and locks. Position the display monitor on the system unit.

2. Facing the back of the unit, plug the far right display monitor cable into the far left connector on the back of the system unit. Check the size of the connectors if you get confused. And make sure the longer edge of the cable connector is up. Hand twist the screws on both sides of the connector to keep the cable in place.

3. Plug the middle display monitor cable into the next connector to the right of the connection that you just made on the back of the system unit. Twist the screws into place by hand.

4. If you have a printer, attach it to the connector located roughly in the middle of the back of the system unit. A graphic of a printer appears above the connector. The connection is a common RS 232-compatible connector.
5. Connect the keyboard into the leftmost round connector on the back of the system unit. Look at the location of the pins and box on the connectors to make sure you line up the connectors appropriately.

    You can adjust the height of the keyboard. Just turn the keyboard over carefully and raise the legs on the bottom until they snap securely.
6. Connect the mouse into the rightmost round connector on the back of the system unit. Again, consider the location of the pins and box on the connectors for correct joining.
7. Connect the telephone cord from the jack on the back of the system unit into your telephone jack. A dual telephone adapter should be supplied so that you can connect both your computer and a telephone or telephone answering machine in the same wall jack. If you need a longer telephone cord or an extension to an existing cord, check out your local electronics store.
8. After you have everything securely attached, you can plug in the computer using the power cord coming out of the display monitor. Make sure to connect your computer to a properly grounded 3-wire electrical outlet.

If you later add other options, such as another diskette drive, or have user-replaceable parts to set up, always turn off the computer and unplug it before beginning work. Then follow the instructions supplied with the add-on or user-replaceable part.

> **Caution:** During lightning storms you can get power spikes through the telephone line or the electrical outlet. To rest easy during storms, unplug both your computer and the line to the telephone jack to escape harm to your system.

> **Caution:** Some add-on parts and all user-replaceable parts are intended for you to work on. The manufacturer has designed these parts to be easy to add or replace and will provide complete instructions. DO NOT assume other parts are as easily added or replaced. DO NOT try to service the machine yourself. Take it to an authorized service center for quick and cost effective servicing.

Using the Hardware

Once the hardware is set up, you may begin. And setting up is easier than you think.

Using the System Unit and Display Monitor

To turn on the machine, just push the power on/off switch on the lower right of the front of the monitor (see 1 in Figure 2.2). The on/off light to the upper left of the button (see 2 in Figure 2.2) will be green for go, which means your system is on. If you have a fixed disk, the fixed disk in-use light in the system unit directly below the power on/off switch (see 3 in Figure 2.2) will light up as the computer is processing. On a diskette based system, the diskette drive in-use light near the diskette drive (see 4 in Figure 2.2) will light up. Any time this light is on, your computer is in the process of performing an activity. Wait until it is done until you continue your work.

> **Caution:** NEVER remove a diskette from the diskette drive while the in-use light is on.

Once the system is on, the System menu (shown in Figure 2.3) appears. A menu is a screen that allows you to select more than one option. You will see many menus when using your PS/1. The System menu allows four choices: Information, Microsoft Works, IBM DOS, and Your Software.

Chapter 2

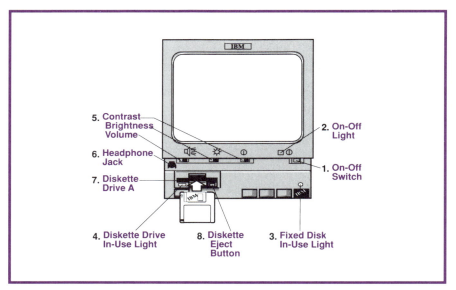

Figure 2.2 PS/1 controls

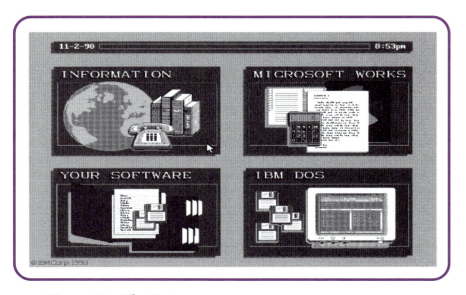

Figure 2.3 The System menu

> **Caution:** Experienced personal computer users should NOT format the hard disk. The software comes loaded. Fully explore the setup of the software before altering anything.

Take a moment to adjust the three tabs left of the power on/off switch. From left to right these are the volume, the brightness, and the contrast (see 5 in Figure 2.2). Pushing any of these three levers right increases the setting. Pushing them left decreases the setting. To hear a sample of the volume, press the Esc key in the upper left corner of your keyboard. Pressing it will cause a beep because the key is not used on this screen. Notice that there is a headphone jack to the left of the volume control (see 6 in Figure 2.2). This jack is especially handy if you play a lot of games and don't want to disturb others.

Your system unit will have one or more diskette drives (see 7 in Figure 2.2). They are where you will place diskettes when you want to use information from a diskette or copy information to a diskette. Note that the diskette drive is faintly labeled with a letter, such as A or B. This is the *drive designation* (name). There is also a diskette eject button (see 8 in Figure 2.2). Press this button to release a diskette once it is in the drive.

Using Diskettes

There are a few rules to remember when using diskettes.

Diskettes are used to store information. Before you can use a new diskette with your PS/1, it must be formatted. See Chapter 3, "DOS—Using the Main Group," for information on formatting a diskette.

You may use high or low density 3.5" diskettes. A high density diskette is labeled as such and has two holes in the bottom corners of the diskette. You format it with your 1.44M diskette drive to hold that amount of information. If you have a low density diskette identified with only one hole in the bottom corner and format it, you will have only 720K of space to store data. As a rule of thumb, 720K equals about 720,000 characters of information.

You can format a low density diskette in a high density diskette drive. But don't format a high density diskette with a low density drive or you may have reliability problems. Also, you cannot use diskettes formatted for high density in a 720K diskette drive.

When using a 3.5" diskette, always place the label side up and the metal end away from you. When the diskette is all the way in, it will click into place. To remove a diskette, press the diskette eject button on the right of the drive.

When preparing to place a 5.25" diskette in the appropriate drive, make sure the lever is turned counterclockwise to the up and horizontal position. Then place the label side up and the opening exposing the diskette magnetic media away from you. Push the diskette in until it is secure; then turn the lever clockwise down to a vertical position. With the lever in this "locked" position, you may use the drive.

 Caution: Again, never remove a diskette from the drive while the drive in-use light is on.

You may *write-protect* a diskette. This way, you can use the diskette, but you cannot change its contents. To write protect a 3.5" diskette, slide the write-protect tab in the lower corner of the diskette to open the hole in the diskette. If you later decide you want to change the contents of the diskette, close the holes with the tab. When using 5.25" diskettes, write-protect them by placing a write-protect tab supplied with the diskettes over the single, square notch on the edge of the diskette. Remove this tab if you want to alter files on the diskette.

Using the Keyboard

The keyboard is much like a typewriter keyboard but modified with additional options.

The section of the keyboard containing the alphabetic keys includes some special keys. Press Shift with a letter for a capital letter. Press Shift with a number (or symbol key) to get the symbol shown at the top of the key. The *Caps Lock* key, when pressed, enables you to type in all capital letters. Notice when you press Caps Lock, the Caps Lock light in the upper right corner of the keyboard lights up if Caps Lock is on. The light remains unlit if Caps Lock is off.

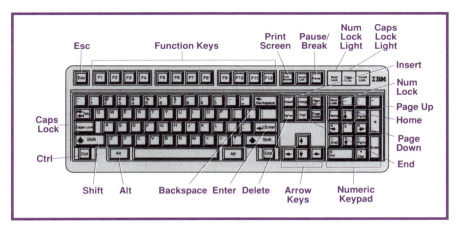

Figure 2.4   The keyboard

The *Ctrl* key stands for Control and *Alt* stands for Alternate. These keys are used in combination with other keys for special purposes. As you learn to use your computer, you will discover their purposes. When you use these keys with other keys, always press the Ctrl or Alt key and hold it down while you press the remaining key(s) specified. In other words, all keys identified are to be pressed simultaneously.

The *Enter* key is used to end a paragraph when you use word processing and also is often used to indicate to the computer that you have finished typing in a command. As you type in commands, you sometimes will notice that the *Backspace* key is used to delete characters right to left.

To the lower right of the alphabetic key area are four *arrow* keys with arrows pointing right, down, left, and up. These keys are used to move the symbol marking your spot on the display (which may be an arrow called a *pointer* or small blinking line called a *cursor*).

Above the arrow keys are keys with the following labels and common uses (customary functions may vary depending on the software you are using):

▶ *Insert* is normally used to control inserting text among existing text versus typing over existing text.
▶ *Delete* is typically used to delete existing text.
▶ *Home* often is used to move your pointer or cursor to the top of a document or the display.

- *End* usually is pressed to move your pointer or cursor to the bottom of a document or the display.
- *Page Up* is commonly used to move a screenful of information backward.
- *Page Down* is typically used to move a screenful of information forward.

There is a numeric keypad on the far right of the keyboard. This keypad is available for those fluent with high speed entry of numbers in this configuration. Notice the *Num Lock* key in the upper left corner of the numeric keypad. Press Num Lock on and off to switch between using the numbers and symbols on the top of the keys and the uses shown on the lower part of the key. When Num Lock is on, the Num Lock light in the upper right of the keyboard is lit.

Finally, take a look at the keys across the top of the keyboard. The first is the *Esc* (Escape) key. The common use of this key is to get out of performing a function you have begun—a very handy key indeed! The next 12 keys are marked F1 through F12 and are called *function keys*. These keys are assigned special uses for every software package you use. Often prompts will appear on your display telling you which function key, or combination of keys including a function key, to press for a specific outcome.

A useful key to discover is the *Print Screen* key to the right of the function keys. Press this key and, assuming you have a printer set up and turned on, the contents of a text—not graphic—display will print.

The *Pause* key typically stops screen action, such as lines of text scrolling up your display. The Ctrl and *Break* keys can be pressed together to stop some programs from processing.

Using the Mouse

Although most, if not all, functions the PS/1 can perform may be accomplished using the keyboard, you can use a mouse to perform many activities. Try out the mouse. You may find it quicker, easier, and more fun.

Generally, any activity involving picking out a selection from a group of selections can be performed using the mouse. To use the mouse, slide it on your desk to move the arrow pointer on or over the item to select. If you run out of desk space, just pick up the mouse and set it down where you have space again; the pointer remains in the same location on the screen while you reposition the mouse on the desk by picking it up and setting it down. To make a selection, press down the left button on the mouse and then release the button. In mouse lingo this is called "clicking." You sometimes will be asked to "double click," which means pressing and depressing the left button twice, quickly. When you are asked to click the mouse, assume this is a press down and up of the left button. For the rare cases where the right button should be clicked, it will be specifically stated.

Using the Modem

Your PS/1 has a modem built in. This modem allows you to communicate through the telephone line with other computers for reservations, stock information, computer users groups, shopping, classes, game playing, and a host of other activities. You can't use your telephone line for calls when your modem is in operation using the line. If you even pick up the phone, your modem connection may be interrupted.

Whether you are very technical or not, you may need the following modem information when you try to hook up with friends, colleagues, or commercial services. (Your modem settings must match the equipment with which you are hooking up.)

- ▶ The PS/1 modem communicates at speeds of 300, 1200, and 2400 bits per second (bps) in full duplex.
- ▶ The modem supports up to eight data and parity bits.
- ▶ The Microsoft Works default modem speed is 1200 bps.
- ▶ In Prodigy and the Users' Club, the default modem speed is 2400 bps.
- ▶ Your telephone company may require you to supply the FCC registration number, USOC, and Ringer Equivalency Number (REN) for your equipment. To do so, slide off the front bezel of the PS/1 system unit (the cover plate on the front) and slide the top cover forward to see the label with this information.
- ▶ The PS/1 modem commands are compatible with the Hayes AT command set. A limited list of these commands is shown in Appendix B of the *User's Reference for PS/1*. A complete list is available in the *Technical Reference for IBM Personal System/1 Computer* manual.

> **⊘ Caution:** If you have "call waiting," you will want to disable it before using your modem. An incoming call signal can disrupt your modem operation. Most systems allow you to disable call waiting by entering *70 with touch tone service or 1170 with regular dial service. After entering this prefix, enter ,,, and then the phone number for the modem to call. For example, this entry for a phone number will first deactivate call waiting, pause, and then dial the phone number shown here: *70,,,6029981444

Call waiting is reactivated when your computer hangs up. If using *70 doesn't work, read the instructions in your phone book or call your telephone company to find exact information about your call waiting feature.

Using a Printer

The PS/1 does not come with a printer. As mentioned in Chapter 1, you may select among several popular types of printers. These are a dot-matrix printer (typically lower print quality, high speed, and lower cost), a letter-quality impact printer (customarily higher print quality, lower speed, and lower cost), or a laser printer (usually higher print quality, higher speed, and higher cost). No matter which printer you choose, you will want to make sure the software you use recognizes the type (usually right down to the brand and model) of printer you use. Instructions in this book and in manuals describing software identify how to set up the software to recognize your printer.

You also will want to learn the basics about your printer. These basics may include how to turn the printer on and off, change pitch (characters per inch) and fonts (type styles), clear paper misfeeds, change ribbons or toner cartridges, turn the printer on- and off-line (available to not available), perform "form feed" (to advance the page), and perform "line feed" (to advance one line). Consult your printer manual to learn about these and other features.

Using the System Menu

Your PS/1 comes "ready to go" from a software standpoint. If you have a fixed disk, the software is already loaded in directories called *folders*. If you have a diskette drive only system, you start your system from the diskette in the drive. Whichever kind of system you have, you will come to the System menu (see Figure 2.5) to get started. Notice that the arrow pointer is on the lower right corner of the Information box.

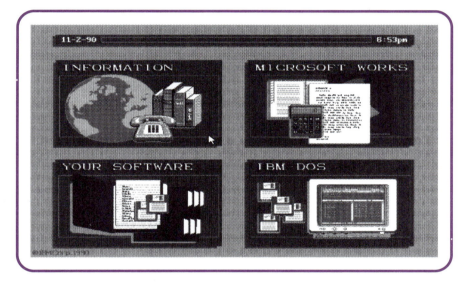

Figure 2.5   The System menu

There are four selections on the System menu. The first, Information, is your gateway to the PS/1 Users' Club, Prodigy service, PS/1 System Tutorial, and the Microsoft Works Tutorial. The second selection (moving clockwise) is Microsoft Works, the third is IBM DOS, and the last is titled Your Software which leads you to a screen showing each program folder for each software program—somewhat the equivalent of a DOS directory—and will show folders for any software you may add at a later date.

You can make selections from the System menu using the mouse by sliding the mouse on the desktop to position the arrow pointer. Then press and release (click) the left button. The next screen in the series appears.

To use the keyboard to make a selection from the System menu, use the arrow keys to position the arrow pointer; then press Enter. The next screen appears.

 Selecting from the System Menu with the Mouse

1. Move the mouse on the desktop to position the arrow pointer.	The arrow is positioned on your selection.
2. Press and release (click) the left mouse button.	The next screen appears for your next selection. ☐

 Selecting from the System Menu with the Keyboard

1. Press the arrow keys as necessary to position the arrow pointer.	The arrow is positioned on your selection.
2. Press the Enter key.	The next screen appears for your next selection. ☐

Backing Up Your Software

A good habit to get into immediately is backing up your software. Backing up means that you make one or more additional copies of your software on diskettes. This protects you from losing use of your software from damage or theft. Backing up your software will take a little time, but remember that your software is, at best, difficult to replace.

> ▶ **Tip:** Always keep your backup diskettes in a safe place. Make sure the temperature is controlled and there are no strong magnetic fields to damage the contents of your diskettes. If the software and information on the diskettes is very critical, you may want to keep the diskettes off-site in case of fire, flood, or theft.

Backing Up a Fixed Disk

The software on your fixed disk comes already loaded. However, what would happen if you damaged your fixed disk? You could lose that software and related files forever. Before you go further, back up the fixed disk. To learn how to use other backup options, see Chapter 3, "DOS—Using the Main Group."

> **Caution:** Always back up your fixed disk before moving the computer or sending it in for repair. That way, if any damage is done or if a technician needs to remove all the files from your hard disk, you haven't lost all your software and data.

Here is the general procedure. Make sure you have at least six diskettes with 1.4M capacity. Label the first diskette "IBM DOS Backup-PS/1" and the others numerically starting with "PS/1 Fixed Disk Backup #1." When you make this backup, your DOS files will be backed up on the specially marked diskette. ABSOLUTELY label the diskettes and number them. If you don't, you cannot restore the diskette contents at a later date because the restore process asks for diskettes in order. Don't worry about formatting the diskettes to be recognized by your machine. As you perform the backup, the system formats the diskettes. So, you can use the diskettes right out of the box.

After you have labeled all diskettes, place the first diskette (IBM DOS Backup-PS/1) in drive A by pushing it in label side up and metal first until it clicks into place. From the System menu, select IBM DOS. On the Main Group menu, highlight the following option and press Enter, or move the mouse pointer to the option and double-click the left mouse button:

```
Backup and Restore Your Fixed Disk...
```

You want to back up everything on your fixed disk, so make sure the following option is highlighted on the new screen that appears and press Enter:

```
Backup your entire fixed disk
```

Then the following message appears:

```
A DOS backup diskette will be created first.
Insert new diskette for drive A:
and press ENTER when ready...
```

> **Caution:** All information—if any—on the diskette will be lost and the backup of your fixed disk will be replaced. If this is okay with you, press the Enter key.

A message showing the percent of the diskette in drive A which is formatted appears as the PS/1 works. Once the diskette is formatted, the following message appears:

```
Format complete
```

Then you'll see this message telling you that DOS has been copied:

```
System transferred
```

This message asks for your response:

```
Volume label (11 characters, ENTER for none)?
```

Don't worry about naming the diskette with a volume label. Just press Enter. A lengthy informational message like this appears telling you the total disk space, the amount used, and the amount available:

```
1457664 bytes total disk space
109568 bytes used by system
1348096 bytes available on disk
512 bytes in each allocation unit
2633 allocation units available on disk
Volume Serial Number is 1D12-1ADA
Format another (Y/N)?
```

This message simply indicates that the diskette is formatted. However, your DOS files have not yet been fully copied. You want to move on and back up the files, not format another diskette. So press N for No and then press the Enter key. This message appears while the DOS files are copied to your diskette:

```
Copying DOS files to the backup diskette...
```

When the files are copied, this message appears:

```
Remove the diskette from the drive and label it
DOS BACKUP.
Press any key to continue...
```

Remove the DOS Backup diskette; make sure it is labeled. Next, put the diskette labeled "PS/1 Fixed Disk Backup #1" in the drive and press Enter. You see this message which contains a warning that any existing files on your diskette will be erased:

```
Insert backup diskette 01 in drive A:
WARNING! File in the target drive
A:\root directory will be erased
Press any key to continue...
```

Press Enter to go ahead. As each file is backed up, this type of screen scrolls by:

```
*** Backing up files to drive A: ***
Diskette Number: 01
\AUTOEXEC.BAT
\CONFIG.SYS
\WORKS\CHECKS.WDB
ETC.
```

You may watch as each software file is copied. Continue this process until the system is backed up. You return to the menu when the backup is complete. Store the backup diskettes in a safe place. You may want to keep a set of backup diskettes with your system in "untouched" form. Then make one or two other sets of backup diskettes to rotate as you add more files to the system. You also will need to back up these sets periodically.

> **Caution:** If you see an `Insufficient Disk Space` message while you work, put in a new diskette while the diskette drive's in-use light is off and continue.

Backing Up a Diskette-Based System

The software for your system came on diskettes. But, if you lost or damaged a diskette, you would be out of luck when you want to use the software. Don't keep using the diskettes that came with your system. Copy them to working copies and use those diskettes. That way, if you lose the use of a working copy, you can always make a new copy from the original master diskette.

To make copies of your diskettes, make sure you have the same number of diskettes and capacity for copies as you have master diskettes. Label each working diskette carefully with the same name as is on the master diskette. Don't worry about formatting the diskettes. As you perform the disk copy, the system will format the diskettes.

Once all diskettes are labeled, place the first master diskette in drive A by pushing it in label side up and metal first until it clicks into place. From the System menu, select IBM DOS. Highlight this option on the Main Group menu and press Enter:

```
Disk Copy (Copy a diskette)
```

A *pop-up* (a window on your screen) appears asking you to enter the *source* and *target* drives. The source drive is where you will place the master diskette to be copied. The target drive is where you will place the working copy diskette to be copied to. If you have just one drive, enter **A:** for both and press Enter. If you have two drives, make the source drive A: and the target drive B: (the source and target drives must be the same drive type—both 3.5" or both 5.25"). Make sure to put the master diskette in drive A and the working copy diskette in drive B. Many users have horror stories about being tired, placing the wrong diskette in the wrong drive, and copying old files or nothing, thus formatting and losing the contents of the diskette with the desirable files.

> **Caution:** It can't be said enough. Always be careful that the master diskette is in the source drive when designated and the working disk is in the target drive at all times. Otherwise, you risk copying over and ruining your master diskettes.

Once you have entered the source and target drives, inserted diskettes appropriately, and pressed Enter, a message such as the following appears reminding you where to place your diskette. Make sure the diskettes are in the correct drives.

```
Insert SOURCE diskette in drive A:
Press any key to continue...
```

Press Enter. This message appears:

```
Copying 80 tracks
18 Sectors/Track, 2 Side(s)
```

If you have two drives, the copying will take place. If you have only one drive, once the information is copied into memory, this message appears:

```
Insert TARGET diskette in drive A:
Press any key to continue...
```

For one drive copying, remove the master disk (the source diskette) and place the working copy diskette (the target diskette) in the drive. Press Enter. Whether you're copying with one drive or two drives, the following message appears during copying if the disks are not already formatted:

```
Formatting while copying
```

Continue with this process (swap source and target diskettes as indicated on your display if you have one drive) until a message like the one below appears:

```
Volume Serial Number is 1BC7-4048
Copy another diskette (Y/N)?
```

Press Y and continue following the prompts to copy other diskettes in this fashion until working copies of all are made. Then respond N to the `Copy another diskette (Y/N)?` prompt to be returned to the menu.

Chapter 2

Turning Off the PS/1

Never turn off the PS/1 while within a program. Always select the Exit option from a menu (or press Esc) to go back to the System menu. From the System menu, you can turn off the machine with the power on/off switch.

Troubleshooting

If you have trouble using your system as described, take some time to walk through this troubleshooting guide. It will help you isolate what might be the problem. When you troubleshoot, relax. Follow a logical, step-by-step assessment of the problem. Identify what does work and what doesn't work for clues about what to do.

When you alter the conditions of your computer, try again and alter only one condition at a time. This way, you can walk through possible solutions and know what works and what doesn't. Here's a simple example. Suppose the display doesn't appear when you push the power on/off switch. The machine may not be plugged in. You plug in the machine and wiggle the display connection. The display still doesn't appear. After you plugged in the machine, you accidentally loosened the connection. And you believe you have now checked both the power and connection.

Also remember the rule of taking one step back. If a condition isn't working, consider what has to work before the condition can work. Stepping backwards in this fashion can often be a fairly direct path to a solution. Continuing with the earlier example, if the display doesn't come on when the power on/off switch is pushed, a good question to ask would be, "What does the power on/off switch need to operate?" Since power is needed to fuel the display, electricity would be the answer.

Here are some other troubleshooting tips:

1. Make sure the system is plugged in and all cables are securely attached.

2. Make sure the power outlet is active. Check it with another electrical device such as a hair dryer if necessary.
3. Make sure the system is turned on and the power light (near the on/off switch) is on.
4. Check the brightness and contrast controls to make sure the display monitor can display the screen. Make sure the volume control is turned up to alert you to system beeps.
5. As the system powers up, it performs a self test and then beeps if everything is okay. If it does not beep, a problem with the hardware or system software is suggested. Turn the machine off and try again. Watch for and write down any messages as the machine tries the tests again.
6. Always carefully read and write down any error messages you may see on your display. General types of error messages are covered in Chapter 5, "Changing the DOS Group and Your Software," as well in other PS/1 reference manuals.
7. If you have trouble reading or writing to a diskette, try a diskette that you know is good. Throw out any diskettes that display performance problems. They are inexpensive compared to the cost of your software and the cost of your effort in developing files.
8. If you can't write to a diskette, make sure it is formatted, that the diskette is not write-protected, that you are reading the correct drive, and that there is plenty of room on the diskette for the information you want to add to the diskette.
9. If you have trouble with the keyboard or mouse, make sure the connectors are secure. Check to be certain the screen allows selection or typing.
10. If you have communications trouble, make sure the phone outlet works. Make a call from a phone using it. Check the number and the way the number is entered. Make sure no one but you is using the telephone. Check the configuration including the bits per second you are using relative to the receiving modem.
11. If you have printer problems, make sure the printer works by running a self-test (see your printer manual for instructions). Then try to print a screen with the Print Screen key on the PS/1 keyboard to test the connection between the PS/1 and the printer. After that, check your software manual and make sure you are using the correct files for your printer and that you are sending the file to the printer in the correct manner.

Chapter 2

12. When in doubt about how to fix a problem, return to the System menu, turn the machine off for 5 seconds, turn the machine on, and try to perform the function again. It's amazing the types of problems this will solve. Remember: only turn the machine off from the system menu.
13. If you have checked out troubleshooting steps 1-12 and still see an error code, you can consult your User's Reference Manual for PS/1. You may need expert technical assistance. Jot down all error messages, the conditions you are experiencing, what you were doing just prior to the error condition, and then call an authorized service representative for assistance.

What You Have Learned

In this chapter you've learned to

- ▶ Place your PS/1 in a safe and accessible area.
- ▶ Secure each connection tightly when setting up hardware.
- ▶ Set the display controls for easy viewing and listening.
- ▶ Never force disks into diskette drives.
- ▶ Store diskettes in safe, climate-controlled places.
- ▶ Make menu selections with a mouse by pointing and clicking the left button.
- ▶ Make menu selections with the keyboard by using the arrow keys and then pressing Enter.
- ▶ Follow basic technical information when you need to make modem connections.
- ▶ Always back up software to protect your investment.
- ▶ Always exit the PS/1 system from the System menu.
- ▶ Follow the logical, step-by-step troubleshooting procedures before calling for technical support. Don't panic.

Chapter 3
DOS—Using the Main Group

In This Chapter

- *Performing DOS functions including setting the date and time, formatting a diskette, copying a diskette, and backing up and restoring a hard disk*
- *Going to the DOS command prompt*
- *Translating PS/1 operations for the DOS familiar*
- *Customizing display colors, system startup, and how your hardware is configured*

The What and Why of DOS

DOS stands for Disk Operating System. It is the traffic cop of your system because it makes sure the hardware and software work together. There also are several DOS program commands which you will find necessary to take care of your PS/1 system. These DOS program commands are available through the IBM DOS selection on the System menu and are the subject of this chapter and the next, Chapter 4, "DOS—File Handling." You may add other DOS program commands to your screen or use them from a DOS command prompt. These commands and how to add them are described in

Chapter 5, "Changing the DOS Group and Your Software." (The BASIC Programming Language also appears on this screen. See Chapter 15, "Basics of BASIC," for information about the language.)

DOS and Your PS/1

The PS/1 menu system places the most often used DOS program commands in a handy menu. It is part of the DOS Shell which surrounds the DOS program commands and related software, making them easier for you to use. The often used commands are accessible through the IBM DOS selection on the System menu. This group of program commands is referred to as the *Main Group*. Figure 3.1 shows the Main Group menu which appears once you select IBM DOS from the System menu.

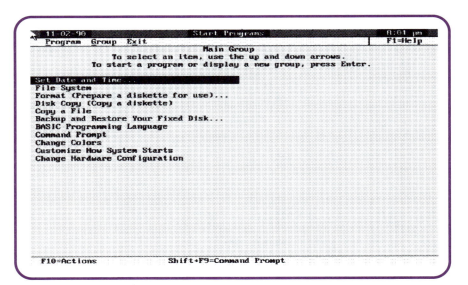

Figure 3.1 The IBM DOS Main Group menu

The ellipses (...) that end many selections on the Main Group menu identify there are more selections to be made on the next screen once you make the selection from this screen.

For the DOS familiar, notice that the DOS program Command Prompt is available through this menu as a selection. The DOS prompt is your gateway to DOS in its more natural form. The Command Prompt is also readily available from any DOS menu by simultaneously pressing Shift with F9. This prompt for Shift+F9 is shown on the bottom of the screen.

You can follow some general procedures to move around the IBM DOS set of menus. To select an option from the IBM DOS Main Group menu using a mouse, simply highlight the selection by pointing at it and clicking. Then point and click on Program in the upper left corner of the screen. A pull-down menu appears. Point and click on Start. To select an option from the IBM DOS Main Group menu using your keyboard, use the arrow keys to select a menu option, and then press Enter. You also can point and double-click to start a selection.

To "back out" of any DOS related screen, use the mouse to point to and then click on Exit which pulls down a menu; then select Exit to leave the DOS Shell and return to the System menu. Using your keyboard, press F3, or press Esc to cancel out of the last screen and return to the previous screen. If ESC appears at the bottom of the screen, you also can click on that to back out.

The DOS screens allow you to yell "help" at any time. The F1=Help prompt in the upper left corner of each screen reminds you to press F1 to call for Help. When you press F1, a pop-up like that shown in Figure 3.2 appears. You also can point at F1 with the mouse and click. When you select Help, you see a description of the highlighted command. You may read through the information in the Help pop-up by pressing Page Down or Page Up to move a "pop-up window full" at a time or the down- or up-arrow key to move a line at a time. You also can click the mouse on the bar making up the right side of the pop-up to designate how far to travel through the pop-up information.

The bottom of the Help pop-up reminds you that you can press Esc to Cancel out of Help at any time. When you leave this pop-up —or any pop-up within your PS/1 system—your screen goes back to business as usual. The bottom line of the Help pop-up also tells you that you can press F1 to get "Help about Help" (which is how to use Help). Further, you may press F11 for an index of all topics for which help exists. When you press F11 from the Help pop-up, you see that there is help for option commands not shown on the Main Group menu. You can look at Help here for a variety of topics. Also, notice that you can press F9 for a description of the keys to be used with a given DOS program command.

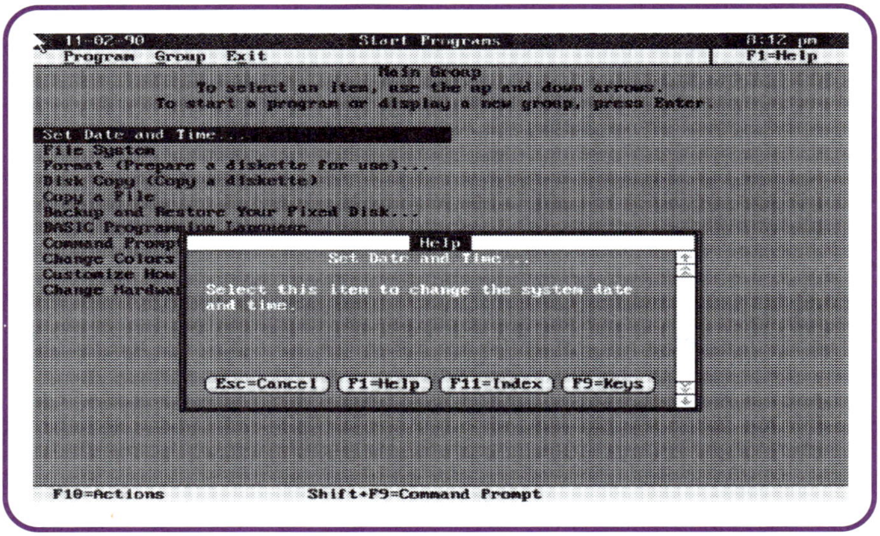

Figure 3.2   Help pop-up

Setting the Date and Time

When you first get your PS/1, you should set the date and time. This date and time is battery-powered, and it remains with the system even when you shut off the machine or unplug the power cord. Setting the date and time is critical for handling your files, which may include any document such as a letter. Whenever you stop using a file, DOS attaches the date and time to the file. The date and time are useful when you have two files with similar names on a diskette or the same name on two diskettes and you want to know which file is the most current.

To set the date and time, select Set Date and Time... from the DOS Main Group menu. This takes you to a submenu where you select Set the Date or Set the Time. Either selection takes you to a pop-up where you enter the new date or time. See Figure 3.3 for the Set the Date pop-up.

These pop-ups show you the proper format in which to enter the date or time. Enter the date with two numbers for the month, a dash, two for the day, a dash, and four numbers for the year. For example, enter September 30, 1993 as

09-30-1993

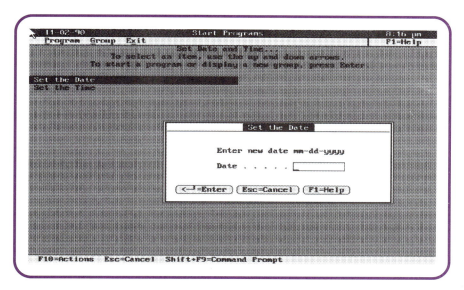

Figure 3.3   Set the Date pop-up

Enter the time with the hour, a colon, the minutes, and the a.m. (morning) or p.m. (afternoon) designation. For example, enter five minutes after eight in the morning as

8:05am

Once you enter the date or time, press Enter to save the entry. From either the Set the Date or Set the Time pop-up, you may press Esc to cancel at any time or press F1 for Help.

Preparing a Diskette for Use by Formatting

Another DOS program command you'll use early on in life with your PS/1 is the *Format* command. You may recall that any diskette you purchase must be formatted before you store files on the diskette. Formatting with DOS makes the diskette "readable" by DOS.

> **Caution:** When you format a diskette, all the information already on the diskette is erased.

Chapter 3

To format a diskette, select `Format (Prepare a diskette for use)....` You go to a menu with the following options:

```
Format a 3 1/2" 2.0 MB diskette (1.44MB)
Format a 3 1/2" 1.0 MB diskette (720 KB)
Format a 5 1/4" 360 KB diskette
Format a 5 1/4" 1.2 MB diskette
```

First, consider the size of diskette you want to format. You work with 3.5" diskettes or 5.25" diskettes according to the type of diskette drive.

Next, consider the storage capacity of the diskette and the ability of your drive to create and read from a diskette. The PS/1 3.5" diskette drive can format for and read 2.0M diskettes. When formatted, this capacity diskette holds 1.44M of information. You may notice that 1.44 is printed on the eject button of your 3.5" diskette drive. When you purchase diskettes with this capacity, they may be labeled as HD (High Density), and they have two holes on the bottom of the diskette, away from the metal part.

Your drive also can *format down*, which means it can format for and read diskettes of a lesser capacity. For example, one Format menu option is to use a 3.5" diskette and format for 720K of information. These diskettes have only one hole at the bottom.

>  **Caution:** Don't format a 2.0M diskette to 720K; it may be undependable.

> **Caution:** If you swap diskettes between two machines, such as a machine at home and one at work or school, make sure that you know the capacity of each drive and that they are compatible. You can't use a 2.0M diskette in a 720K drive. If you try to use a diskette in an incompatible drive, the diskette just won't work.

After you have determined the diskette to format and its capacity, select that option from the menu. You go to a screen with a message like this:

```
Insert a new diskette for drive A:
and press ENTER when ready...
```

A message showing the percent of the diskette formatted appears. The in-use light on the diskette drive is lit as the drive is in use. Remember to never remove a diskette from the drive while this light is on. After the formatting is done, a message like the following appears:

```
Format complete
Volume label (11 characters, ENTER for none)?
```

You may enter a *volume label* by typing in up to 11 characters. The volume label is nothing more than a name identifying the diskette. Because you identify diskettes to the PS/1 by the drive the diskette is inserted in—and to yourself by the title you will hand write on the diskette label—press Enter to skip the volume label. A message like this appears:

```
1457664 bytes total disk space
1457664 bytes available on disk
512 bytes in each allocation unit
2847 allocation units available on disk
Volume Serial Number is 4347-10D7
Format another (Y/N)?
```

This message shows you how much space is available for your files on the diskette along with technical information which is unimportant to most users. Respond to the Format another (Y/N)? message by pressing Y and then Enter if you want to format another diskette (you will receive prompts to begin the process again) or N and then Enter to stop formatting the diskette. When you respond with N, you return to the DOS Format menu.

> **Tip:** Always keep several formatted diskettes on hand. This way, if you ever run out of space on a diskette when storing your files, you will have a diskette ready for storage. Otherwise, you may get in a jam and have to go out of your way to format a diskette or otherwise lose your file information.

Formatting a Diskette

1. Select IBM DOS from the System menu.

   The DOS Main Group menu appears.

2. Select Format (Prepare a diskette for use)....

   The diskette size and capacity options appear.

3. Select the diskette size and capacity that is appropriate.	The message `Insert new diskette for drive A: and press ENTER when ready...` appears.
4. Place the diskette in the drive and press Enter.	The percent formatted appears. DO NOT disrupt the machine or drive until the `Format complete Volume label` message appears.
5. Press Enter at the `Volume label` message.	Disk information appears along with the `Form another (Y/N)?` message.
6. Press Y to begin the process again with a new diskette, or press N to return to the DOS Format menu.	The process begins again or you go to the DOS Format menu. □

> ▶ **Tip:** If you are in the process of formatting a diskette and want to stop, press the Control key with the Break key while the diskette drive is not in use. You return to the Format menu.

Copying a Diskette

There are several reasons you may want to copy the contents of one diskette onto another diskette.

- ▶ You may want to give the information to a colleague or friend or take a copy to work or school.
- ▶ You may periodically want to put a new copy of irreplaceable information in a safe place such as a bank deposit box or off-site from your computer to protect your information from an accident like a fire or flood.
- ▶ You may want a second copy of the information on the diskette to keep near your computer in case the diskette is damaged or wears out.

▶ You may want to keep working copies of software diskettes and keep the master diskettes in a safe place. That way, if you damage the working copy, you always can make a new copy from your master.

When you copy a diskette, both the diskette you are copying from and the diskette you are copying to must be the same size and capacity. See "Preparing a Diskette for Use by Formatting" in this chapter for information about diskette size and capacity.

> **Caution:** When you copy an entire diskette, the diskette is formatted so that any existing contents of the diskette are erased. Another option is to copy a single file onto a diskette, thus maintaining the other contents of the diskette. See "Copying a File" in this chapter for more information on that option.

From the System menu, select IBM DOS to copy a diskette. You transfer to the Main Group menu. Highlight Disk Copy (Copy a diskette) and press Enter, or double-click on this selection with the mouse.

A pop-up appears in the screen asking you to enter the source and target drives. The source drive is where you will place the diskette to be copied. The target drive is where you will place the diskette to be copied to. If you have just one drive, enter A for both and press Enter. If you have two drives, make the source drive **A:** and the target drive **B:**. Make sure to put the source diskette to copy from in drive A and the target diskette to copy to in drive B.

When copying diskettes, you are wise to write-protect your original diskettes. On 5.25" diskettes, place a small piece of tape—generally provided with your diskettes—over the notch in the side of the diskette. On 3.5" diskettes, push the tab, or lock, open in the corner of the diskette. This action will prevent you from writing or copying over the information on your diskette.

> **Warning:** Be alert and make certain that the diskette to copy from is in the source drive when designated and the diskette to copy to is in the target drive when designated. Otherwise, you risk copying over and ruining your original diskettes.

The following message appears reminding you that the diskette to copy from should be in drive A:

```
Insert SOURCE diskette in drive A:
Press any key to continue...
```

Press Enter and the following message appears:

```
Copying 80 tracks
18 Sectors/Track, 2 Side(s)
```

If you have two disk drives, the copying takes place. If you have one disk drive, once the information is copied into memory, this message appears:

```
Insert TARGET diskette in drive A:
Press any key to continue...
```

Remove the disk to copy from (the source diskette) and place the diskette to copy to (the target diskette) in the drive. Press Enter.

Whether you have one drive or two, this message appears if the disk is not already formatted:

```
Formatting while copying
```

Continue until a message like this appears:

```
Volume Serial Number is 1BC7-4048
Copy another diskette (Y/N)?
```

Press Y for Yes if you want to repeat the process to copy other diskettes. Otherwise, respond N for No to the `Copy another diskette (Y/N)?` prompt. You return to the menu.

 Copying a Diskette

1. Select `IBM DOS` from the system menu.   The DOS Main Group menu appears.
2. Select `Disk Copy (Copy a diskette)`.   The Disk Copy pop-up appears.

3. Enter the drive of the source diskette (to copy from) and a colon and then the target diskette (to copy to) and a colon; these may be the same drive. Press Enter.

   This message appears:
   `Insert SOURCE diskette in A: Press any key to continue....`

4. Press any key on the keyboard.

   Copying messages appear. If you have one disk drive, you are prompted when to swap the source diskette and target diskette in the drive.

5. Swap the diskettes in one drive if necessary. Otherwise, just wait for copying to complete.

   When copying is complete, the `Copy another diskette (Y/N)?` message appears.

6. Press Y to begin the process again or press N to return to the menu.

   The process begins again or you go to the menu.

Copying a File

You may want to copy a file between two diskettes. When you copy a file, the file remains on the diskette you are copying from and an identical copy is placed on the diskette you are copying to. As with copying diskettes, you may want to copy a file to take a copy to work or school, give it to a coworker or friend, or place a second copy in a safe place in case the original disk or diskette becomes damaged. Many PS/1 users like to make a copy of a file once the file has been significantly updated. That way they are sure to have the backup copy if something happens to the original.

> **Note**: You use the copy function described in this section to copy between diskettes, not between a hard disk and a diskette. To copy between a hard disk and a diskette, see the copy function in Chapter 4, "DOS—File Handling."

If you copy a file onto a diskette where the file already exists, the existing version is replaced with the newer version. DOS matches up files by file name and extension assigned. Both the file name and the extension must match exactly for a hit. A file name may be made up of eight letters, numbers, or the following characters:

! @ # $ % & ( ) - _

The optional file extension is three characters. The name and extension is separated by a period. Some software programs, like Works, automatically add file extensions when you name files. For example, this may be a file full of memos. The .WPS extension is automatically added by Works to identify the file as a word processing file:

MEMOS.WPS

To copy a file between diskettes, select `Copy a File` from the DOS Main Group menu. A pop-up appears asking for the name of the file to copy. If you have one drive, place the diskette with the file to copy from in the drive. If you have two drives, place the diskette to copy the file from in drive B and the diskette to copy the file to in drive A. Whether you have one or two drives, after `From:` use the arrow keys to move past and keep the B: drive designation. Then enter the file name and the file extension. For example, to copy the file MEMOS.WPS from either drive A or drive B, use the arrow key to pass the B: drive designation and then type:

B:MEMOS.WPS

> ▶ **Tip:** This use of the B: drive designation for drive A in a one drive system is pretty unusual. Typically, you identify the drive by the actual letter of the drive.

After you have typed in the name of the file to copy, press Enter. The pop-up message asks you to enter the new drive to copy to and the file name. `To:` and the `A:` drive designations appear. To keep the same file name during the copy, keep the A: drive designation and just press Enter. To copy the file under a new name, use the arrow key to move past the A: drive designation, enter that new name and extension, and press Enter.

If you have a one drive system, the following message appears:

```
Insert diskette for drive B: and press any key when
ready
```

Make sure the diskette to copy from is in the drive labeled A and press any key on your keyboard. The file is copied to memory. A message like the one below appears:

```
Insert diskette for drive A: and press any key when
ready
```

Swap diskettes in your single drive now. Make sure to insert the "copy to" diskette. Press any key. Keep swapping diskettes if similar messages continue to appear; your file is too large to be in memory at once, so it is being copied in pieces.

Whether you have a single drive or more than one drive, once the file is copied, the following message briefly appears and then you are returned to the menu.

```
1 File(s) copied
```

If DOS looks for your file and cannot find it, the message `File not found` appears. If this happens, try the process again. You probably entered a typographical error when typing in the file name or you may have forgotten the extension. Or the file is not on the diskette in the drive indicated. You can check the contents of diskettes to see what files are on the diskette. See Chapter 4, " DOS—File Handling" for more information on how to check out the contents of a diskette.

Q Copying a File Between Diskettes

1.	Select `IBM DOS` from the System menu.	The DOS Main Group menu appears.
2.	Select `Copy a File`.	The Copy a File pop-up appears.
3.	If you have one drive, place the diskette with the file to copy from in the drive. If you have two drives, then place the diskette to copy the file from in drive B and the diskette to copy the file to in drive A.	The diskettes are in the proper drives to perform copying.
4.	Keep the B: drive designation whether you have one or two drives and type in the file name and extension of the file to copy from. Press Enter.	The pop-up asks you to enter the new drive to copy to along with the file name.

43

5. Leave the A: drive designation. Press Enter to keep the same file name or enter a new file name; then press Enter.

   If you have a two drive system, the file is copied. If you have a single drive system, you are instructed when to swap diskettes to perform the copy. When the file is copied, `1 File(s) copied` appears. □

Backing Up and Restoring a Fixed Disk

If you have a fixed (hard) disk inside your system unit, you will want to regularly create a backup copy of the contents of the disk. That way, if there is a hardware or software failure or the machine is somehow damaged, you will not lose all your software and every file you have created. You will, however, lose the information entered since your last backup. If you have a backup, you can copy the contents of the disk stored on diskette back onto the disk—a process called *restoring* the fixed disk.

Backing up and restoring your fixed disk once every year or two, depending on use, is also a good idea. This way you can clean up little items like "lost clusters" which are bits of data that have gotten copied into "never never land" and are taking up space on your disk.

To back up a fixed disk, select `Backup and Restore Your Fixed Disk...` on the DOS Main Group menu. The following options appear:

▶ `Backup your entire fixed disk`; this option erases any information on your diskettes and copies each file from the fixed disk to the diskettes.

▶ `Backup changes on your fixed disk`; this option skips files that have not changed since the last time you backed up the fixed disk onto this set of diskettes and only copies those files that have changed since the backup on the diskettes was performed.

▶ `Restore your fixed disk`; this option enables you to copy the files from your backup diskette copy back onto your fixed disk.

Backing Up Entire Fixed Disk

To begin, make sure you have plenty of diskettes to handle the information on your fixed disk. If your disk was full and you were backing up from scratch, you could conservatively estimate using as many as 20-30 3.5" diskettes with 2.0M capacity. (The storage space on every diskette does not get fully consumed due to the varying size of files.) The rule of thumb: always have many more diskettes than you expect you'll need.

The diskettes are formatted as part of the backup. All contents of the diskettes are lost when formatting takes place.

Label the first diskette "IBM DOS Backup-PS/1" and the others numerically starting with "PS/1 Fixed Disk Backup #1." Make sure to label the diskettes because they can't be restored at a later date unless they are in the correct order of backup. Put the first diskette, "IBM DOS Backup-PS/1", in drive A. From the System menu, select IBM DOS. Select Backup and Restore Your Fixed Disk.... To make a copy of every file on your fixed disk, select Backup your entire fixed disk. This message appears:

```
A DOS backup diskette will be created first.
Insert new diskette for drive A:
and press ENTER when ready...
```

Press Enter. You'll see a series of messages showing the percent of the diskette formatted, the completion of formatting, copying the DOS system, and an inquiry asking for a volume label. Press Enter to skip naming the diskette with a volume name.

After you skip the volume name process, a message identifies the total disk space, the amount used, and the amount available. The question Format another? (Y/N) appears. You want to continue backing up, not formatting more diskettes. Press N for No and then Enter. A message appears indicating that DOS files are being copied. Then the following message appears:

```
Remove the diskette from the drive and label it
DOS BACKUP.
Press any key to continue...
```

Remove the DOS Backup diskette. Put the diskette labeled "PS/1 Fixed Disk Backup #1" in the drive and press Enter. You see a message and warning that any existing files on your diskette will be erased. Press Enter.

Each file name appears as it is backed up. Continue the process of following the prompts and inserting diskettes as instructed until the system is backed up. You return to the menu.

> **Caution:** If you see an `Insufficient Disk Space` message while you work, put in a new diskette—with the in-use light off—and keep going.

Backing Up Changes on the Fixed Disk

If you have critical information on your fixed disk, you should take extra care. Some users like to have two sets of backup disks—the old set and the most recent set. That way, when it is time to back up, they use the earlier of the two backups to make the new backup. If the system should fail AND damage the backup set, the most recent backup would still be available to be restored.

When you start a new backup using an existing set of backup diskettes, remember that your storage requirements may well have grown. In addition to the backup diskettes, you'll want extra diskettes to allow for this expansion of your files since the last use of the backup diskettes. Put the last diskette that was backed up (the highest numbered) in drive A. From the System menu, select `IBM DOS`. Select `Backup and Restore Your Fixed Disk`.... **To make a copy of every file on your fixed disk, select** `Backup changes on your fixed disk`. This message appears:

```
Insert last backup diskette in drive A:
Press any key to continue...
```

Press any key on the keyboard. You see a message like this:

```
*** Backing up files to drive A: ***
```

The diskette number and list of each file as it is backed up appears. You are prompted to insert other diskettes if necessary. When the backup is complete, you return to the menu. If you attempt to back up changes and there are no changes to back up, this message appears:

```
WARNING! No files were found to back up
```

Restoring Your Fixed Disk

When you need to restore your fixed disk, you finally reap the benefits of all the backing up. Restoring the fixed disk enables you to copy from the backup diskettes to your fixed disk.

Put the first diskette that was backed up (the lowest numbered diskette) in drive A. From the System menu, select IBM DOS. Select Backup and Restore Your Fixed Disk.... To restore, select Restore your fixed disk. This message appears:

```
Insert backup diskette 01 in drive A:
Press any key to continue...
```

Press any key on the keyboard. You see a message like this:

```
*** Files were backed up 02-08-91 ***
*** Restoring files from drive A: ***
Diskette:01
```

The list of files being restored follows the message. Once the files on the diskette are restored, you are instructed to insert the next backup diskette in numeric order and press any key. Continue restoring the diskettes following the prompts until all backup diskettes have been restored. You return to the menu.

> **Tip:** If you have wiped out DOS or the DOS Restore command, you cannot use the command from the menu. Use the RESTORE command from the DOS backup copy diskette you produced. Type **RESTORE A:\ C:*.* /S /P** at the DOS prompt which becomes available after starting up from that diskette, and follow the prompts.

Going to the DOS Command Prompt

Many DOS program commands are not available through the Shell. And there are ways to add parameters to some of the DOS program commands with which you are now familiar to slightly alter their use.

Chapter 3

To use commands outside of the menu Shell or add parameters to commands you're familiar with from the IBM DOS menu system, you need to go to the DOS command prompt. To do this, select `Command Prompt`. The screen shown in Figure 3.4 appears.

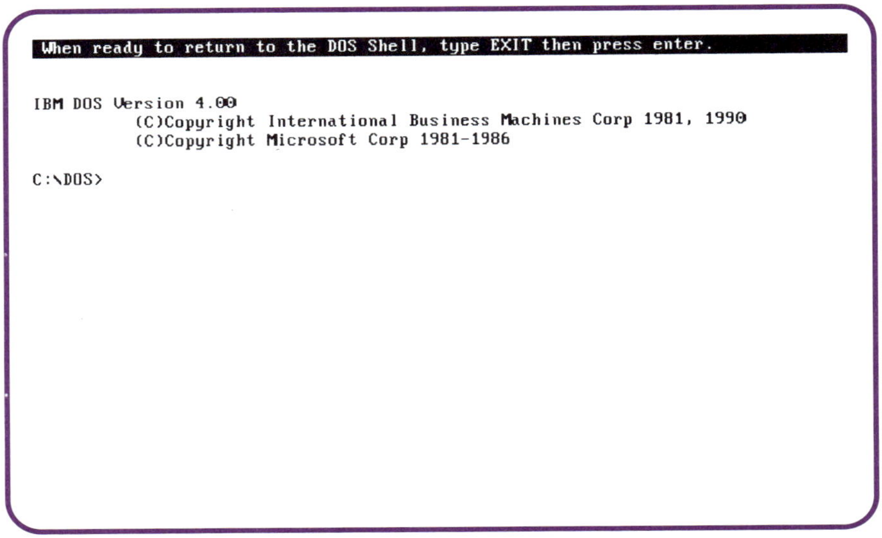

```
When ready to return to the DOS Shell, type EXIT then press enter.

IBM DOS Version 4.00
          (C)Copyright International Business Machines Corp 1981, 1990
          (C)Copyright Microsoft Corp 1981-1986

C:\DOS>
```

Figure 3.4   The command prompt

Notice the prompt at the top of the screen states:

```
When ready to return to the DOS Shell, type EXIT then press enter.
```

You may use any DOS program commands from the prompt. When you are done, type **Exit** at the command prompt and press Enter. You return to the menu.

> ▶ **Tip:** The quick way to go to the command prompt is to press Shift with F9 on the screens where that option is presented at the bottom. When you select Exit and press Enter at the command prompt, you return to the screen you left before selecting the command prompt.

Changing Colors on Your Display

If you have a color display, you can change the colors that are used. Four options are available. Choose colors with contrasting foreground and background hues for easy reading in the light you are using.

To change colors, select IBM DOS from the System menu. Select Change Colors. Press the left or right arrow to see the selections. When the color combination you want appears, press Enter. Press Esc to leave the screen and keep the last color setting you were using before entering the Change Colors screen. You also can use the mouse to press the arrows on-screen and select ESC at the bottom of the screen.

Customizing How Your System Starts Up

Changing certain built-in selections concerning how your system starts up is easy. Any changes you make stay in place—even when the system is turned off—until you make further changes.

To change how the system starts up, select IBM DOS from the System menu. Select Customize How System Starts. You see the screen shown in Figure 3.5.

From this screen, you can control certain keyboard options, the location of the operating system, as well as the first screen, files, and disk locations. Each selection is described in this section.

The current selections are marked with a directional pointer. To change a selection, point to the selection with the mouse and click. Or use the up- and down-arrow keys to highlight the selection and press the space bar. Once you have made all your selections, press Enter. If you make some selections and then decide to go back to the original settings present when you entered the screen, simply press Esc.

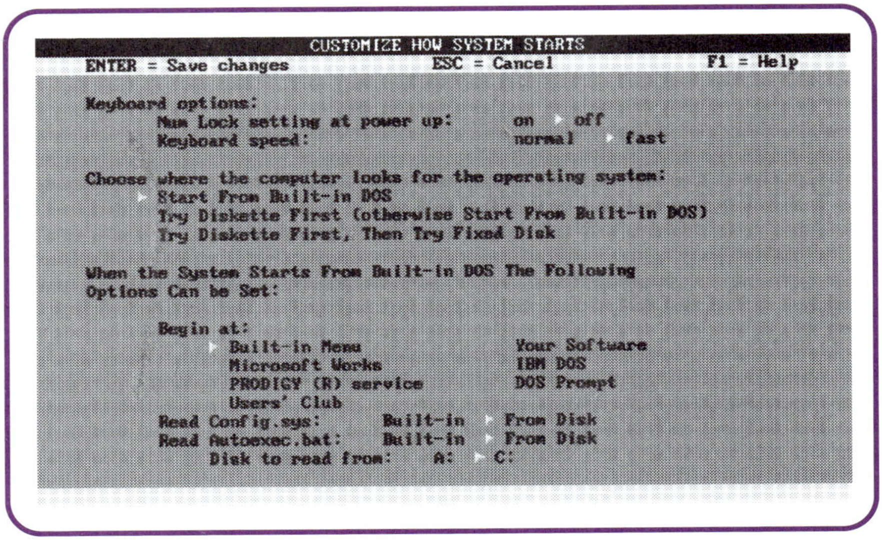

Chapter 3

Figure 3.5 Customize How System Starts screen

> ▶ **Tip:** To go back to the values first in place when you got the system, turn off the PS/1 and turn it on with both mouse buttons held down. Although this procedure sounds odd, it works.

Keyboard Options

The first set of options on the Customize How System Starts screen is the keyboard. You may set Num Lock on or off when the system comes up. If you usually use the numeric keypad at the right of your keyboard for numbers, set Num Lock on. If you usually use the bottom labels on the keys (arrow keys, etc.), set Num Lock off.

The keyboard speed can be normal or fast. The speed refers to how fast the system repeats a key when you hold it down. For example, if you want to use an arrow key to move across the text in a letter, you may want that arrow key to move your cursor as fast as possible. Using a system with a slow cursor is a little like sitting in rush hour traffic. You know where you want to go, but it's frustrating going. So, set the speed to fast.

Location of Operating System

When you boot your PS/1, it starts from the DOS built into the system which is called *Built-in DOS*. This DOS is not the copy of DOS on your fixed disk or diskette. You may want to have PS/1 first look for and use DOS on the diskette in drive A and, if there is not a diskette in drive A, then go to Built-in DOS. Or you may want to have the system check the diskette and then the fixed disk. These options are handy if you want to use some special DOS features when you start up.

First Screen, File, and Disk Reading

When you start from Built-in DOS, which is the last option discussed, the PS/1 is set up to start at the Built-in menu (the System menu). If you use another application most of the time, you may want to skip this menu and start somewhere else in the system. If you keep the Start From Built-in DOS option, you may choose to start at the first screen for any of these options: Microsoft Works, Prodigy service, Users' Club, the Your Software, IBM DOS, or the DOS Prompt.

You also have a *CONFIG.SYS* file and *AUTOEXEC.BAT* file built into your system in *ROM* (Read Only Memory versus on the disk or diskette). If you want to use another CONFIG.SYS file (some software requires other configuration settings) or a different AUTOEXEC.BAT file (to execute other DOS program commands when you turn on your machine) you can set the `From Disk` reading and then indicate the `Disk to read from:`. This way, you can change the contents of CONFIG.SYS or AUTOEXEC.BAT, a common requirement if you are using software other than that supplied with your PS/1.

Changing Your Hardware Configuration

Most, if not all, the new components you add to your system can be handled without changing the hardware configuration. These components include added memory, an additional diskette drive, a fixed disk, a mouse, an internal modem, as well as an audio card and joystick. The PS/1 is smart. It can sense what you have added to the system and make the necessary adjustments.

Chapter 3

> ▶ **Tip:** To change the contents of a built-in ROM CONFIG.SYS file, see the next section "Changing Your Hardware Configuration." To change the contents of the CONFIG.SYS file and/or AUTOEXEC.BAT file on the IBM DOS diskette or on your fixed disk, use Microsoft Works. Select Works, go into File, and select Open Existing File. In the File to Open field, type in the drive and path to the file you want. Press Enter. Word processor should be the file type shown in the pop-up. Save the file under a new name in case you want it again. Select File and then Save as.... In the Save File As: field, keep the drive and path information and type in the new name. Once the file is saved, edit the file and save it under the appropriate CONFIG.SYS or AUTOEXEC.BAT name; then exit Works. This command must be in your CONFIG.SYS file for the System menu to appear (assuming SHELLSTB.COM is in the root directory):
>
>   INSTALL=SHELLSTB.COM
>
> Restart the PS/1 to use the CONFIG.SYS file or AUTOEXEC.BAT file.

However, the PS/1 isn't so smart when it comes to removing hardware. If you detach hardware from your system, you may need to update the configuration by simply entering the Hardware Configuration screen or else you may experience error messages. You also can use this screen to change between serial and parallel port settings to accommodate other printers or modems.

To go to the Hardware Configuration screen, select IBM DOS from the System menu. From the DOS Main Group menu, select Change Hardware Configuration. The screen shown in Figure 3.6 appears.

The following settings are automatically sensed and updated by the PS/1:

- ▶ Installed Memory; lists the total amount of base and extended memory.
- ▶ Fixed Disk; distinguishes whether a fixed disk is installed.
- ▶ Diskette Drive A type and Diskette Drive B type; identifies the diskette size and the maximum capacity of the diskette drives installed.

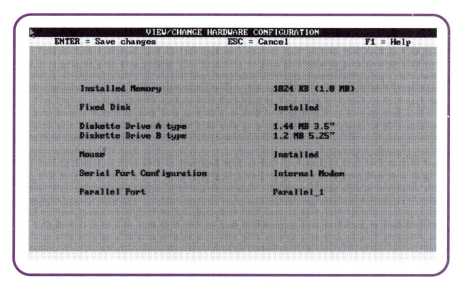

Figure 3.6 Change Hardware Configuration screen

- Mouse; recognizes whether or not a mouse is installed.
- Audio Card and Joystick; appear as installed on the screen only if they are present.

The following two settings are sensed by the PS/1, but you can override them. To change the settings, select the option with the up- or down-arrow key; then change to a new setting using the left- or right-arrow key. Or use a mouse to point and click on the option setting.

- Serial Port Configuration; the status may be Internal Modem, Disabled, or Serial 1. If there is an adapter card installed and it conflicts with the setting, the port is disabled.
- Parallel Port; the status may be Parallel 1, Parallel 2, Parallel 3, or Disabled. If the adapter card conflicts with the Parallel Port, the system goes ahead and changes the board address and sends you an error message. Check out this screen to accept or change the setting.

What You Have Learned

In this chapter you've learned

- ▶ You can use the most practical DOS program commands from the Main Group.
- ▶ You must format diskettes before they can be used with your system.
- ▶ Keeping backup copies of your work is important in case the original files are lost or damaged.
- ▶ When using diskettes in other computers or when copying from diskette to diskette, you must make certain the diskettes and drives are compatible.
- ▶ You can change colors, system startup, and hardware configuration settings.

Chapter 4
DOS—File Handling

In This Chapter

▶ *Organizing your file system*
▶ *Creating, rearranging, and deleting directories*
▶ *Identifying the location and contents of files*

Handling Your File System

Many of the DOS program commands in the Main Group covered in Chapter 3, "DOS—Using the Main Group," are related to files. The commands are pretty straightforward as long as you know which file to work with, what's in the file, what's on your disk, and where the file is located. But what if you don't know those details? Diskettes and disks are not like books. You can't just glance in a room and see how they are organized or physically open them up and peruse the contents. This is when the Main Group File System option becomes important. The File System enables you to see the contents of your disk, diskettes, and files. You also can see information about each and manipulate the contents and organization.

Chapter 4

To go to the File System screen, select IBM DOS from the System menu. From the Main Group menu, select File System. The File System screen like the one shown in Figure 4.1 appears.

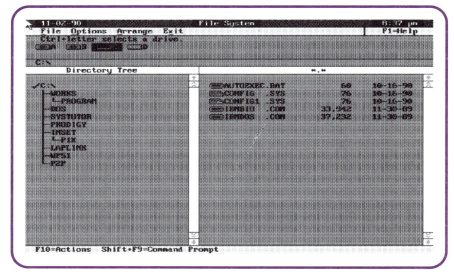

Figure 4.1 The File System screen

You have several options in moving around the File System screen. You can select items with the mouse by pointing and clicking. With the keyboard, press the Tab key to move from area to area and then use the arrow keys or Page Up and Page Down to move within an area. To select a drive, directory, or program, press Enter. To select a file, press space bar. The scroll bar (see Figure 4.2) appears in two places on the screen. Point and click the mouse button on the arrow to move a line up or down, on the double angles to move a page up or down, or in the center of the scroll bar for partial page moves.

Directory Tree

The *directory tree* consumes most of the left side of the screen. You can set up a directory with DOS to separate your software and files into areas on a disk. Therefore, all the files related to a given software package, like Microsoft Works, can be contained together. Further, all your files created with Works, such as letters and reports, can be in their own directory related to Works. Because there is so much space on a fixed disk, separating the disk into directories to store software and information files is necessary for better organization.

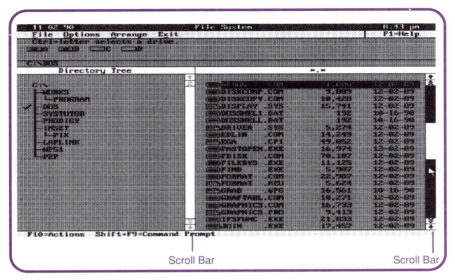

Figure 4.2 The scroll bar

The directory tree illustrates the organization of your disk. The *root* of the tree points to the drive designation; in the figure, C:\ is the root. All directories and subdirectories are connected to this root directory (see Figure 4.3).

The files on the root directory are shown on the right side of the screen (again, see Figure 4.3). This is called the *file list* area. The file name, extension, size in bytes (a byte is roughly a character), and the last date the file was opened appear. To see the files on any of the directories off the root, use the mouse to point and click on the directory, or use the up- or down-arrow key to highlight the directory and press Enter. The list of files on the right of the screen will be that directory's contents.

If the number of files or the directory tree is too large to fit in the area of the screen designated, use the mouse to point and click on the scroll bar on the right edge of each area of the screen. Or you can use the Tab key and arrow keys to see more files.

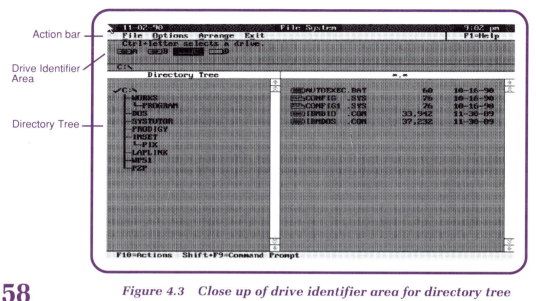

Figure 4.3   Close up of drive identifier area for directory tree

Drives and Directories

The upper left corner of the File System screen is the *drive identifier* area. You can see *icons* (illustrations) of drives. In Figure 4.3 a fixed disk (drive C) with both A and B diskette drives is installed. The D: drive designation is the ROM (Read Only Memory) location where Built-in DOS is stored. On systems without a fixed disk, this location is called drive C. The directory tree and list of files appear for the drive selected. You can look at the directory and files contained on other drives by pressing the Ctrl key with the letter of the drive.

Make sure a diskette is in the diskette drive. If one is not, a pop-up will appear informing you Drive not ready and asking you to press 1 to select Try to read this disk again or press 2 for Do not try to read disk again. Because the in-use light is not on after this warning comes up, you can put a diskette in the drive and press 1 or just stop the process by pressing 2.

The drive you have currently selected and are using is commonly called the *current directory*. The current directory is located on the screen below the drive identifier area and above the directory tree. If you are in one directory and want to use a file in another directory, type in the path of the file you want to locate. Include the root, each directory and subdirectory, and the file name in the path. For example, if you have a fixed disk with Works files in a Works directory and the Works program files as a subdirectory to the Works files, part of your directory tree will look like the following:

```
C:\
   Works
      Program
```

If you had a file called MEMOS.WPS in the Works file, the path to that file would appear as

```
C:\WORKS\MEMOS.WPS
```

The Program subdirectory is not included in the path because the Works documents you create are in the Works directory, not in the subdirectory with the Program files.

 Note: Only make the path from the root to the file you want to access and no further.

The Action Bar Selections

The *action bar* is in the upper left of the File System screen. The selections are File, Options, Arrange, and Exit.

Press the Tab key or F10 to get to the action bar area. Once there, press the underlined letter to get to the pull-down menu selections. Or you may point and click the mouse on a selection to see the pull-down menu rather than use the keyboard.

When you pull down a menu, the options in dark, bold print are those that are available for use. The light, wavy printed options are only available under certain circumstances. An ellipsis (...) after a selection indicates that there are more activities to follow on subsequent screens.

The selections available through the action bar sometimes require that you select files. For example, you may copy several files at once; however, you must first select the files and then perform the copy. To select files using the keyboard, use the Tab key to go to the file list area. Highlight a file name to select and press the space bar. The symbol near the file name is highlighted. To deselect the file, highlight the file name and press the space bar again. You can also use the Select All or Deselect All options on the pull-down menu to affect file selection. Or with the mouse, click on the file name to select or deselect.

Action Bar: File

The first action bar item is File. Following is a description of each option you may select.

Open (start): Files with .COM, .BAT, or .EXE extensions are executable, which means that they can run on their own. When you use Open, only a file with one of these extensions can be run successfully. When you select Open, you go to a screen which enables you to enter options which are DOS parameters to further define how the file operates. You can enter parameters or leave the area blank and press Enter to execute the file as is.

Print: The Print option enables you to print selected files. Before you print, you must enter this DOS program command either at the DOS command prompt (Ctrl-F9 to go there) or by selecting Print from the DOS folder in Your Software. Enter the Print command after the DOS command prompt (in this case C:\) as follows:

C:\print/d:prn

Once you have entered the command and pressed Enter, this message appears to let you know the print program is in memory and ready for use:

```
Resident part of PRINT installed
Print queue is empty
```

When you select Print on the File pull-down menu, the file selected is immediately sent to be printed.

Associate: You use this File option to *link* (or associate) the selected files—which are probably program files—to files with a certain extension. Then every time you select a file with that extension, the selected program file is started. When you enter the extensions, enter three letters and separate each extension with a space. You cannot associate an extension with more than one program file.

`Move`: The Move File option copies the selected files to the location you identify and then erases the original versions. Enter the path if necessary.

`Copy`: The Copy option copies the selected files to the location you've identified. The original file is left intact. If you are copying a file to a destination where the file already exists, you are asked whether you want to replace the file. Then you are asked to confirm the action if you have not turned off the confirmation option which is discussed later in this chapter.

`Delete`: This option erases the file or directory. The PS/1 gives you a pop-up and again enables you to choose to delete or not delete. This second step is for your protection. Make sure you do not need the file or directory before you delete it. Sometimes the PS/1 will stop you from deleting a directory or file all together. For example, you may try to delete a directory and see the message `Access denied`. Before you can delete a directory, all the contents, including subdirectories, must be deleted. If you see `Access denied` when you try to delete a file, the file is probably *read only* which means you cannot change or delete the file. Note for the DOS familiar: This Delete function resembles the DELETE, ERASE, and RMDIR (Remove Directory) DOS program commands. The PS/1 provides one stop for getting rid of things.

`Rename`: The Rename option lets you change the name of a file or directory. If you try to name a file or directory with a name already in use on the disk or diskette, a message such as `Access denied` will appear. Try again with a unique name.

`Change Attribute`: Files may have three attributes associated with them. A *Read Only* file means the file can be read but not changed or deleted. A *Hidden* file is not displayed when the DIR (Directory) DOS program command is used although it will appear on the Shell lists. An *Archive* attribute means the file will be backed up when the Backup command is used. To change attributes, select the attributes and a pointer will appear to the left of each attribute selected. To deselect an attribute, repeat the selection process.

`View`: The View option enables you to see the contents of a file. Press F9 to switch between *ASCII* display (text) and *Hex* display (numeric values for the computer to interpret the characters; used by programmers).

Create Directory: For the DOS familiar, this option is like the well known MKDIR (Make Directory) command. You can create a directory to contain new software or special files. For example, when you add new software to your system, create a directory and then copy the files into the directory. Or follow the installation procedures for the software which will result in the creation of a new directory.

The name of the new directory you type in will be used to create the new directory. It will be placed under (subordinate to) the directory you have selected on the directory tree. The directory will appear as a folder when you select Your Software from the System menu. A directory name can contain up to eight characters and may be followed by a period with an extension of up to three characters. The system will automatically stop you from using reserved characters and names. Give directories names to suggest their contents.

Select all: This option selects all the files in the current directory. This is handy to perform operations as a whole. For example, you may want to copy all the files in a directory or subdirectory to a diskette. Rather than marking each file, use Select all. Timesaver tip: If you want most but not all the files, use this option and then deselect the files you don't want by clicking on each one.

Deselect all: If you select all or some of the files in a directory and then change your mind, you may use Deselect all to start from scratch.

Action Bar: Options

The second action bar item is Options. A description of each selection follows.

Display Options: This selection enables you to control how the file list appears on the display. You can display certain files by entering a partial file name and using asterisks (*). When you use the asterisk, any number of characters or symbols may replace the asterisk position. For example, if you wanted to display only the files that start with P and end with the .WPS extension, you could enter

p*.wps

Files with the following names would appear because they start with P, end in .WPS, and have up to seven characters in between. Remember, the maximum file name is eight characters.

```
PCH3.WPS, PIPER.WPS, P.WPS
```

Files with the following names would not appear because one or more of the required characters is missing.

```
TIMESHT.WPS, PIPER.WPP, P
```

Using the asterisk is handy if you want to perform a function, such as copy or move, on a group of related files with similar names.

The Display Options selection also enables you to sort files by name, extension, date, size, or disk order. This helps you organize files to expedite functions. For example, you may want to clear some space off a disk by moving unnecessary files to a diskette. If you sort the files by size, you can identify which files will be the most significant to move to free space.

`File Options`: The File Options selection enables you to set or omit the step to confirm deletions or replacements. For example, when you identify a file for deletion, the system essentially asks "are you sure?" You have the chance to back out of the deletion and save the file. The same query is used for replacing files on copies. You are asked whether you want to replace an existing file with the new copy. If you feel these queries are more hassle than protection, omit the query. However, most users think the query is a good check and leave it alone.

The File Options selection also enables you to select files from more than one directory. That is, you can select a directory to display the files, select the files from that directory, select another directory, and then select files from that directory, and so on. To "X" or "de-X" the options you want, click the mouse on the option or highlight it with the arrow keys; then press the space bar. The Xs as you set them are only valid until you leave the Shell. When you reenter, they are set back to their original values. To select across directories at any time, see the System File List function described under the Arrange option.

Show Information: The Show Information option enables you to see information about the file highlighted last and its related directory. You see file information including the name of the file, its extension, if any, and the attributes which may be Read Only, Hidden, or Archive. (See Change Attribute under File options in this section for more detail.) The drive selected is shown along with the number and size of files selected. The name and size of the directory is indicated with the number of files in the directory. Finally, you see disk information including the volume label, capacity, and space still available, as well as the number of files and directories on the disk.

> **Caution:** If you have a fixed disk, one good practice is to periodically select the root directory and then select Options, Show Information to check the available space on the entire disk. The rule of thumb is: Don't let the available space drop below 20% or you may experience space problems that could lead to losing information. If you get close to a full disk, move some files or software to diskette storage.

Action Bar: Arrange

The third action bar item is Arrange. The selections in the Arrange option enable you to pick from three ways to display file lists. You may display

- ▶ A single file list for a single directory.
- ▶ Two file lists for two directories which may be on the same or different drives. A drive identifier area for each list appears for you to change drives. Change directories by selecting a new directory from the directory tree.
- ▶ The System file list for a list of all directories on the current drive. The file information shown is for the first file or the highlighted file if there is one.

► **Tip:** By choosing System file list under the Arrange item and then Display Options under the Options item, you can sort and select files across directories. The system file list includes all files on the system. Then you can sort by any criteria you enter as Display Options.

Figures 4.4, 4.5, and 4.6 show the file list for each of these three options.

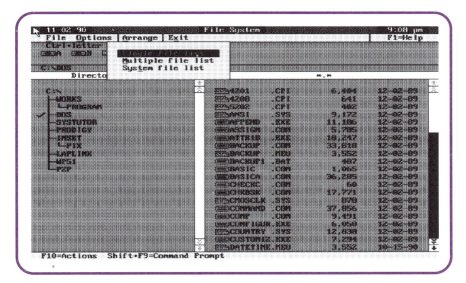

Figure 4.4   Single file list

Action Bar: Exit

The fourth action bar item is Exit. Select it to leave the File System option (DOS Main Group) or, if you made a mistake when you selected Exit File System, pick Resume File System to continue your work with the file system. As indicated in the upper right corner of the pull-down Exit menu, press F3 to Exit; this works even when Exit is not selected.

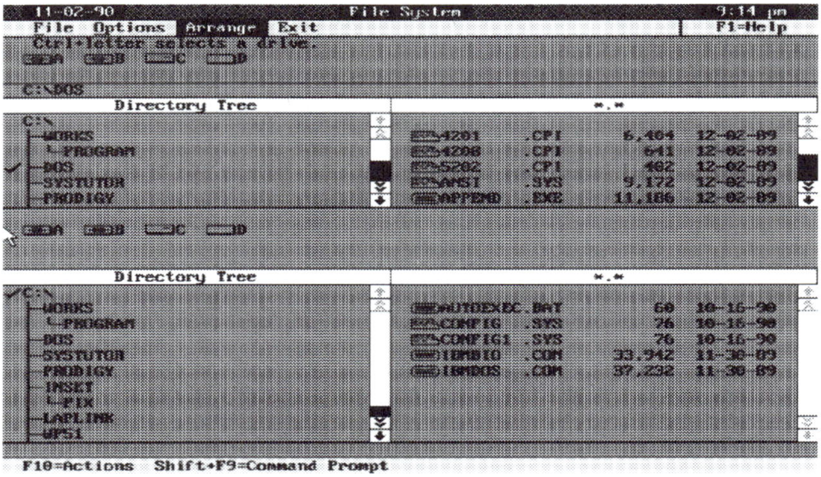

Chapter 4

Figure 4.5   Multiple file list

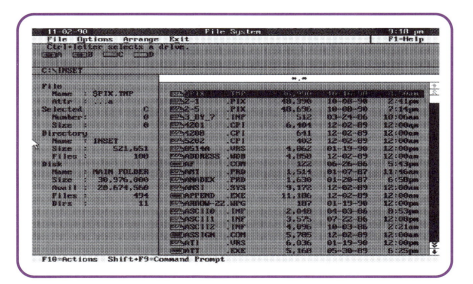

Figure 4.6   System file list

Creating a New Directory and Adding Files

If you have a system without a fixed disk, your "file organization" will primarily consist of controlling the contents of well labeled diskettes. However, if you want, you can create directories on diskettes. You can, therefore, group files into defined directories. As you read the instructions in this section, substitute the letter of the appropriate drive for C:\ and swap diskettes as necessary to accomplish the tasks described.

If you have a fixed disk, you should create new directories to hold your own programs and files. The earlier discussion in this chapter about the file system covered the functions needed to create a directory and place programs and files in the directory. In this section you learn the step-by-step process of combining those functions.

First, you must create the directory. Then you can copy files into the directory. To create the directory, start at the File System screen. Make sure the current directory shows the root directory for the fixed disk (C:\). If not, select this drive from the drive identifier area. In the directory tree, make sure the directory under which you want the new directory to appear is selected; a check mark should appear before the directory. For example, if you are adding a new software program, such as a tax package, you may want the directory for the program to appear off the fixed disk root directory. A check mark should be before the C:\, and the directory you create will sprout off C:\.

Once the location for the directory you create is identified, select File (look in the upper left corner of the File System screen) and then Create directory.... A pop-up appears asking you to enter a name for your new directory. Make the name as descriptive as possible and press Enter. The new directory is created and appears on your directory tree. (If the directory exists with other directories at the same level, it will be reordered to the end of the list once you select the drive again.) Congratulations are in order. However, your new directory is not useful until you copy files into the directory.

To copy files into the directory, place the diskette with the files in drive A. Then select drive A in the drive identifier area. The files you want should appear on the right of the screen. If you need to select a subdirectory on the diskette to see the correct files, do so

Chapter 4

now. Select each file you want to copy to the directory you have just created. The symbol to the left of each file name is highlighted after you select it.

When all files to copy to the new directory are identified, select `File` and then `Copy`. A pop-up appears listing all the file names to copy; these names may extend past the field entry area in the pop-up if there are several. Fill in the drive designation, path, and directory name which is the destination of the copy. For example, if you are copying the files from drive A to drive C into a subdirectory called DOCS which is subordinate to a directory called SOFTRITE, the drive and path would look like the following:

```
C:\SOFTRITE\DOCS
```

The drive designation is followed by a colon, a slash, the directory name which is linked to the root, a slash, and the new subdirectory name which is subordinate to the directory.

Press Enter when the path to copy the files through is complete. A pop-up appears as each file is copied. The message `n of n` appears which tells you the number of files (of all files) that are copied. When the copy is done, the pop-up disappears. If you want to check that the files were copied, select the drive and directory. The names of the files appear on the right of the screen.

After files are copied into the directory, you can access the directory and files through the Your Software option. A folder is created for each directory and the executable files are listed in its contents. See Chapter 5, "Changing the DOS Group and Your Software," for more information.

Creating a New Directory and Adding Files

1. If you have a fixed disk, select `IBM DOS` from the System menu.	The Main Group menu appears.
2. Select `File System`.	The File System screen appears.
3. Select the drive and directory under which the directory will be added.	A check mark appears before the directory on the directory tree.
4. Select `File`.	The File pull-down menu appears.

5. Select `Create directory....`   The Create Directory pop-up appears.

6. Type in the name of the new directory and press Enter.   The newly created directory appears on the directory tree.

7. Locate the files to copy into the directory. Place the diskette in the drive, select the drive letter, and go to any subdirectory on the directory tree as necessary.   The files to copy into the directory appear on the right of the screen.

8. Select the files to copy into the new directory by clicking on the file names.   The symbol to the left of each selected file is highlighted.

9. Select `File`.   The File pull-down menu appears.

10. Select `Copy`.   The Copy File pop-up appears.

11. Enter the drive, path, and new directory name, for example, **C:\SOFTRITE\DOCS**. Press Enter.   The files are copied into the directory.

☐

What You Have Learned

In this chapter you've learned to

▶ Control the files and directories by using the File System option.

▶ Add new software to your system by creating a new directory and then copying the files into that directory. Or follow the installation instructions of the software which will result in the creation of a new directory.

▶ Use the File Systems File command to affect the contents and existence of directories and files.

▶ Use the File System Options command to control functioning of certain file system functions.

▶ Use the File System Arrange command to control how the display of your files looks.

Chapter 5

Changing the DOS Group and Your Software

In This Chapter

▶ *Altering the Main Group functions*
▶ *Using the Your Software option on the System menu*
▶ *Finding out about other DOS commands*
▶ *Interpreting DOS error messages*

Changing the Main Group

Although the "typically most used" DOS program commands and program functions are included in the Main Group, you may want to change the program commands and functions in the Main Group to meet your special needs. Usually this change is a question of adding DOS program commands or other programs; however, you can delete or reorganize the order of the information as well.

What DOS program commands or other programs might you add and why? You can add any program you want to start from the Main Group menu. For example, you can add programs for investments or games. Putting the program on the Main Group menu enables you to start up the program with a click of the mouse or a press of a key. The alternative for starting a program is to go through the Your Software option on the System menu. You also can start a program by double-clicking the mouse on the program in the File System option under the IBM DOS selection. The Main Group menu is also a good place to put DOS program commands for execution. Check out the quick reference list of DOS program commands later in this chapter for inspiration. You can add new program commands that are not covered in the Main Group or add variations on existing ones.

> **Note:** When you add or delete Main Group options, you are not affecting directories or the files in directories. You are simply adding or deleting the descriptive name for the option, the associated execution instructions, and related information. How to control directories and files is covered in Chapter 4, "DOS—File Handling," in the "Handling Your File System" section.

When you first select IBM DOS from the System menu, you go to the Main Group menu. The *action bar* (Figure 5.1) on this menu is your gateway to changing the Main Group. You can select Program, Group, or Exit. The Program option enables you to add Main Group entries that will execute a single program. The Group option enables you to add a single title which will lead to another screen of selections for single programs under the group. And the Exit option enables you to leave the screen.

> **Tip:** To use the action bar, press F10, the arrow keys, and press Enter on a selection. Or just click on an option with the mouse. A pull-down menu appears. Options on the pull-down menu that are available are in bold print. Those that appear in faded print are available with other selections. To leave a pull-down menu, press Esc.

Changing the DOS Group and Your Software

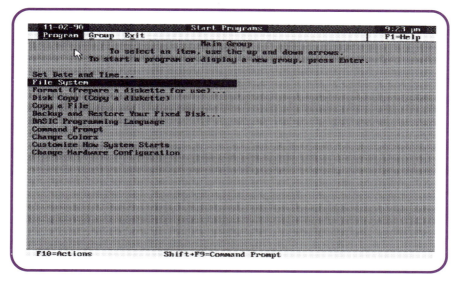

Figure 5.1   Main Group action bar

Add Program

The Program pull-down menu is used to control a single Main Group entry which may execute a single or multiple programs. These may be DOS command programs or other programs. To add options for a group of programs which lead to a menu of several entries to select among, see the "Add Group" section.

Select Start on the Program pull-down menu, and you start the selection that is highlighted in the group, such as Set Date and Time....

> **Caution:** If you have a one drive system with no fixed disk, make sure you have the diskette for the program in the diskette drive when you start a program. Otherwise, you get a Bad command or File Name message, and you'll have to begin again.

To add a single program entry, select Add from the Program pull-down menu. As with any entry on the Main Group screen, this can be a DOS program command or any program. When you select Add, a pop-up appears (see Figure 5.2).

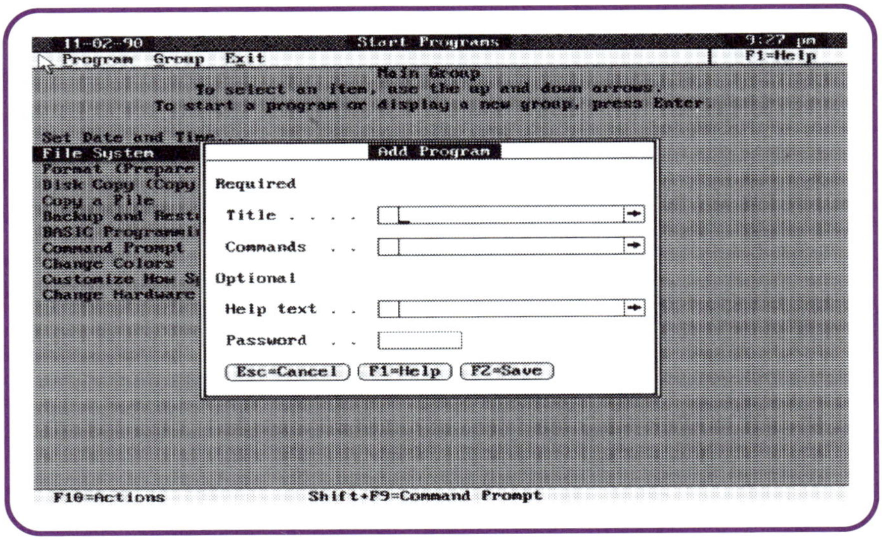

Chapter 5

Figure 5.2   Add Program pop-up

Title

On the Add Program pop-up, you must type in the title of the program selection. Make the title as descriptive as possible and enter anything that will help you identify the option. The title may be up to 40 characters (including spaces).

Commands

Next, in the Commands area, enter the program startup command for that specific program. See the documentation for the software to identify the correct program startup command or, for DOS, use the actual DOS program command described later in this chapter. You may need to enter the drive, path, and command in this special way. Type in the letter designation of the drive where the program resides followed by a colon. Then press F4. A special bar appears. Enter the letters **CD** (for Change Directory), a space, and the full path (starting with the drive designation) to the directory with programs. Then press F4 again for the special bar. Finally, type in the program startup command. For example:

C:|CD C:\SOFTRITE\DOCS|SR

To execute several programs in order if there is more than one command, press the F4 key between each command. You can enter up to 500 characters in the Commands area.

Batch files may be used as program startup commands. Put the CALL command before the batch file name followed by the .BAT extension. For example, on the Add Program pop-up screen, you could type this text in the command entry field:

Commands . . [CALL BATCH1.BAT   ]

In the command area, you can enter prompt options to get pop-up prompts each time the program selection is made. This is like designing your own pop-up with the PS/1 providing the framework. The prompt options enable you to control the text on the pop-up, the length of the area you may type in text (called the *entry field*), and other characteristics. You can use one or more of the prompt options which follow. Type in the brackets, slashes, quotation marks, letters, and/or symbols as shown. The text you type between the quotation marks—replacing the two dots (..) shown—appears on the screen. Substitute a number for the letter n shown. If you are stringing several prompt options together, you need only enter one set of brackets enclosing all prompt options.

[ ]	To get the default pop-up prompt. It enables you to enter parameters to the command to further define the command. Following is the text on the pop-up: Program Parameters Type the parameters, then press Enter. Parameters... [->
[/T".."]	To enter a title for the pop-up prompt.
[/I".."]	To identify an instruction at the top of the pop-up prompt.
[/P".."]	To identify the word(s) before the entry field in the pop-up prompt.
[%n]	To save any value in the Parameters field with the assigned n equaling any number 1 through 10.
%n	To save the value entered to use in the next program startup command. For example, the value n in [%n] can be used within another command by entering the same n value in %n.
[/D".."]	The default value that will appear every time in the entry field (which can be typed over when you use the pop-up prompt).
[/D"%n"]	A default value appears in the entry field with %n substituted by the value saved with [%n] described earlier.

Chapter 5

[/R]	To clear the default value in the entry field when any key other than a key for editing is pressed.
[/L"n"]	To make the maximum length of the entry field less than 127 characters.
[/M"e"]	To make sure the file name entered from the keyboard is valid before continuing.
[/C"%n"]	To use the value in a preceding task, if any, as the value in the current task.
[/F".."]	To identify whether the file exists in the path specified. Enter the path and file name for the two periods (..) between the brackets.
/#	To put the drive letter and colon from which the Shell was started into the program startup code.
/@	To put the root and path from where the Shell was started into the program startup code.

> ▶ **Tip:** Press F4 for the special bar and then enter PAUSE at the end of each command so that you can see any DOS error messages that may appear before you go back to your screen. The system will display the following prompt which allows you time to view any messages:
>
> ```
> Press any key to continue . . .
> ```

> ▶ **Tip:** Typing **ECHO** and then a message enables you to add any message you think is appropriate for your program. For example, ECHO may be the first entry in the command area followed by the message—not in quotation marks. Then press F4 for the special bar, enter PAUSE, press F4 for the special bar, and enter the program startup code.

Help Text

Entering help text is optional. The text you enter appears when you press F1 with the program line highlighted on the Main Group menu. Useful help text includes a description of what selecting the line will do along with reminders of other functions to perform, such as putting a diskette in the drive.

> **Tip:** A good way to see the prompt options in action is to learn from existing options. Select an existing Main Group option, select Program and then Change, and view how the prompt options are set up. For example, the Disk Copy (Copy a Diskette) option on the Main Group has the following text in the command line. Notice the use of the brackets.
>
> ```
> diskcopy [/t"Disk Copy (Copy a diskette)"/i"Enter source
> and target drives"/p"Drives . ."/d"a: a:"/l"5"]|pause
> ```
>
> The command line means: The program startup command (the DOS DISKCOPY command) should be executed. The title (/T) of the pop-up is
>
> ```
> Disk Copy (Copy a diskette)
> ```
>
> The instruction (/I) for the pop-up is
>
> ```
> Enter source and target drives
> ```
>
> The prompt (/P) for the entry field is
>
> ```
> Drives . .
> ```
>
> The default (/D) value that appears and can be changed is
>
> ```
> a: a:
> ```
>
> The maximum length (/L) of the entry field is five characters. Setting this maximum length limits the possibility that you will enter incorrect values. The special bar created with F4 follows the options. Finally, the PAUSE command appears for you to be able to read any DOS messages which may appear if there is a problem.

Password

Entering a password is also optional. Use a password only when you have sensitive information you want to protect. You or a particular group which requires access to the program selection can use the password. Type in a password up to eight characters. Don't be obvious, for example, using your pet's name, your name, or the name of a relative.

Chapter 5

> ⊘ **Caution:** Don't forget or lose the password. Write down the password and store it in a safe place. Every time you want to make the selection you are adding, you must type the password. If you forget the password, you cannot change anything about the program selection. If you decide later to remove the password requirement, use the Main Group Program Change option to delete the password.

Once you have made all the entries on the Add Program pop-up, press F2 to save. Then take a moment to test the program selection. If the program does not execute as you anticipated, use the Program Change option to check and edit your entries.

Using Add Program

1. Select `IBM DOS` from the System menu.	The Main Group screen appears.
2. Select `Program` from the Start Programs screen.	The pull-down menu appears.
3. Select `Add....`	The Add Program pop-up appears.
4. Type in the title of the program selection (up to 40 characters).	The title appears.
5. In the command area, enter the drive designation; press F4, enter CD, a space, and the path; press F4; enter the program startup command.	The drive, path, and startup command are entered.
6. If desired, enter help text.	The help text is complete.
7. If desired, enter a password.	The password is complete.
8. Press F2 to save the program selection.	The program selection appears on the Main Group menu. □

Program Change, Delete, and Copy

To change a program selection, highlight that program selection. You cannot, however, change several of the Main Group selections that come with the system. Once you have highlighted the change, select `Program` and then `Change`. The Change Program pop-up appears. You can change the title, commands, help text, or password. (See the description of the Add Program pop-up earlier in this chapter for details on the conventions to follow for each entry.) Press F2 to save your changes. If you make changes and then have second thoughts before pressing F2, simply press Esc to cancel the entries and return to the original settings.

To delete a program selection, highlight it and choose `Program` and then `Delete`. Continue with the prompts if they are presented to delete the program selection.

You can copy a program selection to the Main Group or a subgroup of the Main Group. Copying a program selection is a quick way to create a program selection similar to an existing selection. Instead of starting from scratch, you can copy the program selection and then change it. Using this copy function is also good if you want to change an existing program selection and test it before deleting the original program selection. That way, if you make a mistake, you can always go back to the old program selection.

To copy a program selection, highlight that program selection. On the action bar, select `Program`. From the pull-down menu, select `Copy`. This type of message appears:

```
To complete the copy, display the destination group,
then press F2. Press F3 to cancel the copy.
```

Go to the group or subgroup to copy the program selection to. The program selection will be automatically added to the screen that appears—not within the highlighted selection on the screen. Once the screen for the Main Group or subgroup appears, press F2. The program selection is added to the Main Group or subgroup.

Add Group

The Group pull-down menu enables you to add, change, or delete groups of program selections. This allows you to control program selections from the Main Group that lead to subordinate groups. You also can change the order of the program selections in a group using the Group pull-down menu.

To add a group with subordinate program selections, select `Group` and then `Add` from the Main Group screen. The Add Group pop-up contains the following field entries.

Title: Enter the title of the group program selection. Make the title as descriptive as possible up to 37 characters. The ellipsis (...) is added automatically, showing that the program selection leads to a group of other program selections.

Filename: Enter the file name (up to eight characters) where you will keep the information for the group. You must make an entry here. However, you can enter any file name whether the file exists or not. The group program selection will be created, and you can choose the group program selection and go to the next level to add subordinate program selections. This process is like adding any program selection (select Program and then Add).

Information in a file should follow the conventions for commands—like those identified for completing the Commands option when you use Add Program. To see an example of the contents of a file, select any group program selection, identify the file name, and then view the contents of that file through the File System, File, View option. For example, the Set Date and Time... group program selection uses the file named DATETIME. When you go through the File System program selection on the Main Group, select DATETIME.MEU, select File, and then select View. You can see the contents of the file containing the information used in the help window, the program selection options for the subgroup, the program startup commands, and the prompts for executing the option.

> ▶ **Tip:** As a beginner, you may find adding subordinate program selections with the Program Add option on the Main Group screen easier than creating a file for execution. See "Add Program" in this chapter for more information. You also can copy program selections from one group to another and then keep them as is or edit them for use. See "Program Change, Delete, and Copy" in this chapter for more information.

Help text: Entering help text is optional. The text you enter will appear when you press F1 and the program line is highlighted on the Main Group menu. Enter up to 478 characters.

Password: Entering a password is also optional. Passwords are easy to forget or misplace. Only use a password if the function is highly sensitive. Type in a password up to eight characters. Write down the password and keep in a secure place. You can omit the password at a later date by changing the group (using the password to get into the Change Group pop-up) and deleting the Characters Password field.

> **Caution:** Passwords appear when you type them in or when you access a Change pop-up. When you enter passwords, make sure no one is standing nearby to see the password.

After you have made all the entries on the Add Group pop-up, press F2.

Group Change, Delete, and Reorder

To change a group program selection, highlight the group program selection. You are, however, prohibited from changing several of the Main Group selections. After highlighting the selection to change, select Group and then Change. The Change Group pop-up appears. Feel free to change the title, file name, help text, or password. (See the description of the Add Group pop-up earlier in this chapter for more detail.) Press F2 to save your changes. If you change some fields and then change your mind about your changes, you can press Esc to cancel the entries and return to the original settings.

To delete a group, select the group and choose Group and then Delete. Respond to any prompts which appear until the group program selection is deleted.

> **Caution:** If you delete a group program selection, all the program selections under the group are deleted. You aren't given any are you sure? message. Make certain that you copy any program selections you want to keep from the group to other groups before deleting the group program selection.

You can reorder any program selection in a given group on a single screen. You accomplish this by moving program selections one at a time. To reorder a program selection, highlight the program selection to move. Pick `Group` and then `Reorder`. The following message appears:

```
To complete the reorder, highlight the new position,
then press Enter. Press Esc to cancel.
```

Highlight the program selection that the move should go above. Then press Enter. The program selection is moved above the last program selection highlighted.

Exit

The Exit option in the action bar gives you the options of exiting the DOS Shell or, if you accidentally got this menu by mistake, resuming what you were doing earlier. As is shown on the pull-down menu for Exit, you can press F3 any time to exit the DOS Shell.

Your Software

So far this book has covered how to use DOS program commands and other programs through the System menu (`IBM DOS` selection) or by pressing Shift+F9, when available, to go to the DOS command prompt. Another way to use DOS program commands and other programs is through the Your Software option on the System menu.

From the System menu, select `Your Software`. You go to the screen like that shown in Figure 5.3.

A folder appears for each directory on your system, such as DOS. If you add directories containing the files for other software programs, each directory appears on this screen as a folder. You may select any folder on this screen. You go inside the folder (see Figure 5.4) where each program is displayed.

Changing the DOS Group and Your Software

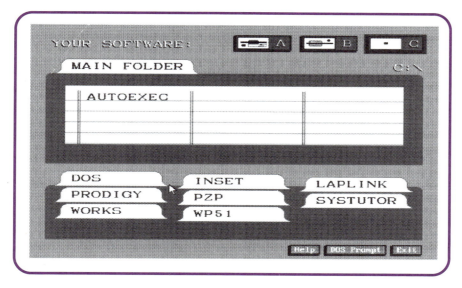

Figure 5.3   Your Software screen

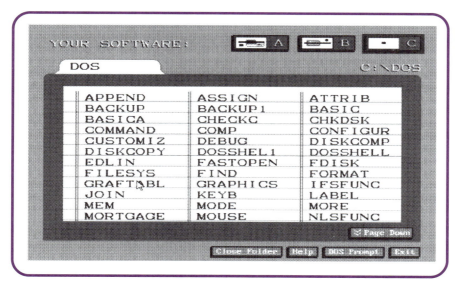

Figure 5.4   Inside the DOS folder

You can select any program to start. You go to a screen like that shown in Figure 5.5 where you may start the program by selecting Start or add options before selecting Start. Press Page Up or Page Down to see programs in the folder that don't appear on this screen.

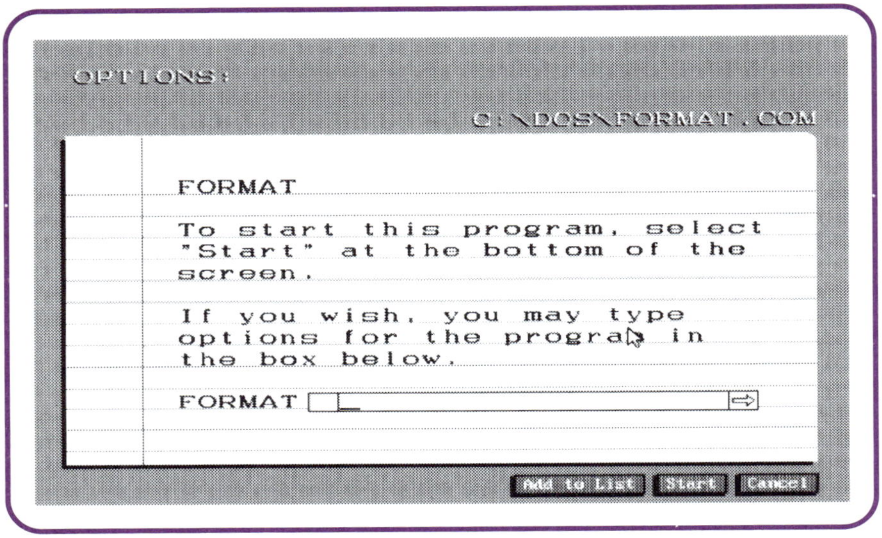

Figure 5.5   Starting a program

Your Software is the quick route to the commands and programs listed in your DOS folder as well as to programs you may add to your system.

The DOS Folder in Your Software

The typical DOS functions 99% of users need are included in the DOS Main Group. As a result, you may never need to use the DOS commands in the DOS folder.

If you are familiar with DOS, you may notice that not every DOS program command which exists appears in the DOS folder. Some commands that are handled through the IBM DOS Main Group option are not included, such as COPY. Others that are used in the IBM DOS Main Group are also here, such as FORMAT.

If you want more information about these DOS commands, you may secure a publication from IBM describing these commands (see your *PS/1 User's Reference*, "Related Publications" for more information) or purchase a book on DOS from your local bookstore. Most introductory books identify the possible parameters you can add to DOS commands to make them operate specific to a particular need you may have.

Before purchasing additional publications, make sure you know the version of DOS you are using and purchase a publication for that version. You can see the version number by pressing Shift+F9 from an IBM DOS screen. Jot down the version number. To return to your screen, type **Exit** and then press Enter.

DOS Error Messages

DOS sends a variety of messages to alert you to problems that might exist. Following is a list of some of the more common messages and their resolution. Many of the messages will ask you whether you want to

```
Abort, Retry, or Fail?
```

Enter **A** to abort (escape) the process, **R** to retry the process, or **F** to fail and return the error to the application program.

▶ Error codes when you start up the PS/1: There are a variety of messages that may appear when you turn on your PS/1. Watching your machine start up is a good way to pay attention to the health of your machine. If there are problems, turn off the machine, wait five or more seconds, check all connectors and add-ons (as applicable to the message), and then turn the machine back on. If the message is `163 Set Date and Time`, set the date and time through IBM DOS. If another message appears and you cannot easily correct the problem, you may have a failing system unit or other serious problem. Contact your authorized service center or call IBM at 800-765-4747.

▶ `Access denied`: You may have tried to write to a file that can only be read. Try another file.

▶ `Out of memory`: Your operating system uses memory as do some DOS commands such as PRINT or GRAPHICS. Going to the DOS prompt from Microsoft Works requires more memory than going there by selecting `Your Software` or `IBM DOS`. If you have an out of memory problem, you can exit the system and turn it off to clear memory. If this does not solve the problem, check to see what programs may be automatically loading when you start up (see your AUTOEXEC.BAT and CONFIG.SYS files). Delete any programs that are not necessary. If the problem persists, add more memory to your system or use software that takes up less memory.

▶ `Insufficient disk space`: The diskette or disk doesn't have enough space to store your file. Save the file to another diskette. Make sure to keep formatted diskettes around for this use. Caution: If the fixed disk is low on space, move files from the disk to create an at least 20% *space vacancy rate*.

▶ `Not ready`: Not Ready messages usually apply to diskette drives but can apply to most hardware options. If you retry, make sure there is a diskette in the drive, that the diskette is inserted appropriately, and that the diskette is formatted. Sometimes diskettes aren't seated properly. Reseat the diskette by removing it and inserting it again. Test out the drive by using a diskette you know is good. If the `Not Ready` message involves the letters PRN, check out your printer. Make sure it is turned on, is on-line, is available, and has paper.

▶ `Invalid` anything: This message may proclaim: `invalid device, invalid directory, invalid path, invalid parameter,` or `invalid drive` or `file name`. Check the entry to make sure you have typed in the correct information and that the entity you say exists does exist in the location specified.

▶ `File not found`: The process you were using involved looking for a file. This message tells you one of several conditions: 1) the file doesn't exist; 2) you entered a typographical error, hence an incorrect file name; 3) the file is on a different drive or directory and you failed to enter the path or a correct path; or 4) the file is hidden and cannot be found. Check your work and try again.

▶ `Bad command or file name`: The command cannot be recognized by the system. Check that you have spelled the command correctly and that you are in the drive or directory where the command or file exists.

▶ `Insert diskette with batch file`: The system is looking for the diskette with the batch file from whence you came. Insert the diskette which loaded the software back in the drive and try again.

▶ `Program too big to fit in memory`: The file with the external command program is too big to fit into the available memory. Reduce the use of your memory or reduce the number in the FILES or BUFFERS command in CONFIG.SYS. You also may want to try the old standby—turn off the machine and turn it back on to clear memory.

What You Have Learned

In this chapter you have learned

▶ You can change the Main Group by adding, changing, deleting, copying, and reordering program selections or groups.

▶ A variety of useful DOS program commands and other programs are available through the DOS folder in Your Software.

▶ Error messages give you clues about what to do to perform the function desired.

Chapter 6
Using Information (Especially Prodigy)

In This Chapter

- *Options available through Information*
- *Using tutorials for the PS/1 and Microsoft Works*
- *Using on-line services*
- *Starting up Prodigy*
- *Getting around in Prodigy*

Investigating Information

The PS/1 welcomes you to the information age by putting an abundance of information literally at your fingertips. Therefore, the first selection on the PS/1 System menu is Information.

Select Information and you see these broad categories—several of which are simply the tip of an iceberg:

- Users' Club which you reach through the modem telephone connection. This option enables you to learn about your PS/1 and communicate with other PS/1 users. The Users' Club is available through the Prodigy information service.

▶ The Prodigy information service (reached through your modem and telephone connection). Selecting `Prodigy` is your entrance to a wide variety of services for shopping, playing games, making travel reservations, talking to other users, and the list goes on and on. How to initially sign onto Prodigy is covered in this chapter. For information about the wealth of services Prodigy has to offer, see Chapter 7, "Prodigy Services (Users' Club and Others)."

▶ System Tutorial and Works Tutorial (software programs which are part of your PS/1—no modem or phone connection required). Both tutorials are free lessons in how to use your PS/1 and the powerful Microsoft Works. There is more information on these programs later in this chapter.

Another popular service comes with your PS/1. It is called Promenade. Consult Chapter 14, "Promenade," for details on this education, information, and entertainment service you can reach with your modem and telephone connection.

Free Class: System Tutorial

Learn to use your PS/1 while using your PS/1. Sound weird? Select `Information` from the System menu and then `System Tutorial`. Choose topics from the menu that appears:

```
Introduction
Hardware
Software System Care
```

Or select `Index` and pick the topics that most interest you from the over 60 presented.

When you are ready to leave the System Tutorial, press the Escape key to go back to a previous menu or simply press F10 to exit to the System menu.

Free Class: Works Tutorial

The Microsoft Works Tutorial gives you a "bookmark." That is, you can identify the lessons you have completed by entering your name on the first screen. Once you've entered your name, these options appear:

```
Works Essentials
Word Processing
Spreadsheets & Charts
Databases & Reports
Communications
Using Tools Together
```

Each topic has a submenu so that you can hone in more specifically to your area of interest. Press a key on the keyboard (no mouse) to pick the topics that most interest you, or start at `Works Essentials` and do it all. You can go back to the main menu any time by pressing Ctrl+M when that prompt appears. Press Q to quit when that prompt appears.

> ▶ **Tip:** You can use this tutorial from within Microsoft Works. Get to the Works Tutorial from within Works with these steps:
>
> 1. Select the Help pull-down menu.
> 2. Select `Works Tutorial` from the Help pull-down menu.
> 3. Enter your name and continue to use the Works tutorial as desired.
> 4. When done, exit the tutorial with Q. You return to Works.

Notes on Using On-line Services

The word for using services through your modem and phone line is *on-line*. It means your computer is communicating over a line to

Chapter 6

another computer where the service software is located. Basically, you are using the software on the other computer, and the two computers talk to each other according to your instructions.

To benefit from the Users' Club, Prodigy, Promenade, or any other on-line service, your modem connection on the back of the PS/1 must be attached to a telephone jack (see Chapter 2, "Get Set" for more information about your modem and connections). You also need an ID and password to get into the services. These are supplied with the information about the service you will use. Finally, you need to identify the access phone number for the computer to dial up. These numbers must be supplied by Prodigy (for the Users' Club and Prodigy), Promenade, or the service you plan to use.

With the services that come with your PS/1, you'll have some *free time* as a new user. Then you are billed according to the product agreement. If you have questions about the charges involved, check out the fees on the service itself or call the on-line service information number. Also, if there are telephone line charges, such as long distance, you are responsible for those charges.

When you connect with another computer over the phone lines, it is important that the telephone line connection not be interrupted or corrupted. The most common ways to lose your telephone connection, once established, are 1) someone picks up a telephone on the same line, 2) the connection is interrupted with an incoming call allowed through call waiting, or 3) there is simply a bad connection like you occasionally get with any phone call.

To ensure a continuous, clean connection, don't pick up the telephone on the same line your computer is using. If you share the line with others at your home or office, make sure they know when you are on the computer using the phone line. It's easy to forget, so, if necessary, put a sticky note on each phone saying "Don't use ... computer on-line." That way, they may reach for the phone, but they'll think twice before picking it up.

Call waiting is the service which allows you to answer a second call while you're already on the line. It's good for people but bad for computers. It can mess up the signal going to and from your computer. If you have call waiting, you should disable it temporarily before completing the call with your computer to the on-line service. The way to do this with most call waiting services is to press *70 before making a call on a touch-tone service or 1170 on a rotary dial service. After the call is completed, call waiting is automatically activated again without any action on your part. However, your call

Using Information (Especially Prodigy)

waiting service may be different. Consult the directory supplied by your telephone company for more information. As you'll see later, when you make the on-line connection, the computer actually dials the phone number to connect with another computer for you by sending the appropriate signals. So when you type in the phone number to call for the on-line service, you can precede it with the symbols and/or numbers to disable call waiting, followed by a comma (,) to pause before the actual on-line service is called.

The remedy for a bad connection is the same as with a bad phone connection: hang up and try again. With the computer, simply go off line by leaving the on-line service. Then try connecting again.

Signing On and Off Prodigy

Signing on to Prodigy for the first time takes a while. After you are enrolled, you can shortcut the process.

Keyboard and Screen Tips

As of this printing, mouse support is not available with the PS/1 Prodigy version. Mouse support is available with version 3 and higher of Prodigy. Try your mouse to see if you can use it to make selections. Otherwise, use the keyboard.

When you enter information, simply use the keyboard as you normally would. You can enter capital or small letters. The case doesn't matter for the ID or password. Use the following keys in Prodigy.

Tab	To move consecutively from option to option.
Shift-Tab	To move consecutively backwards from option to option.
↑, ↓, ←, →	To move in any given direction allowed.
Delete	To delete the character under your cursor.
Backspace	To delete characters to the immediate left of your cursor.

Chapter 6

Insert	To toggle the Insert symbol (^) on the top right of the screen. When it appears, you can insert among existing characters; when it is gone, you can type over existing characters.
Home	To jump to the top of the screen.
End	To jump to the end of the screen.
Enter	To process the selection that is blinking or keyboard entry.
Esc	To close an open window.

 Tip: The Print Screen key does not work in Prodigy. You can only use Print if it shows up as an option on a screen.

In Prodigy, you can make menu selections by pressing the appropriate number or > symbol. Throughout Prodigy, you can make selections suggested at the bottom of the screen. Select the option, or type in the first letter of the option. See the section on "Prodigy Commands" later in this chapter for details. For now, just remember that HELP gives you a description of what you are doing and EXIT takes you out of Prodigy.

 Tip: When a pop-up window appears, you may need to select OK or press the Escape (Esc) key to continue.

Signing on to Prodigy—First Time

To sign on to Prodigy for the first time, make sure you have

- ▶ The Prodigy ID and password supplied with your PS/1.
- ▶ The Prodigy service phone number appropriate for your area along with the network designation for that phone number; look in the Prodigy-supplied Phone Book.

If you have trouble finding any of this information, call 1-800-284-5933 for help from Prodigy.

If you are using a fixed disk system, select Information from the System menu and then select the Users' Club or Prodigy. If you have a system with no fixed disk, place your working copy of the IBM Users' Club and Prodigy service diskette in the diskette drive and then select Information.

Whether you select the Users' Club or Prodigy, you see a screen with the Prodigy Services Company copyright notice asking you to wait while the Prodigy software on your computer is loaded.

When you sign on for the first time, Prodigy asks you to provide some information. You are asked to select Tone or Pulse for your type of phone system. If you have push button phones, select Tone, or if you have older fashioned rotary dial phones, select Pulse. If you are uncertain, Pulse will work or call your phone company for the information. The type of phone service currently selected is marked with an arrow (=>) before it. Mark the correct type of phone service so that it blinks; then press Enter. Even if the correct information appears, don't select EXIT. This will knock you out of Prodigy entirely and back to the PS/1 System menu.

On a separate screen, Prodigy asks you to identify the network for the appropriate Prodigy phone number for your area. Use the Prodigy Phone Book to find the phone number for the city closest to you—a local number rather than long distance, hopefully. The network symbol is on the far right column. Enter the network symbol in the box and press Enter. Again, don't exit or you'll leave Prodigy.

A screen appears for you to enter the phone number for the Prodigy service. This is the phone number shown in the Prodigy Phone Book. As discussed earlier in "Notes on Using On-line Services," if you have call waiting, enter the symbols and/or numbers to disable it, a comma to pause, and then the phone number. You don't have to enter the area code if the call is local. If you must dial one or more numbers to get an outside line—9 with many office phone systems—or a long distance line, enter those numbers as well. For example, enter the following line to disable call waiting, pause, dial 9 for an outside line, pause, and call the local Phoenix-based Prodigy service:

*70,9,9551400

The PS/1 now has all the information about your phone system necessary to make the phone connection. Next, it needs to know who YOU are through the Sign-on menu.

Chapter 6

Select 1 Sign on the service. Prodigy asks for your ID and the password supplied by Prodigy. Type in your ID, press the Tab key to go to the next input field, and type in your password. Do this carefully. Your ID and password must be exact.

Next, Prodigy asks you to enter a new, secret password between 4 and 10 characters in length. You can use letters and/or numbers. Don't use spaces or punctuation. Be careful when you enter the password so that you don't accidentally enter a typographical error. Write down your password and keep it in a secure place. Asterisks may appear when you enter your password. This is to keep the password secure in case someone else is looking over your shoulder.

> **Caution:** Always guard the passwords you use with any on-line service. If anyone finds your ID and secret password, he can access the service and you'll be handed the bill. This can be particularly expensive if long distance calls are involved or if you are enrolled in services that are authorized to use your credit card. You may want to periodically change your password for security. You can use the JUMP command, described later in this chapter, and then select change pw to change your password. If you lose your password, you must call the Prodigy Member Services group. They will verify your membership and mail your password. For your security, the group will not give your password over the phone.

As you complete enrollment, Prodigy asks you for information about yourself including your address, age, and sex. Not all the information is required. You also will be able to sign up other household members (up to six people) to use the service. Each household member will get an ID—write them down when Prodigy gives them to you—and will need to sign on with the supplied password and then create his own password. Each household member gets his own electronic mailbox for personal messages.

After you have entered all the required information, the Prodigy software on your computer dials the phone number and attempts to make the connection with the Prodigy service's computer. Assuming the volume on your PS/1 is turned up, you hear the dialing, ringing, and connection just like the sounds when you make a regular phone call.

Using Information (Especially Prodigy)

> ▶ **Note:** If you have any trouble signing on to Prodigy, go back to the System menu and begin again. If you repeat the steps several times with no success, you may have a problem with your ID or password. Usually a message will inform you of this fact. If this may be the case, call Prodigy for a new ID and password. After you are on-line with the Prodigy service, you go to the Highlights screen for Prodigy (see Figure 6.1).

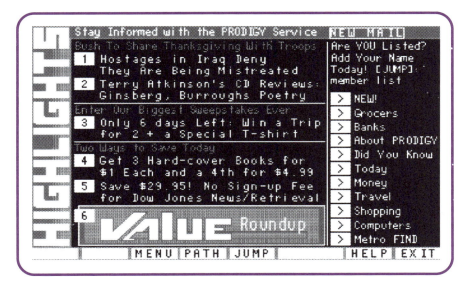

Figure 6.1   The Prodigy Highlights screen

Exiting Prodigy

When in Prodigy, you can exit at any time. Just select EXIT as required until you reach the Exit screen (see Figure 6.2). Select 1 End This Session. The message Now disconnecting appears. Once you are off line, you return to the PS/1 System menu.

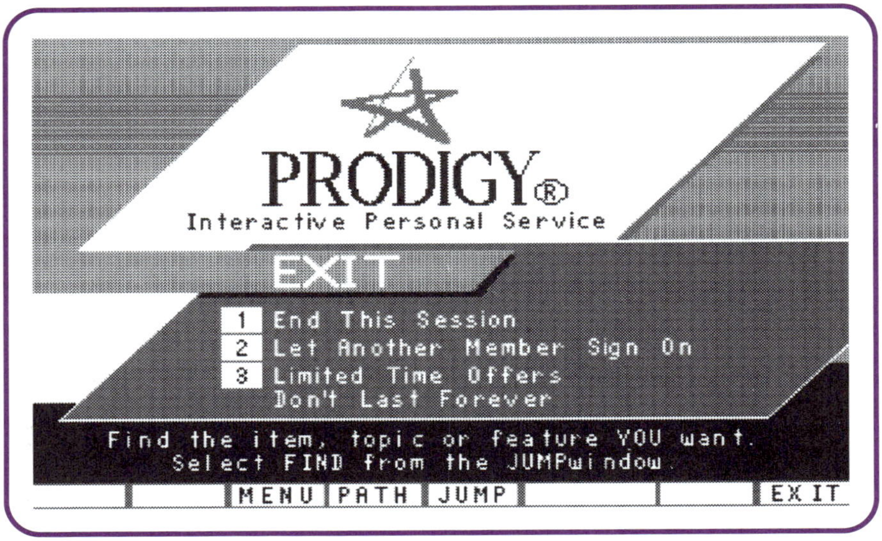

Figure 6.2   Prodigy Exit screen

Prodigy Sign-On Shortcut

After you have signed on to Prodigy for the first time—and enrolled—you can sign on using selection 1 Sign on from the Sign-on menu. This selection walks you through typing in your ID and password. To avoid having to enter your ID and, optionally, your password, set yourself up on the Sign-On Shortcut List. In either case, use the phone system information and number setup in Prodigy.

Select 3 Create or change the Sign-On Shortcut List from the Sign-on menu. The Sign-On Shortcut List screen is shown in Figure 6.3.

Select Add to list and press Enter. A pop-up appears for you to enter your name and ID. Do this and then select OK and press Enter.

> **Caution:** Each person must have his own unique ID assigned by Prodigy. The system will not allow you to enter the same ID for two people, nor will it allow an invalid ID.

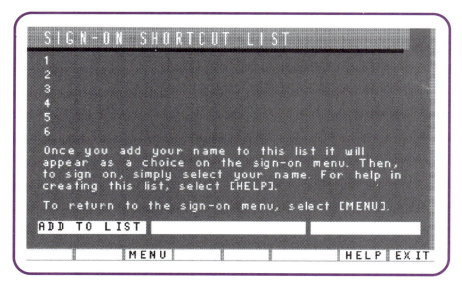

Figure 6.3   Sign-On Shortcut List

Next, you can enter your password, if desired. If you do, enter it, select OK, and then press Enter.

> **Caution:** Only enter your password in the system if there is no danger of an unauthorized person signing on with your password by using the shortcut sign-on or learning your password by using the Change List feature on the Sign-On Shortcut List screen. If you are concerned about the security of your system and password, leave the screen blank and continue by selecting OK.

Once you have completed the Password screen, your addition is complete. Select MENU to see the selection. In Figure 6.4 the most recent addition is shown as selection 4 Sign on Kate Barnes.

You can remove sign-on selections if they become out of date. To remove a selection, start at the Sign-on menu. Choose 3 Create or change the Sign-On Shortcut List. Select Remove from list. Enter the member number which is the number before the name of the person for which you want to remove the sign-on. Then select OK and press Enter. A confirmation pop-up appears allowing you a double check of the name and ID to remove. If you still want to remove the selection, select OK here.

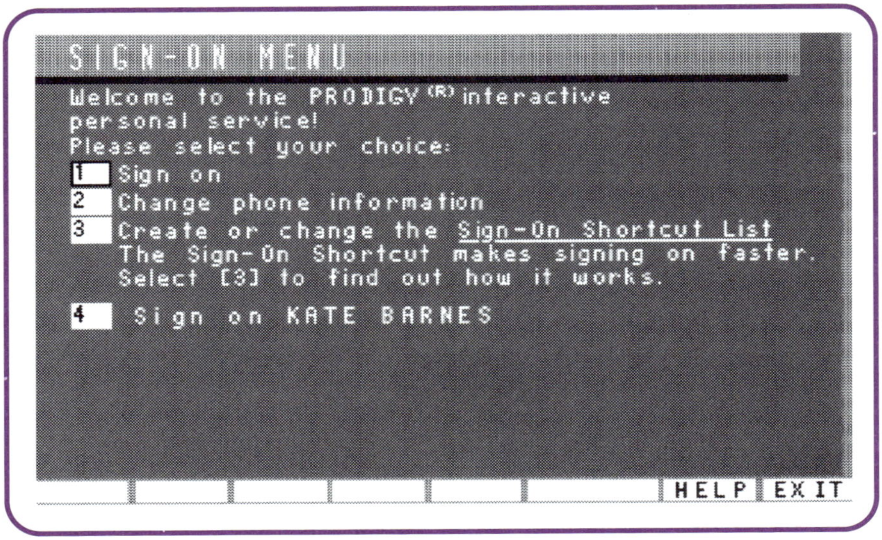

Figure 6.4   Prodigy Sign-On menu with sign-on selection added

You also can change the list. For example, you may want to change how a person's name appears or need to change an ID or password. Select `Change list` on the Sign-On Shortcut List screen. Enter the number of the member to change and select `OK`. The name and ID appear. Make any changes and select `OK`. Change the password information, if applicable, and select `OK`.

The following quick references summarize how to create, remove, and change sign-on shortcuts.

Adding a Sign-On Shortcut

1. From the Sign-on menu, select `3 Create or change the Sign-On Shortcut List`. — The Sign-On Shortcut List screen appears.
2. Select `Add to list`. — The Add pop-up appears.
3. Enter the name and ID; then select `OK`. — The Password pop-up appears.
4. Add the password, if desired, and select `OK`. — The selection is added.

Q Removing a Sign-On Shortcut

1.	From the Sign-on menu, select `3 Create or change the Sign-On Shortcut List`.	The Sign-On Shortcut List screen appears.
2.	Select `Remove from list`.	The Remove pop-up appears.
3.	Enter the number for the member to remove and select `OK`.	A confirming pop-up appears.
4.	To confirm the removal, select `OK`.	The selection is removed. ☐

Q Changing Sign-On List

1.	From the Sign-on menu, select `3 Create or change the Sign-On Shortcut List`.	The Sign-On Shortcut List screen appears.
2.	Select `Change list`.	The Change pop-up appears.
3.	Enter the number for the member to change and select `OK`.	The Name and ID pop-up appear.
4.	Enter the desired name and ID and then select `OK`.	The Password pop-up appears.
5.	Change the password, if desired, and select `OK`.	The selection is changed. ☐

Changing Prodigy Phone Information

The phone information in your Prodigy software may need to be changed from the information you entered during the initial enrollment. To change information, select `2 Change phone information` on the Sign-on menu and follow the prompts. This is the information you may change through this option:

▶ Type of phone service; Pulse—usually rotary dial phones—or Tone—usually push button phones or a whir instead of a tone when you press a button.

▶ Network symbol—as shown next to the phone number you have chosen to use from the Prodigy Phone Book.

▶ Prodigy phone number—include any call waiting disabling, outside line, long distance characters, and the phone number along with a comma for pauses between each.

Using Prodigy

Using Prodigy is easy. You can move around quickly with commands, JUMPwindow options, and JUMPwords. A handy template for the PS/1 is shown later in this chapter to help you remember the commands. Read on for more information.

Prodigy Commands

The Prodigy Commands shown at the bottom of the screen are your means of getting around in Prodigy. This section describes each command. However, not all commands are available from all screens. What you see on the screen is what you get. You may call up each command by pressing a letter followed by Enter. Alternatively, you can select the command box and then press Enter or use the other options described here.

ACTION— Press A-Enter or F2	When you are shopping, this option appears for you to place an order. It is available only when you are shopping.
BACK— Press B-Enter or Page Up	The BACK command enables you to go back to the previous screen.
EXIT— Press E-Enter	Use the EXIT command to leave Prodigy. It is a good way out for a beginner if you get really lost and want to reenter through the Prodigy Highlights screen.
FIND— Press F-Enter or F8	The FIND command gives you a quick route to finding products, services, and information you want.

Prodigy asks you to enter one or more key words and select from there. Use this option (versus JUMP) if you know what you want to find (not a specific Prodigy location).

HELP—
Press H-Enter or F1

HELP supplies details on the screen or option you are using.

?—
Press A-Enter or F2

This command shows information about the command or text but is not available from all screens.

INDEX—
Press I-Enter or F7

The INDEX command opens the JUMPwindow with INDEX selected. Choose INDEX to see a list of all valid JUMPwords which you can select to go to certain locations in Prodigy. INDEX is *the* way to get around. You may press I any time to go to the INDEX through the JUMPwindow (whether INDEX appears as a command at the bottom of your screen or not). You can move through the index quickly by entering one to five letters and pressing Enter. Use NEXT (or the Page Up key) and BACK (or the Page Down key) to move through the index words "page by page." Select any index word to go to that Prodigy location. You can print the Prodigy index by selecting PRINT at the lower right corner of your screen. Because the index is so large, printing will take some time. No other information than the JUMPwords appears, so you may find viewing the list on the screen just as effective. Figure 6.5 shows a sample of a printed index page.

```
        PRODIGY  (R)  interactive  personal  service  10/29/90  2:57  AM

               Index of JUMPword sm Listings

               1990S                   AMA
               20TH CENTURY            AMC DAILY
               49ERS                   AMC GOSSIP
               76ERS                   AMC WEEKLY
               A'S                     AMERICA ONLIN
               AA ONLINE               AMERICAN AIR
               AADVANTAGE              AMERICAN WOME
               ABEL                    AMERICANA
               ABLE                    AMERICANWOMEN
               ABOUT CR                AMERICAONLINE
               ABOUT MAC               ANDERSEN
               ABOUT PRODIGY           ANDERSON
               ABOUT TECH              ANGELS
               ABOUTPOLICIES           ANOTHER WORLD
               ACCESSWORLD             AOL
               ACTION VIDEO            AP FOOT ODDS
               AD INFO                 AP FOOT RANK
               AD REVIEW               AP FOOT SCHED
               ADD MEMBER              AP FOOT SCORE
               ADDMEMBER               APPLIANCEPLUS
               ADDRESS BOOK            AQUARIUS
               ADVICE                  AREA NEWS
               AFC LEADERS             ARIES
               AFC STANDINGS           ARROW KEYS
               AGREEMENT               ART GALLERY
               AIR FRANCE              ARTS CLUB
               AL LEADERS              ARTS VIDEO
               AL SCHEDULE             ASK BETH
               AL SCORES               ASK PRODIGY
               AL STANDINGS            ASTROS
               ALAMO                   AT HOME
               ALEX                    ATHLETIC SUPP
               ALL CLUB                ATHLETICS
               ALLSTATE                ATHLETICSUPPL
               ALLSTATE AUTO           ATKINSON
               ALLSTATE HOME           ATL FALCONS
               ALLSTATE LIFE           ATLANTA
               ALLSTATE MOTO           ATLANTA EVENT
               ALLSTATEMOTOR           ATLANTA GUIDE
               ALTERNATIVEHS           ATWT DAILY
               ALTERNATIVES            ATWT GOSSIP

        Copyright  1988,  1989,  1990  Prodigy  Services  Company.  All  Rights  Reserved.
```

Figure 6.5 Printed index page

JUMP—
Press J-Enter or F6

Select JUMP and the JUMPwindow opens for you to enter a valid JUMPword which is essentially a command to go somewhere in Prodigy (see "JUMPwindow" and "JUMPwords" later in this chapter).

Using Information (Especially Prodigy)

Use JUMP rather than FIND when you know the specific location to go to in Prodigy.

MENU—
Press M-Enter or F9

This command returns you to the last menu you used.

NEXT—
Press N-Enter or Page Down

The NEXT command moves you forward to the next screen.

PATH—
Press P-Enter or F4

You can create a path of up to 20 locations in Prodigy. Whenever you select PATH (or press F4), you go to the next location on your own list. (See VIEWPATH in this list for more information.)

REVIEW—
Press R-Enter or F10

This command enables you to see and select from the last 12 places you've been in Prodigy.

TOOLS—
Press T-Enter or T

Press T from any screen to go to the JUMPwindow with TOOLS highlighted. Use the TOOLS command to change personal data such as name, address, and your password; optional features; credit card information (some services also have you enter credit card information when you sign on); test patterns for shades or colors on your display; and member addresses and phone information for adding new members.

VIEWPATH—
Press V-Enter or F3 or V

VIEWPATH enables you to look at, go to, or change the Prodigy locations you have set up in your personal path. Press V from any screen to go to the JUMP window with VIEWPATH highlighted. To change your path, select CHANGEPATH from the VIEWPATH Your PATHlist screen. You go to a CHANGEPATH screen (shown in Figure 6.6) which shows your current path in order.

Chapter 6

Change the path using these VIEWPATH screen options:

ADD	The previous location or another location. Make sure the JUMPword you want shows up, and assign a number 1 through 20 for the new location in the path.
DELETE	Enter the number assigned to the JUMPword on this screen to delete the JUMPword from the path.
REARRANGE	Identify the number of the JUMPword to move and the new number to assign; the other JUMPwords are renumbered accordingly.
ZIP— Press Z-Enter	If you use LOOK to read more about an advertisement, select ZIP to return to your original location before using LOOK.

> **Tip:** If you learn to use only a couple of commands, don't miss JUMP and INDEX. These are your most powerful means of maneuvering in Prodigy.

Once you make changes, the CANCEL CHANGES command appears for you to return to your original path. The GO TO option doesn't change your path, but you can use it to go to any location, including your previous location or any other location you identify by the number assigned on this screen.

Using Information (Especially Prodigy)

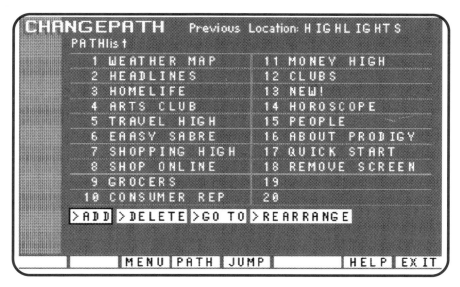

Figure 6.6   CHANGEPATH screen

JUMPwindow

Selecting JUMP at the bottom of the screen (by pressing J and Enter or F6) takes you to the JUMPwindow (see Figure 6.7).

From the JUMPwindow, enter a JUMPword to take you to a particular location in Prodigy. Or select a Prodigy Command, such as FIND, or one of the following options.

GUIDE shows you where you are in Prodigy. For example, Figure 6.8 shows the GUIDE pop-up windows indicating SPORTS, which is part of NEWS & FEATURES, which is a subset of the main guide. You may press G any time to get the JUMPwindow with GUIDE highlighted.

UNDO is the same as REVIEW. You may see and pick from the last 12 places you've been. You may press U from any screen to go to the REVIEW list.

READ MAIL jumps you to your mailbox if you have mail. If not, you are informed there is no mail. The message NEW MAIL appears when you sign on if you have new mail. If you receive mail while you are working on-line, you must check your mailbox to see that mail has arrived. Otherwise, the NEW MAIL message will appear the next time you sign on.

Chapter 6

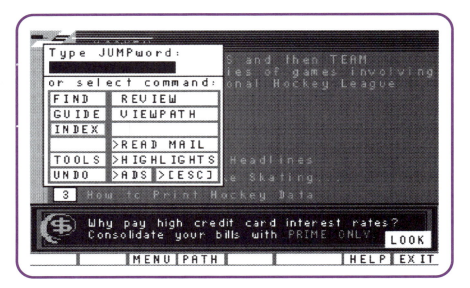

Figure 6.7 *JUMPwindow*

Figure 6.8 *GUIDE Pop-up window from the Prodigy Highlights screen*

HIGHLIGHTS takes you back to the first Prodigy screen (the Highlights screen). This is a familiar spot to travel to if you feel really lost.

ADS takes you to the AD REVIEW screen which allows you to see previous advertisements which have appeared during this on-line session. Or you may see ads that have not yet appeared. Use LOOK to see more about an ad and ZIP to leave detailed ad information. (If you're a compulsive shopper, keep a firm grip on that credit card. There are some deals offered!) Use ESC when you want to leave the JUMPwindow. Just press the Escape key to go back to what you were doing before entering the JUMPwindow.

JUMPwords

Prodigy has a tremendous number of JUMPwords, which should not be surprising considering the number of services provided through Prodigy. Because printing the index of JUMPwords takes plenty of time—and the index can quickly go out of date—skimming through the JUMPwords when you have time to spend is the best way to see what is available.

> **Tip:** You may not have to type an entire JUMPword to identify that JUMPword. All you have to enter are enough letters to uniquely identify the JUMPword.

Some of the more useful and fun JUMPwords are listed in Table 6.1; however, there are plenty more where these came from!

> **Tip:** You can get to many of the Prodigy locations by more than one route. For example, when you need an update on love in the single lane, you can get to advice for singles through the **advice** or **single life** JUMPwords.

Table 6.1   Useful JUMPwords

JUMPword	Description
about cr	Peruse a description of *Consumer Reports* magazine on Prodigy; the JUMPwords that start with CR are consumer reports.
about prodigy	Get information about the Prodigy service.
ad info	Discover how to advertise on Prodigy.
ad review	Review the last advertisements you've seen in this on-line session or look at other ads that will appear; use LOOK and ZIP to look at and return from an ad.
add member	Go to the TOOLS option to add new members of your household (same as the **addmember** JUMPword).
address book	Create and change your own address book of Prodigy IDs and the nickname you use when you address a person; if your address book gets long, use LOCATE to find people quickly; you can create a mailing list including people you regularly send the same piece of mail to and name the list for quick mailing.
ask prodigy	Read about Prodigy and/or send a question to Prodigy, such as billing errors, connect problems, or issues with merchants that you haven't been able to straighten out with the merchant directly.
basics	Go to the Prodigy HELP menu for a review of the basics of cursors, menus, screens, windows, etc.
change pword	To head out for the TOOLS option to change your password.
changepath	Takes you to the CHANGEPATH screen (otherwise maneuvered to through the VIEWPATH command) to change your personal path through Prodigy locations.
clubs	See a list of the clubs on Prodigy; clubs are a good way to connect with others that have your interests.
coming soon	Look at the new features coming on Prodigy.
commands	Learn about Prodigy commands.
communication	Learn about communications—how to write a message, use the message center, use the address book, create a mailing list, use the member list, etc.
computer club	Go to the computer club quickly (not the same as the PS/1 Users' Club).

(continued)

JUMPword	Description
email	Go to the same Prodigy Communication screens as with the communication JUMPword; email stands for electronic mail; learn to handle messages and mail with Prodigy.
ev (city)	Enter a valid city and see the events for that city.
get started	Learn a mixed bag of information about the Prodigy service.
getting help	Learn more mixed bag information about Prodigy.
help desk	Another way into the Ask Prodigy option of reading about or sending a message to Prodigy.
help hub	Get help about how to use Prodigy; it's a good overview place to start.
highlights	Go back to the first Prodigy screen (called the Highlights screen).
ibm ps/1	See an ad for the PS/1 (same as **ps1**).
ibm ps/1 club	Participate in the club for PS/1 users (same as **ibm usersclub**).
input fields	Learn how to type data into Prodigy.
jump	Read a description of the JUMP command.
jump tip	Discover how to use JUMPwords.
jumpwindow	Identify how to enter JUMPwords.
jumpwords	See how to move around with JUMPwords.
keyboard keys	Review how to use the keyboard.
mail	See the mail in your mailbox (same as the **messagecenter** JUMPword).
member list	See names and Prodigy ID of other people using Prodigy; locate the person by last name or city and state; a good way to locate people and then send a message to them.
membership	Get to Prodigy Membership Services for assistance with Prodigy problems or questions.
messagecenter	See messages in your mailbox (same as **mail** JUMPword).
message tips	Learn how to use electronic mail.
mousetool	Control mouse sensitivity, if the mouse feature is available.

(continued)

Table 6.1 *(continued)*

JUMPword	Description
navigating	Use the Prodigy HELP service.
new	See what is new on Prodigy this week.
path	Learn how to use or change your personal path through Prodigy (related to theVIEWPATH command).
prodigy help	Same as **ask prodigy.**
prodigy poll	Cast your vote on issues of political and social concern.
prodigy star	Read Prodigy's own weekly service for news.
questions	See the most frequently asked questions ... and answers.
quick start	Learn how to move around Prodigy.
screens	Learn how to read a Prodigy screen.
service hours	Check when Prodigy is available in your area.
service sched	See when certain services update their information on Prodigy, such as when banks post their new rates.
shop online	Use the How To Shop tutorial to learn how to shop with Prodigy.
short cuts	How to move around Prodigy quickly.
target	Learn about using the JUMP command.
today	Examine news for the day.
tutorials	See how to practice using tutorials.
w (city)	Type **W** and then a valid city name for the weather in the city.
window tip	See how to use pop-up windows.
write	Send a message through Prodigy.

> ▶ **Tip:** Many of the JUMPwords take you to a commercial or a commercial service. Some of the ads are pretty cute. "Come and Get It" is fun in a goofy way.

Using Information (Especially Prodigy)

Prodigy Keyboard Template

Figure 6.9 is a quick reference template you may want to keep near your keyboard to prompt you about the commonly used Prodigy function keys and single letter commands. The template is designed to be used with the function key layout of your PS/1. For more information on any one of these commands, see the "Prodigy Commands" and "JUMPwindow" sections earlier in this chapter.

Figure 6.9 *Prodigy keyboard reference for the PS/1*

What You Have Learned

In this chapter you have learned

- ▶ You can get tutorials for your PS/1 system or Microsoft Works through the Information selection on your System menu.
- ▶ You must enroll in Prodigy to use the Prodigy service or the IBM PS/1 Users' Club.
- ▶ Guard your password because it is your key to using your computer for a variety of on-line services, including ones storing credit card information.
- ▶ Two of the most powerful commands in Prodigy are JUMP (to enter a JUMPword and move to the location) and INDEX (to see the various JUMPwords you may use).
- ▶ If you have problems with Prodigy, use the JUMP command and enter **ask prodigy** as the JUMPword; send a message about your problem for quick response.

Chapter 7

Prodigy Services—Users' Club and Others

In This Chapter

▶ *How to find and use tutorials for various services*
▶ *A quick look at popular Prodigy services including the Users' Club*
▶ *Hints and cautions when using Prodigy services*
▶ *Solving Prodigy problems*

Tutorials

Several tutorials for Prodigy services are available through Prodigy. Select About Prodigy from the Highlights screen; then pick the Help Hub. Or select JUMP and then enter **help hub** as the JUMPword. From the Help Hub, select Tutorials. Current tutorials, such as EAASY SABRE, Grocery, Control Fin, and Quick Start, are listed for your selection.

Chapter 7

IBM PS/1 Users' Club Services

The IBM PS/1 Users' Club exists as a give-and-take information exchange with IBM and other PS/1 users. The quickest way to get into the IBM PS/1 Users' Club for the first time is to press J (for JUMP) and enter either of these JUMPwords:

ibm ps/1 club
ibm usersclub

> **Note**: The IBM PS/1 Users' Club is not the same club as the computer club which you select through `3 Computer Club` on the Prodigy Highlights screen. That club includes bulletin boards, news, expert comments, computer games, popular software lists, and more. To check it out, make the selection and look at the `Quick Intro/Rules` for the club.

When you enter the Users' Club for the first time, you need to accept the IBM PS/1 Users' Club Service Agreement through the Agreement screen. Once you've gone through the initial acceptance screens, the IBM PS/1 Users' Club screen shown in Figure 7.1 appears.

> **Tip**: After you enter the Users' Club for the first time, you can use the selection for the Users' Club from the `Information` selection on the PS/1 System menu to access the club. You go directly to the screen shown in Figure 7.1.

Each of the services which appears on the IBM PS/1 Users' Club screen is described here.

`ANSWER BANK` is where you may read answers to commonly asked questions on specific PS/1 related topic areas, such as hardware or Microsoft Works.

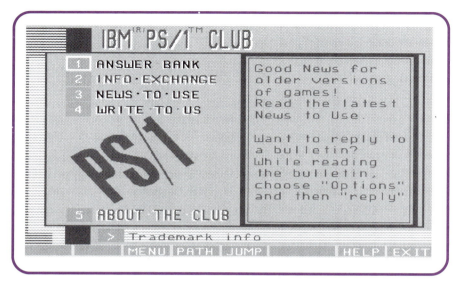

Figure 7.1 IBM PS/1 Users' Club

INFO EXCHANGE is a bulletin board where you can browse or select specific bulletins from other members. Or you can pose your own questions to or provide answers to other PS/1 users. Use the Subject Search Window to quickly see the bulletins available. IBM experts occasionally join in the exchange.

To reply to an Info Exchange bulletin, select Options and then Reply. When you develop a reply, you may make it public (to all members) or private (to the member IDs you enter). To post your own bulletin, select Topic and then Subject and just type away. When you enter your own bulletins, using topics that already exist is a good idea. That helps keep the length of the Subject Search Window under control. Bulletins you enter will stay on the bulletin board for 30 days if there is no reply or 60 days if there is a reply.

NEWS TO USE is IBM's commercial message sprinkled with tips. Give it a glance to keep up on the latest software releases and other developments.

WRITE TO US is *the* way to communicate directly to the IBM PS/1 Users' Club headquarters. Write whatever is on your mind. Just enter a subject, your message, and send away. You can even print your own copy of your message.

For more information on the Users' Club, examine the ABOUT THE CLUB option.

Mail and Messages

Prodigy's mail and message system is a fun way to connect with others for business or fun. If you have a new message, NEW MAIL appears as a selection in the upper right corner of your screen when you sign on. If you get mail while you are on-line, you need to check your mailbox; a NEW MAIL message won't appear until you sign on again.

To use mail, you go to (or through) the Prodigy Communications screen (shown in Figure 7.2). This screen is your pathway into all the ways to use messages.

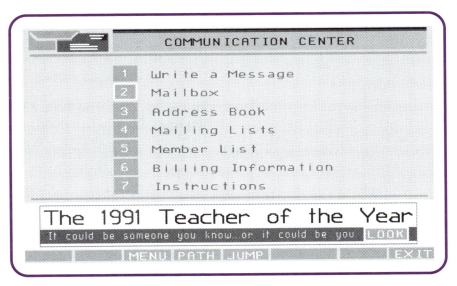

Figure 7.2 Prodigy Communications screen

Reading mail is easy. Just select Mailbox.

Unread messages are marked with an asterisk and are saved for only two weeks. If you want to keep a message longer, select RETAIN. To delete a message, select DELETE. To reply, select WRITE. To print a copy of the message, select PRINT.

> **Hint**: Commercial mail is marked with a # in the subject line. The contents of these messages are like advertisements in a magazine. Keep your cool about this unsolicited junk mail. Remember that fees for mailing you these commercial messages help feed the Prodigy family and help keep your monthly fee low.

When you send mail, you can choose from several options to streamline the identification of the recipient of your mail. The first is the *single person/easy method*. Just check the Prodigy Member List (select Member List on the Prodigy Communications screen). You can look up member IDs by last name or by city and state.

Another method is to set up your own personal address book through the Address Book selection on the Prodigy Communication screen. Use the Address Book to enter up to 50 IDs and nicknames of people you contact often. This way, you can quickly find them Nicknames are used so that the name used to address your mail to a person may be the name they like to be called, not the formal billing name entered in Prodigy.

The third alternative for identifying mail recipients is useful if you work with various groups, such as special interest groups or clubs, for mass mailings. Use the Mailing List option to create one or two lists of up to 10 people each. The nicknames of people entered on your Mailing List must be in your Address Book before you add them to your Mailing List.

To send mail, select Write a Message. You need to know the ID, nickname, or Mailing List name of the recipient of your message. You can find out that information through Options where you can search for an ID on the Member List (check by last name or city and state). Type the ID, nickname, or Mailing List name in the To: data entry field. The List option on the Write a Message screen enables you to enter distribution lists. As mentioned earlier, this feature is great for small clubs or special interest groups.

Next, enter a descriptive subject. Then enter your message which may be up to four pages. Use NEXT or Page Down to go to the next page. Use BACK or Page Up to go to the previous page. Check out the upper right corner of the screen for a page number. If there is a page number, you can go to the page number box, type in another page number, and press Enter to go to the page you indicated. If you

Chapter 7

make a mistake as you compose the message, edit it using the insert and delete keys or, to wipe it totally out and start again, use the CLEAR command.

Once the message is complete, select SEND to send the message. Electronic mail messages are sent immediately. You may also want to print the message so that you have a hard copy for later use.

The following JUMPwords can be used to go quickly to the Prodigy Communications screen or other related screens—all subordinate to the Prodigy Communications screen.

What you want to do	*Valid JUMPwords*
Communications screen access	email, communication
See the mail in your mailbox	mail, messagecenter, mailbox (You also can select READ MAIL from the JUMPwindow.)
See names and IDs of Prodigy users	member list
Learn about electronic mail	communicating
Send a message	write
See your personal mailing list	mailing list
See your address book	address book
Create a distribution list	list

Checking Your Mail with JUMPwords

1. Press J and Enter or F6. You go to the JUMPwindow.
2. Type in **email** and press Enter. You go to the Prodigy Communications screen for electronic mail.
3. Select Mailbox. Select any message; if there are no messages, a pop-up window lets you know.
4. Read the messages and select RETAIN or DELETE. A message appears confirming the action taken with each message.

5. When done, press U and Enter to Undo. Your REVIEW list appears with the last location highlighted.

6. Select the screen to return to and press Enter. The screen appears.

Writing Mail with JUMPwords

1. Press J and Enter or F6. You go to the JUMPwindow.
2. Type **write** and press Enter. You go to the Write a Message screen.
3. Complete the information; check LIST for member IDs or use the MENU option to back out one level to consult your Address Book or Mailing List for IDs. The ID, subject, and message appear.
4. Select SEND to send the message. A prompt appears for you to double-check the send.
5. Respond affirmatively to the prompt. The message is sent and a confirmation pop-up window appears.
6. Press Escape at the confirmation pop-up window. You go to the Write a Message screen.
7. Press U and Enter to Undo. Your REVIEW list appears with the last location highlighted.
8. Select the screen to return to and press Enter. The screen appears.

Caution: At the time of this writing, Prodigy was setting limits on the number of messages members can send per month for the monthly fee. Messages over the limit would incur a charge. Check out the limit if you will be sending several messages.

Chapter 7

Shopping On-line

Shopping with Prodigy is like visiting the world's largest mall while not leaving the comfort of your home. Of course, the down side is that you can't see, touch, or try on your selection. But the time and hassle saved is often worth it if you have a very busy schedule and generally dislike the mall experience.

Suppose you are shopping for new stereo equipment. Rather than reading ads in the paper and visiting several stores, which is time-consuming, enter the JUMPword **shopping** and go to the categories of types of goods and services you may find (see Figure 7.3). Choose Audio & Video To Buy. Or if you know you want to buy the equipment from Sight & Sound (a Sears specialty store), type in the JUMPword **sight&sound**.

Figure 7.3 Shopping Find screen

> ▶ **Tip**: The JUMPword Listings booklet that comes with Prodigy is a good place to browse the stores available to you by category.

Once at the store, you can browse item descriptions. If the store also publishes a catalog, the catalog identifier and page number where a picture of the item is displayed are given.

To order an item, select ACTION. You are presented with options such as SIZE, COLOR, and QUANTITY. Complete all the necessary information. Then, select ADD to add another item to your order or CHANGE to change an item on your order. To pay for an item, simply enter how you will pay, credit card information (if applicable), billing address, and delivery information. Then just send off the order. If the store you're patronizing has special options, such as gift wrap, you are allowed to choose among them before the send is complete.

> ▶ **Tip**: If you have a problem with an on-line order, contact the merchant directly. Many merchants have ways to contact them on-line through Prodigy. If you cannot resolve the problem, use the JUMP command and enter the JUMPword **ask prodigy** to explain the problem with a note through Prodigy Member Services. For detailed instructions on this feature, see "Solving Prodigy Problems" later in this chapter.

Traveling

Travel is easier with Prodigy. General travel options are yours by entering the JUMPword **travel high**.

You can check out the weather in your destination by entering the JUMPword **weather** for a continental US map or **w (*city name*)** for specific city information. To see what events may be happening in your target town, use the JUMPword **ev (*city name*)**. To see a "best and worst of" several major US cities, check out the JUMPword **city guide**. For area news, type in the city's name as the JUMPword. For a *Consumer Reports Travel Letter*, use JUMPword **cr travel**. Read a column on business travel by Peter S. Greenberg by entering JUMPword **business trav**.

The Travel Club (JUMPword **travel club**) is a bulletin board service for Prodigy members to report on travel experiences. The

Chapter 7

bulletin board works like other Prodigy bulletin boards, such as the Users' Club. You also can access comments from the travel experts and view major travel guides from the Travel Club screen.

Travel options also include memberships in commercial travel activities, services, and information. For example, you can check out American Airlines' Fly AAway Vacations to look at vacation packages, order brochures, and make reservations (JUMPword **fly aaway**). Join TWA's travel club by typing JUMPword **trans world**. Or enroll and pay the fee to belong to a discount travel agency which will pay you rebates on flights and hotels (try out the JUMPword **accessworld**).

Even better than these handy services is the ability to make travel related reservations, such as cars, airlines, and hotels, from your computer. One of the more popular services is EAASY SABRE—that's also the JUMPword. You must enroll in this service. When you enroll, you give the service information, for example, whether you prefer smoking or nonsmoking seats, along with credit card details. You also enter a password to protect your credit card information. And you enter your—or get an—American Airlines AAdvantage frequent flyer number.

> **Caution**: EAASY SABRE uses your credit card when you 1) request Service PLUS to issue your tickets, 2) request American Airlines Tickets By Mail, 3) authorize a hotel deposit, or 4) request a hotel guarantee. When you use EAASY SABRE, you are clearly told when your credit card will be used.

When you enroll in EAASY SABRE, you may enroll to work with a Service PLUS representative who is also on-line and can send you boarding passes with your tickets. The nice thing about Service PLUS is that you can use the JUMPword **eaasy message** to send notes to the agency.

If you use EAASY SABRE, check out the Bargain Finder to find the lowest fares for flights. These fares don't always beat the "bucket shops" advertising in the *Los Angeles Times* or *New York Times*, but the fares are low.

Once you have a fare identified, just make the reservation. For flights, select `Flight Reservations` to go to the Flight Request screen. Enter the days and airports you wish to travel to and from. You must use certain codes. Select `CODES` and jot down the codes you will need before completing the screen. The flights appear (with non-stops listed first) along with the following information:

M	Meals served
ST	Number of stops on the route
EQP	Aircraft type
O	On-time rating for different cities

Once you have completed the reservation, an itinerary is developed for you. You can change the itinerary according to typical airline restriction rules. If you made airline reservations outside of EAASY SABRE, such as with a travel agent, you cannot check the reservations since no itinerary is completed.

EAASY SABRE car and hotel reservations work similarly. You can make reservations when you book a flight (make that selection), or you can enter the JUMPword **eaasy cars** to book a car and then book a hotel. Supply the pertinent information and you are all set.

> **Caution**: When you make reservations, always jot down the related confirmation numbers (which are different from your itinerary numbers). These numbers are your way to identify what reservation was made at what time.

Money and Banking

With Prodigy, you may bank and handle finances on-line. Enter the JUMPword **money high** for a list of many of the related services on the Money Highlights screen (see Figure 7.4). You have no more check fees or standing in line or calling brokers if you play your Prodigy cards right.

You can pay bills, transfer funds, see account activity, and "talk" to your bank. If there isn't a bank in your area, you can use a bank out of state. Enter the JUMPword **bank online**.

You may trade stocks on-line and control your portfolio through the Personal Control Financial Network, a discount brokerage service (JUMPword **pcfn**). Check quotes with Dow Jones News/Retrieval (JUMPword **quote check**). Read business news (JUMPword **business news**), company news from Dow Jones News/Retrieval (JUMPword **company news**), or get a market update of your stocks (JUMPword **market update**). You are given options including printing articles or sending for them as well as on-line reading. Prodigy also has a variety of expert advice; use the JUMPword **money talk** or enter the JUMPword for the particular publication service such as **changingtimes** or **block**. In addition to these services, Prodigy is adding banking and financial services on a regular basis.

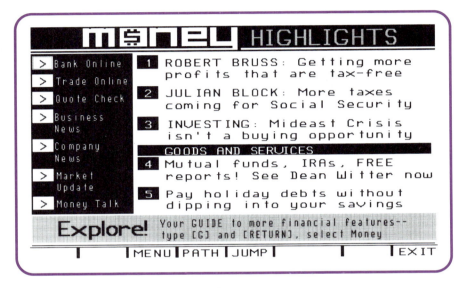

Figure 7.4 Money Highlights screen

Sports and Hobbies

Armchair sport updates are a popular Prodigy feature. Check out the JUMPword **sports**. Use this menu or try out JUMPwords **sports news**, **sports extras**, **schaap** (for Dick Schaap's opinions), and **football talk** by Fred Edelstein.

Sports Games (JUMPword **sports games**) involves you in quizzes and contests. If you pick the most games correctly, you can win a Prodigy service sport bag. To find out sport standings, type the JUMPword for the sport, such as **football**, to see standings and play-related contests. Compare your opinions with others through the JUMPword **sports survey**.

Tired of the armchair? Then take a look at the JUMPword **ski forecasts** to plan your ski trip. Then get up and get involved. After all, Prodigy can't become your only pastime.

Prodigy is as rich with hobby information as sports. Enter JUMPword **victorygarden** for up to the season advice about gardening. The food and wine club (JUMPword **food and wine**) is a good place for bulletin board action about subjects as diverse as desserts and sweets and healthy eating. Try out the JUMPword **cookbook** and you go to The Cookbook Shelf which features recipes, menus, ingredient guides, and special preparation techniques.

There is a general bulletin board for home and hobby communications. Try out the JUMPword **homelife**. Users of this bulletin board center on subjects including home, garage, parenting, pet care, fashion, photography, and genealogy.

The JUMPword **arts club** takes you to many options including a bulletin board, movie, music, TV, video, books, and popular people. News and reviews abound.

Finally, for that favorite pastime, personal advice, try out the JUMPword **advice** for everyone's opinion on anything personal.

Kids' Stuff

Kids can keep busy with Prodigy too! Warning to parents: establish some rules about what to use and when. Keeping kids away from charge-related activities would be wise.

The JUMPword **the club** takes kids to *the place* for fun. The Club screen appears in Figure 7.5. Through The Club, there is a bulletin board for exchanging kid talk. School, music, games, sports, TV and video, and wheels are the types of topics you find here. You also can use this screen as an entrance to activities such as

▶ SCIENCECENTER—uncovering developments in science.
▶ Stories—new installments of stories, contests, adventures, and other features.
▶ Encyclopedia—additional software is required for the Academic American Encyclopedia.

- ▶ Games To Play—chess, maze games, box games, sport games, and more.
- ▶ Art Gallery.
- ▶ Rock Calendar—rock and roll history.
- ▶ Punchline—riddles and jokes.

Figure 7.5 The Club for kids

Another warning to parents: The kids' clubs and activities have advertisements geared just for younger minds. This could be a good opportunity to teach kids about advertising appeals.

Suggestion to kids: If you bug your parents about stuff to buy from the Prodigy advertisements and they get mad, be ready with a joke from Punchline (JUMPword **punchline**).

Solving Prodigy Problems

This section includes some common problems you may experience when you use Prodigy. There is plenty you can do to solve problems; however, if they become unsolvable, you can always use the JUMPword **ask prodigy** and send a message for help.

Q Sending Messages to Prodigy

1. From any Prodigy screen, press J for JUMP and press Enter.
   The JUMPwindow appears.

2. Type **ask prodigy** and press Enter.
   Major subject areas appear.

3. Select a subject area related to your message.
   An informational message appears with the Write Membership Services option.

4. Select `Write Membership Services`.
   The Message screen appears.

5. Type in the subject of your message and the message itself. Be as specific and descriptive as possible.
   Your message appears.

6. Select `SEND`.
   The message is sent. ☐

If you have a problem that can't be sent by **ask prodigy**—maybe you can't even get that far—you can use the Prodigy phone number to call for immediate help. These numbers are

   1-800-284-5933 for installation.

   1-914-962-0310 for billing, diskette, and other problems.

Whenever you call for help

- ▶ Have your ID ready; the operator will ask you for your number.
- ▶ Know your phone number and network symbol.
- ▶ Have notes of error codes or other unusual activity you noticed.
- ▶ Know what version of DOS you are using.

As you troubleshoot on your own before contacting Prodigy, consider what happened before the problem and then trace backward to discover the dilemma. For example, if you attempt to sign on and don't even get a dialing tone, you may want to check the phone number you entered to make sure it is correct.

Following are some common problems:

1. The Prodigy service is not available. Night owls are especially prone to this problem. Be familiar with the times of service in your area. Enter the JUMPword **service hours** to check out the times available to you.
2. You can't sign on; you don't even get to the dialing stage. Your password or ID may be a problem. Carefully check your password and ID to make sure they are correct. Your modem or telephone line connection may be a problem. Check all connections. If the problem persists, call Prodigy or IBM depending on whom you suspect the most.
3. You attempt to connect the phone lines and you hear the tones, but you can't get through. Check the phone number to make sure it is correct, that you have disabled call waiting, and that you have included all numbers necessary. Try again. There may have been a temporary problem on Prodigy's end. Or you are up too late. See number 1 above.
4. You were on the system and then got knocked off. You may have call waiting (disable it according to the instructions earlier in this chapter), someone picked up the telephone sharing the line (educate them), you got a bad connection (try again), or the Prodigy service shut down (again, see number 1 above).
5. You get some kind of `out of memory` message. The Prodigy service doesn't recommend Prodigy use with resident memory software (TSR). You may have run out of memory. Leave Prodigy, turn off your machine, disable any TSR software you're using, and try again.
6. You *time out* of Prodigy. Prodigy is set up to dump you out of the system after 30 minutes of inactivity. You are automatically disconnected and a `CM4` error message may appear. Caution: Writing a bulletin or email message can time out if you spend over 30 minutes during the composition. Prodigy doesn't consider you to be on-line while you write.
7. You think Prodigy is too slow. Don't point fingers so quickly. The speed at which Prodigy works is a function of the speed of your modem, your computer processor, as well as the Prodigy system. Do something else light while you get in and around Prodigy.
8. You have bad dreams about Prodigy giving you a *virus*. A computer virus can infect your software, causing malfunctions. Don't be overly concerned. Prodigy doesn't allow *up* or *down loading* (transfer) of member files, so the opportunity of a virus getting on your machine is remote. However, you should be cautious.

9. You get communications error messages such as CM4, CM5, CM6, OMCM9, OMCM10. These are the result of a bad connection or interruption by call waiting. Stop and start again.

10. You see another kind of error message. Error codes in Prodigy are identified by their first letters:

   CM
   : Identifies there is a communication problem between your PS/1, modem, the phone lines, and the Prodigy service. Possible remedy: try logging on again.

   API
   : Identifies Prodigy service applications. Possible remedy: wait a while—maybe a day or more—and try again. Exception: API8 or API15 may mean you don't have enough memory available. Clear out any resident software or fonts in memory; or get back to the PS/1 System menu, turn the system off, and try again.

   DM
   : Suggests there is not enough memory. Possible remedy: go to the PS/1 System menu, turn off the machine, and try again. Get rid of any TSR (memory resident) software using your memory.

   OMCM
   : Identifies there is a problem with the Prodigy service talking with the Prodigy software you are using on your end. Possible remedy: get the latest version of the Prodigy software from Prodigy Membership Services. Exception: OMCM9 or OMCM10 may mean the transmission was bad. Exit Prodigy and try again.

What You Have Learned

In this chapter you've learned

- ▶ You can use the tutorials about Prodigy's services for more information.
- ▶ Once you have enrolled in the IBM PS/1 Users' Club, you can access it directly from the System menu.
- ▶ You should check your mail regularly, and you can send messages any time.

▶ You may shop, get travel reservations and information, bank, handle investments, play games, check out sports news, and be entertained on Prodigy.

▶ Following common troubleshooting tips can solve most of your problems using Prodigy.

Chapter 8
MS Works—Getting Started

In This Chapter

- *Microsoft Works capabilities*
- *Starting Works*
- *Using menus and commands throughout all Works functions*
- *Using the mouse and keyboard*
- *File handling*
- *Using Works calculator and alarm clock*

Microsoft Works Capabilities

Microsoft Works is where PS/1 users get a lot done. Microsoft Works integrates many functions into one, easy-to-use program. It includes four tools:

1. A *word processor* for developing letters, memos, reports, school papers, and any activity primarily involving words.
2. A *spreadsheet* for creating budgets, financial reports, accounts, and graphs; it is used for any activity predominantly number and calculation based.

3. A *database* to track pieces of information, arrange it in various groups, search, and sort.
4. *Communications* which enables you to talk to another computer over telephone lines; you can connect to a service or directly to another person's computer to swap files.

The beauty of Works lies in the fact that all these tools are designed with the same user interface and can work together. Once you learn some common mouse, keyboard, and menu moves, you can shift information from one tool to another.

For example, you may be part of a group creating a school paper about crime in America. You could create a graph in the spreadsheet and place it in the paper created as a word processing document and then send it to your schoolmates through communications. All this work could be accomplished by learning only one software program instead of several.

Starting Works

To start Works, select `Microsoft Works` from the System menu. If you have a diskette based system (no fixed disk), you will need to have the appropriate Works diskette in drive A. The first screen appears (see Figure 8.1). Notice that there is a menu across the top of the screen (`File`, `Options`, and `Help`) with the commands for File shown. These file commands are common throughout Works regardless of the type of file with which you are working.

Using Menus and Commands

To make a menu or command selection, you can use either the mouse and the keyboard or just the keyboard. Use whatever feels most comfortable to you.

If you use the mouse, you can make menu or command selections by pointing and clicking. If you use the keyboard, you can make selections by pressing Alt to move to the menu options, such as File, if necessary. Then use the arrow keys to highlight the selection and press Enter. An alternative is to press the highlighted letter—or first letter if none stands out—of the selection you want.

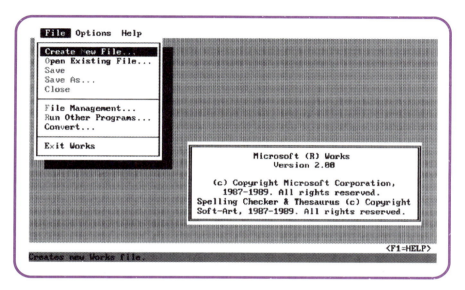

Figure 8.1   Works first screen

If a command has three dots, such as Create New File..., you know that a box appears with more selections. For example, if you selected `Create New File...`, the box shown in Figure 8.2 pops up. This particular box enables you to create a word processing, spreadsheet, database, or communications file. Boxes may ask you to select information, add information, or just confirm the information supplied.

Creating a New File

To create a new file, select `Create New File` and then select the type of file—word processing, spreadsheet, database, or communications. You go to a screen where you begin developing a new document. Works suggests a name for your new file which you may change when the document is saved.

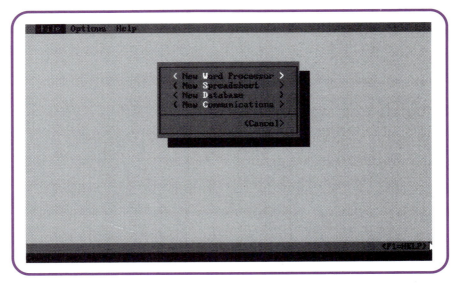

Figure 8.2 Create New File box

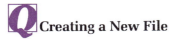 **Creating a New File**

1. Select `Microsoft Works` from the System menu or the File menu option.
   The File commands appear.

2. Select `Create New File`.
   The types of files appear.

3. Select the type of file.
   You go to that Works tool for the file type indicated. □

Saving a File

You must periodically save the file or files you are working on. Otherwise, if you lose power, you risk losing part, if not all, of your work. When you save the file, the information is copied from memory to your disk or diskette for safekeeping. Most users get in the habit of saving every fifteen minutes or so. After you save the file, you can continue working on the file. To leave the tool, see the Close command in this chapter.

When you select Save from the File menu, you go to a box like that shown in Figure 8.3. Press Alt if necessary to go to the File menu selection.

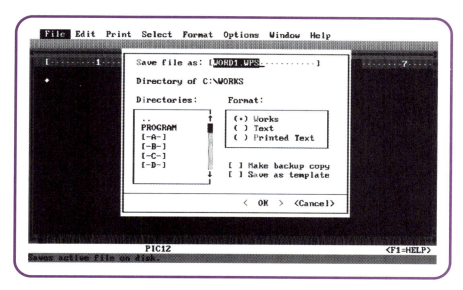

Figure 8.3 Save box

On this screen, Works suggests information which you can change. You can enter the name of the file using up to eight characters except any of the following:

*?.,;[]+=\:|<>

Works adds a period and a three letter file extension to help you identify the type of file. For example, .WPS is a word processing file. The Directory Of option shows the directory where the file will be stored. The Directories option identifies the drives and subdirectories on your system. You can select a new directory for storing the file. The Format option identifies the type of file. Files can be Works, Text (which is a common computer format called *ASCII*), or Printed. When starting out, always use Works. If you select Make backup copy, a second backup copy of your work is created with this different file extension:

Word processing file	.WPS	.BPS
Spreadsheet	.WKS	.BKS
Database	.WDB	.BDB
Communications	.WCM	.BCM

Select OK when all the information is complete.

Saving a File

1. Select File; press Alt if necessary for keyboard access to the File option.	The File commands appear.
2. Select Save.	A box appears.
3. Complete the information in the box and select OK.	The file is saved, and you return to the file to continue working. □

Opening an Existing File

After you have created a file, developed it, and saved it, you may need to open it later to do additional work. Choose Open Existing File. The box in Figure 8.4 appears.

    Enter the name of the file to open. The Directory Of option identifies the directory in which Works will look for the file. Files identifies the files in the current directory listed alphabetically by type (word processing, etc.). You can select the file here. The Directories option shows the directories and drives on your system. You can select a new directory and then select a file from the directory.

Opening an Existing File

1. Select Microsoft Works from the System menu or the File menu option.	The File commands appear.
2. Select Open Existing File.	A box appears.
3. Complete the information in the box and select OK.	The file is opened for your use. □

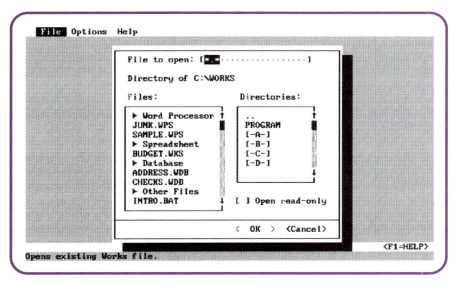

Figure 8.4   Open Existing File box

Closing a File

If you work with a file and decide you don't want to save the changes you've made, you can close the file without saving the changes. Simply select Close from the File menu. A box with this message appears:

    Save changes to: (file name)?

Select No to abandon your work and keep the original file, Yes to save the changes and close the file, or Cancel to cancel this operation and continue working in the file.

Works lets you open more than one file to appear on your screen at a time. If you close the last file which appears on your screen, you are taken out of the tool, such as word processing, and back to the first Works screen.

Exiting Works

When you are done using Works, select `Exit Works` from the File menu. You return to the PS/1 System menu.

If you have changes in a document that have not yet been saved, this message appears:

```
Save changes to: (file name)?
```

Select `Yes` to save the changes before leaving Works, `No` to abandon the changes, or `Cancel` to stop the exit process and go back to what you were doing.

Windows and the Mouse

All Works files appear on your screen in a *window*. You may open one file and then decide to open another file to see the information in it or copy or move information from one file to another. You also can close a file or window by clicking in the upper left corner with the mouse. Works automatically surrounds the information in each file with a window. Figure 8.5 shows one word processing file in a window.

> ▶ **Note**: Using windows is a more advanced function. Most users don't need to use more than one file at a time when beginning. It is good, however, to know how to read the information on a window, know that the capability exists, and to know what happens if you accidentally use your mouse in the wrong place on the screen.

Windows have these common parts:

> A *menu bar*, which lists menu options, such as File; select a menu option and you see the related commands.
>
> The *title bar*, where the name of the document appears.
>
> The *status line*, which shows information such as your location in the file (in the example, page 1 of 1).

The *message line*, which identifies what you can do or describes a highlighted command.

The *help reminder*; press F1 or click on Help for information.

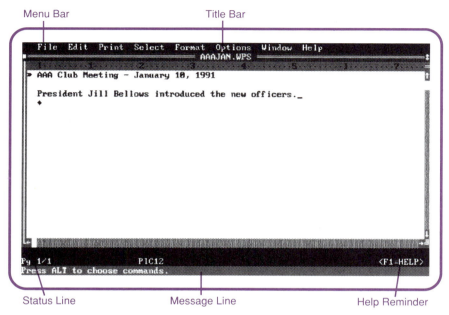

Figure 8.5 A single window

When you use the mouse, you can use the special symbols shown in Figure 8.6 to accomplish the tasks listed here. In addition to pointing and clicking, you may need to *drag* your mouse. To drag, press the left button, hold, move the mouse, and then release.

Title bar: drag to move the window.

Maximize arrow: click on it to make the window the full size of the screen.

Split bar: drag down to split a window.

Scroll box: drag to scroll (move through) the document text.

Scroll bar: click to move to a different part of the file.

Scroll arrow: click to scroll a small amount at a time.

Size box: drag to change the size of the window.

Close box: click to close the file.

Figure 8.6 Mouse activities on the window

Commonly Used Keys

There are several key uses that are common among the Works tools. These keys are identified in Table 8.1. In some cases, you must press two keys at the same time. Both keys are identified and linked with a plus. Don't press the +; just press the keys indicated. Use these keys for getting help, editing, moving your cursor, and selecting text for copying, deleting, or moving. Refer to this list when you begin creating documents. Many of these functions are described in more detail in the chapters devoted to the various tools.

Table 8.1 Works tool keys

Key	Use
F1	Help
Shift+F1	Tutorial for the task
↑,↓,←,→	To move a line, character, or spreadsheet cell at a time

Key	Use
Page Down	To move down in the file
Page Up	To move up in the file
End	To move to the right edge of the file
Home	To move to the left edge of the file
Ctrl+End	To move to the end of a file
Ctrl+Home	To move to the start of a file
F6	To go to the next *window pane* (a portion of a window when split)
Shift+F6	To go to the previous window pane
Ctrl+F6	To go to the next window if you have more than one file on the screen at a time
Ctrl+Shift+F6	To go to the previous window if you have more than one file on the screen at a time
F5	To go to a particular page or location on the screen
F8+arrow	Extend a selection of text, for example, to copy or move
F3	To move the selection
Shift+F3	To copy the selection
F7	To repeat a search
Shift+F7	To repeat a copy or format
Ctrl+;	To insert the current date
Ctrl+:	To insert the current time

File Management

An important File command is File Management. When you select File Management, you have several options for handling complete files at one time. Many of these options perform the same function as DOS Main Group commands.

Copy File: identify the name of the file to copy and the directory; select OK to copy the file. A new box appears; enter the new file and directory to copy to, and then select OK.

Chapter 8

Delete File: identify the name of the file to copy and the directory, select OK to delete, a warning message appears for a double check on your deletion, and select OK again.

Rename File: identify the name and directory of the file to rename, a new box appears, enter the new file and directory, and select OK.

Create Directory: create directories and subdirectories from Works, identify the name of the directory and the superior directory, and select OK.

Remove Directory: make sure the directory contains no files before removing. Identify the name and location of the directory to remove; select OK. Another option is to select Change on this screen to change to another directory.

Copy Disk: identify the drive to copy from and to and then select OK. Make sure you don't reverse the drive designations; if you do, you will lose the contents of the disk you intended to copy.

Format Disk: identify the drive of the disk to format and select OK. Make sure you don't want the contents of the diskette.

Set Date & Time: enter a new date and/or time and select OK.

Calculator and Alarm Clock

Works has a calculator for your figuring and an alarm clock to remind you of special times. You can access both of these options through the Options menu selection.

Calculator

Select Calculator from the Options menu. Type in numbers or click them with the mouse. Selecting CHS changes the sign of the number, CL clears the number, and CE clears the last entry. When you are done calculating, select Cancel. If you select Insert before canceling, the number you calculated is inserted into the location of your cursor in the file.

Alarm Clock

Sometimes you can get really caught up in using Works and forget a meeting or dinner. To prevent time from slipping away, select `Alarm Clock` from the Options menu. Current alarms that are set appear. Enter the message to be displayed. Type in the date and time for the alarm and identify the frequency. Then select `Set`. Your alarm appears as indicated.

There are other alarm possibilities. Simply select the alarm and related information to change with a click of the mouse. Enter the new information. Then select `Change`. The new message appears. To delete an alarm, select the alarm with the mouse and then select `Delete`. The alarm is immediately deleted. When you are done with the alarm box, select `Done`.

> ▶ **Tip**: Make sure the date and time are set correctly in the PS/1. Otherwise, your alarm clock will be operating with the wrong information. See "File Management" earlier in this chapter for information on setting the date and time through Works.

What You Have Learned

In this chapter you've learned

- ▶ There are common key assignments, screens, menus, and commands throughout Works tools, along with special ones tool by tool.
- ▶ You can perform file handling activities similar to many of the DOS Main Group functions through Works, for example, by selecting `File Handling` on the File option.
- ▶ Works gives you a calculator, and you can insert the result in your file at your cursor location by selecting `Options` and then `Calculator`.
- ▶ You may use the Works alarm clock to remind yourself about important events by selecting Options and then `Alarm Clock`.

Chapter 9
MS Works—Beginning Word Processing

In This Chapter

▶ *Entering, inserting, and deleting text*
▶ *Selecting text for deletion, copying, and moving*
▶ *How to undo your last edits if you make a mistake*
▶ *Creating page breaks or using Works automatic page breaks*
▶ *Printing your document*

Entering and Editing Text

To use Works word processing, you first must create a new word processing file or access an existing file. (See Chapter 8, "MS Works—Getting Started," for details on how to do these functions.) After you are in the file, you can change the text as you like.

To start developing a document, simply begin typing. As you type in sentences, don't press the Enter key at the end of a line. The lines will automatically wrap around. This way, when you later insert or delete text, the rest of the text is quickly aligned. When you do want to end a paragraph, press Enter.

> **Caution**: Until you are familiar with Works, follow instructions precisely. Many of the function keys are assigned special uses. If you accidentally press them, you could go into what may seem like outer space and not be familiar enough with Works to get back to what you were doing.

For example, in the letter shown in Figure 9.1, Enter was pressed at the end of each address line. However, Enter was not pressed at the end of the first line of the body of the letter.

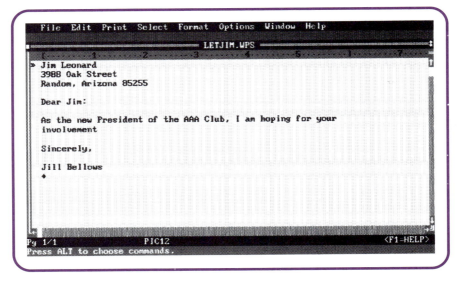

Figure 9.1 **Word processing letter**

As you work, you may want to move quickly around the document. You can press the keys listed in Table 9.1 to get you where you want to go fast.

To insert a character, move your cursor across the existing text to the spot to insert text. Then type in the text. The existing characters move to the right. If you make a mistake, there is one simple way to delete text: press the Backspace key to delete characters to the left of your cursor one at a time. To delete several characters at once, select the text (see the next section on selecting text) and press the Delete key.

Table 9.1 Cursor movement keys

Keys	Action
↑, ↓, ←, →	One character in any direction
Ctrl+→	One word to the right
Ctrl+←	One word to the left
Ctrl+↑	A paragraph up
Ctrl+↓	A paragraph down
Home	Beginning of a line
End	End of a line
Ctrl+Home	Beginning of file
Ctrl+End	End of file
PgUp	Up one window screen
PgDn	Down one window screen
Ctrl+PgUp	To the top of a window
Ctrl+PgDn	To the end of a window

> ▶ **Tip**: As you edit text, routinely and frequently save your text by selecting `File` and then `Save`. Otherwise, if you accidentally lose power, you stand to lose all the edits you have made since the last save. See Chapter 8, "MS Works—Getting Started," for more information on using the Save command.

Selecting Text

Sometimes, rather than affecting text character by character, you may want to affect a lot of text at one time. For example, you may want to delete, copy, or move a block of text. To do this, you first *select* the text to affect and then complete the desired operation.

To select text, place your cursor under the first character or space you want to select. Press the Shift key and hold it down. Press the arrow keys until the text you want to select is completely highlighted. Then complete the operation. For example, to delete, press the Delete key. Figure 9.2 shows selected text. If you press the Delete key, the text will disappear.

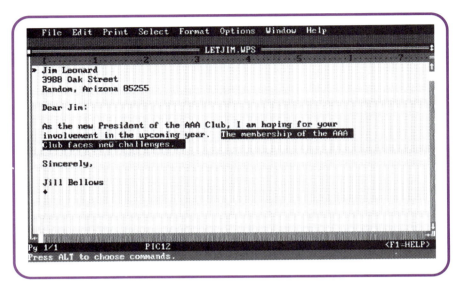

Figure 9.2   Selected text

You also can select text with the mouse. Press the left button at the start of the text to select; then *drag* (hold down the button and move the pointer) to the end of the selection. Release the button at the end of the selection.

If you select some text and then decide against your selection, press any arrow key. The highlighting disappears.

 Selecting Text with the Cursor

1. Place the cursor under the first character or space to select.	The cursor marks the first character in the selection.
2. Press the Shift key and hold it down.	The selection begins.
3. Press the arrow keys to highlight your selection.	The text you select is highlighted.
4. Complete the operation, such as pressing the Delete key.	The selected text is affected as desired. ☐

Selecting Text with the Mouse

1. Point at and press the button under the first character or space to select.	The pointer marks the first character in the selection.
2. Keeping the button depressed, drag the mouse to the end of the selection.	Text highlighting begins.
3. Release the button when the text is all highlighted.	The text is completely highlighted.
4. Complete the operation, such as pressing the Delete key.	The selected text is affected as desired. ☐

> **Tip**: Pay attention to the punctuation and spaces you include in selected text. For example, in Figure 9.2, the spaces after the sentence are included. That way, the correct spacing remains at the end of the sentence. Plus, if you move or copy the sentence, the correct spacing will be taken along with the selection.

Copying Text

Copying text enables you to keep one version of the text and place another identical version elsewhere. Copying text is helpful when you have similar text to repeat in a document, common symbols or lines (possibly when creating a form), or when you want to work with part of a document but keep the original version intact.

To copy text, select it first (see the "Selecting Text" section earlier in this chapter). Then hold down the Shift key and press F3. Put the cursor to the spot where you want to insert the text. The following prompt appears on the bottom of the screen:

```
Select new location and press ENTER. Press ESC to cancel.
```

Press Enter to complete the copy. Existing text after the insertion is moved to the right and down on the page. If you decide not to copy the text, press the Escape key. The copy operation is canceled, and the text is still highlighted as being selected.

> ▶ **Tip**: An alternative to using Shift+F3 is selecting `Edit` and then `Copy` from the menu bar. `COPY` appears on the status bar and disappears once you press Enter to complete the copy.

> ▶ **Tip**: An easy way to copy text from one file to another is to copy text between windows. Simply select `File` to open another file. Then select the text to copy and press Shift+F3. Switch between windows using Ctrl+F6. Place your cursor in the location to copy to and press Enter.

Moving Text

Moving text is useful when you want to remove text from one spot and place it in a new location. To move text, select the text to move (see "Selecting Text" earlier in this chapter). Press F3. The selected text remains in place, and the following message appears at the bottom of the screen:

```
Select new location and press ENTER. Press ESC to cancel.
```

Place your cursor at the new location for the text to be inserted. When you do, the highlight disappears. Don't worry, the text is still selected. Press Enter. The text is moved. If you decide against the move, simply press Escape.

Look again at the selected text in Figure 9.2. If you select the text, press F3, put the cursor under the A in `As the new...`, and press Enter, then the results in Figure 9.3 appear. Since the selection included no spaces before the sentence and two spaces after the selection, the spacing needs no further editing.

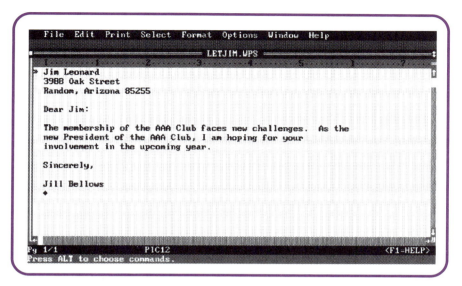

Figure 9.3 Move completed

> **Tip**: Remember F3 as your key to move and Shift+F3 as your key to copy.

> **Tip**: You can move text between two files by opening both as windows on the screen at once and then completing the move. First, select File to open another file. Then select the text to move and press F3. Switch between windows using Ctrl+F6. Position your cursor for the moved text and press Enter.

Undo

Everyone makes mistakes. But your word processing mistakes don't have to be costly if you undo them right away. For example, this option is a lifesaver when you accidentally delete a lot of text. Immediately select Edit on the menu and then Undo. The text you had deleted is restored.

Chapter 9

Undo "undoes" the last activity. This may be a deletion, a copy, a move, format changes, commands just selected, or words corrected by the spelling checker.

Pages

Microsoft Works automatically calculates when to end a page and begin a new page. A chevron (») appears before the first line of a new page. And the new page number appears in the bottom left corner of the screen.

If you want to tell Works where to place a page break, you may do so. Place your cursor where you want the page break. Select `Print` in the menu bar and then select the `Insert Page Break` command. A dotted line representing the page break appears across the screen.

Figure 9.4 illustrates all the page symbols: the chevron inserted automatically by Works for a page break, the page number showing the page on which your cursor resides, and the forced page break dotted line.

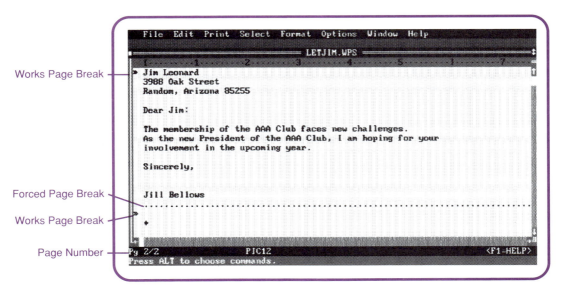

Figure 9.4 Page symbols

To delete a forced page break, place your cursor under the dotted line and in the far left column of the screen. Press Backspace. The dotted line disappears, and the page break is gone.

Printing

Just about everyone who uses word processing needs to print. Before you instruct Works to print your document, make sure that your printer is on and ready to print.

To print, go to the menu bar by pressing Alt. Select `Print`. The box shown in Figure 9.5 appears. Change any of the following options if desired. As with all box entries, you must select the option (use the highlighted letter) to enter an X before the option. Complete additional information, such as pages or file names, as necessary.

The printing options which appear in the box are:

`Number of copies`: enter the number of copies you wish to print.

`Print specific pages`: enter the range of pages of a document to print if you don't want to print the entire document. To print individual pages, put a comma between the page numbers. For example, you would make the following entry to print page 2 through and including page 4 and then print page 6:

> 2-4,6

`Print to file`: Enter a file name here if you want to create a file commonly called an ASCII file or DOS file. This is a special file format that can be used by other DOS-based computers or can easily be sent over the telephone line using Works communications to another computer.

`Draft quality`: Use this option to print quickly, if your printer allows for a draft quality print.

Then select `Print`. Or if you decide not to print, choose `Cancel`.

If you have trouble printing, select `Print` and then `Printer Setup`. Select your brand and model of printer, the *resolution* (density) of printing graphic images, whether pages will be continuously fed by the printer or manually fed, and the port the printer is connected to—LTP1 usually.

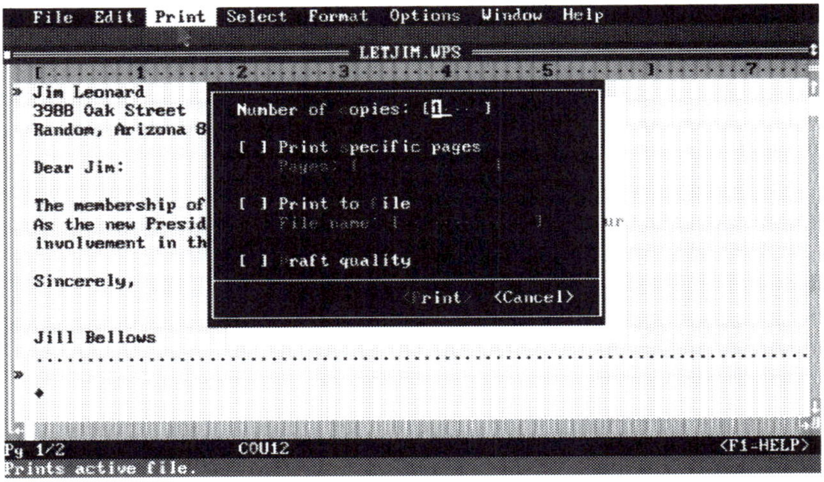

Figure 9.5   Print box

> **Tip**: Once you have finished working on your document, select Close to save the file and then Exit to exit Works. See Chapter 8, "MS Works—Getting Started," for more information on using the Close and Exit commands.

What You Have Learned

In this chapter you've learned

- ▶ Backspace to delete a character; type to insert.
- ▶ Select text by pressing Shift and an arrow key.
- ▶ To copy text, select it, press Shift+F3, place the cursor, and press Enter; to move text use F3 instead of Shift+F3.
- ▶ Other useful menu options: Edit, Undo and Print, Page Break.
- ▶ To print, use the Print option, enter various options, and then select Print.

Chapter 10

MS Works—Advanced Word Processing

In This Chapter

- *Controlling how your document prints on the page, including margins, page length, headers, footers, and page numbers*
- *Using indents and controlling the space between lines*
- *Adding special formats to characters and paragraphs to enhance the appearance of your document*
- *Searching for and, optionally, replacing characters*
- *Spell checking your document*

Page Setup and Margins

Works sets up margins for you automatically. These margins are used by Works to determine how much space to leave at the top, bottom, left, and right of the page. The margins set in Works are shown in Figure 10.1. The left margin is 1.3" and the right is 1.2". The total top and bottom margins are 1 inch each. If you add a *header* and/or *footer* (common text printed on several pages such as a document name or page number), the header and/or footer appears at .5 inch. Works assumes that the paper is 8.5 inches wide by 11 inches long.

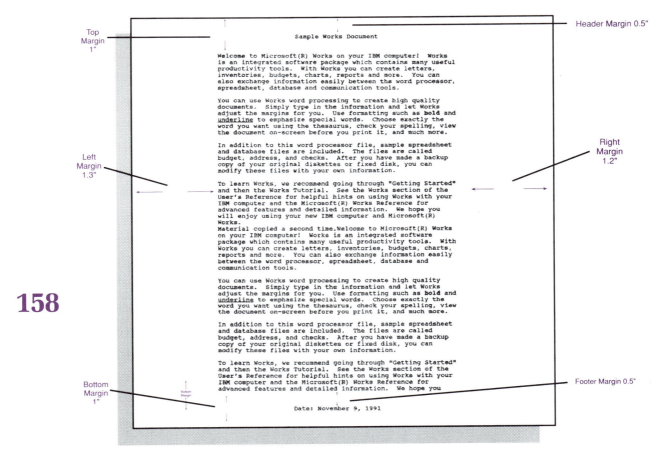

Figure 10.1 Works margins

To change margins, select Print and then Page Setup & Margins. Each of the margin settings along with the page length and width appear in a box. Change the settings as you desire. The settings are attached to your document. If you bring up another document, the original Works settings appear.

> ▶ **Tip**: If you typically use documents with margin settings other than the Works defaults, create a *boilerplate* document with those margin settings. Then, when you create a new document and want those margin settings, you can open the existing boilerplate document, save it under the new document name, and thus avoid always having to enter the new settings.

Indents and Line Spacing

You may want to indent paragraphs. You can control the following variables when indenting:

Left and right indent: the space in inches from the existing left or right margin to the indented left or right margin.

First line indent: the space in inches from the existing left margin—or indented left margin if set—to the indented first line.

Figure 10.2 illustrates two indents. In this example, the quote is set off by entering both the left and right indent at 1" from the existing margins. The numbers (1. and 2.) are set off by using a left indent of .5", a first line indent of −.5" to move the first line back to the existing left margin, and a right indent of 0 which keeps it identical to the existing right margin.

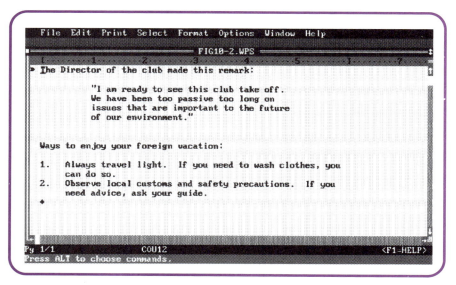

Figure 10.2   Uses of indents

To set an indent, select the text to be affected by the indenting. Select as much or as little text as you like. Then select Format from the menu bar. On the Format menu, select Indents & Spacing. The box shown in Figure 10.3 appears. If you select several paragraphs, there are no values for the indents.

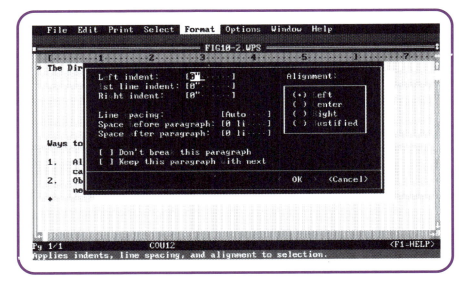

Figure 10.3 Indent & Spacing box

Enter the spacing for the left indent, first line indent, and right indent as needed to get the effect you want. When you finish, select `OK`. The highlighted text is affected. What you see on your screen is what you get (also known as *WYSIWYG*; pronounced "wiz´-z-wig").

 Tip: If the indents and spacing are not what you expect or want, simply select the text again and enter new values.

Use the same Indents & Spacing box to enter the *line spacing* for text (the space between lines). To do this, select the text, select `Format`, and then `Indents & Spacing`. From the Indents & Spacing box, enter the number of lines to skip. Single spacing is AUTO, one and one half space is 1.5, double-spacing is 2, etc.

Settings from the Format menu are attached to the characters or paragraphs you select—not the document as a whole. Therefore, if you want to double-space an entire document, set double-spacing in the first paragraph and keep your cursor before the paragraph symbol at the end of that paragraph. Works comes with the paragraph marks hidden, but you can sneak a peek.

To actually see the paragraph marks containing the format settings and other format characters, select Options and then Show All Characters. You return to your document where format symbols such as paragraph marks, spaces, and indents appear. To get rid of the symbols, select Format and then Show All Characters again. The type of format symbols are shown in Figure 10.4. Most users like to keep this option turned on. It helps to see what you are doing.

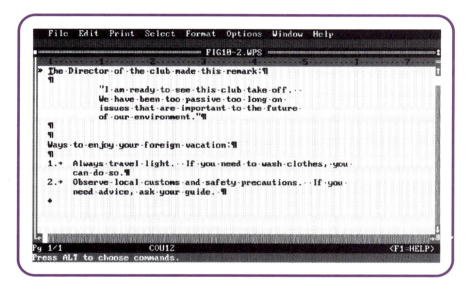

Figure 10.4 Show All Characters turned on

Headers, Footers, and Page Numbers

A *header* is common text that appears at the top of a page. In this book, for example, chapter information is presented in the header to inform you about which chapter you're using. A *footer* is common text that appears at the bottom of a page.

By using headers and/or footers, you eliminate retyping this standard text. But, more importantly, the text in the body of the document can flow from page to page as you edit without your having to constantly readjust text at the top and bottom of pages.

Headers and footers may be multiple lines long. This capability makes headers and footers especially flexible for entering a variety of information. The possibilities are endless, but following are a few:

Page numbers which Works numbers consecutively
Titles
Names of authors
Dates
Copyright notices
Confidential reminders
Notice that the document is a draft
Graphic designs

You control headers, footers, and page numbers through the Print menu. This makes sense because headers and footers only appear on the page when the document is printed. With your cursor anywhere in the document, select Print and then Headers & Footers. The box shown in Figure 10.5 appears.

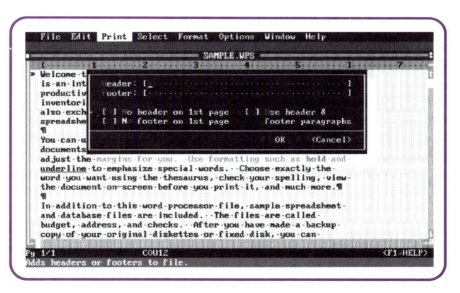

Figure 10.5   Header & Footer box

Place an X in the Use Header & Footer Paragraphs option by pressing U for Use. If you want to skip the header or footer on the first page for some reason, such as the first page being a cover letter, select the highlighted letter to place an X in either of the following options:

```
No header on 1st page
No footer on 1st page
```

After you have entered the appropriate Xs, select `OK`.

You can enter header or footer text in the Header & Footer box after `Header:` or `Footer:`. These fields can be used for word processing documents and must be used for spreadsheet or database headers or footers. The alternative in a word processing document is to enter the text in the document, which is the approach in this chapter. If you do enter the header or footer in the box, use the special characters listed in Table 10.1 if desired.

Table 10.1 Special header and footer characters

Characters	Desired Action
&l or &r	Left or right column alignment
&c	Center characters
&p	Print page number
&f	Print file name
&d	Print date
&t	Print time
&&	Print an ampersand

After you select `OK`, you return to your document. An `H` (for header) and `F` (for footer) appear in the far left column of the window. Both are at the top of the document. Don't worry, Works will place both your header and footer at the appropriate spots during the printing of the document.

To enter the text of your header or footer, move your cursor under the paragraph mark after the `H` or `F`. Select `Options` and then `Show All Characters` to display the paragraph marks. Type the header text using any word processing options you like. If you want the header or footer to be more than one line long, press Shift+Enter at the end of a line instead of just Enter. That way, the header or footer text will stay together. If your header or footer becomes too large to fit in the allowed margin, you can make the margin larger (see "Page Setup and Margins" in this chapter).

When you are done entering header or footer text and want to return to working on your document, press an arrow key to return to the body of the text. You can return to the header or footer area any time to edit the text there. Simply use the arrow keys.

> **Tip**: To omit just the header or footer, leave the line after the H or F blank.

You may have noticed that the footer contained centered text like the following:

```
Page - *page*
```

This is the format used by Works to enter a page number. The characters:

```
Page -
```

will be followed by a consecutive incremented page number on each page.

If you want to keep the page number centered in the bottom footer, leave the notation alone. If you want to put the page number somewhere else, delete *page* from the footer. Place your cursor where you want the page number, select Insert Special on the Edit menu, and then Print page. The *page* notation is entered.

You also can select Insert Special on the Edit menu to print the date, the time of the printing, or the file name in your document. This information can appear in the header or footer—or anywhere in a document for that matter. For example, when you select Print date, the following notation appears in your text where the current date will be printed:

```
*date*
```

> **Tip**: DO NOT type just ***page***, ***date***, or any other notation using the asterisk and letters on your keyboard. If you do, the asterisks and letters will print—not the page, date, time, or file name.

When you use a page number, you may want the page number to begin with a number other than 1. If so, select Print and then Page Setup & Margins. In the 1st Page Number field, enter the page number you want to begin with and select OK.

To delete a header or footer, select `Print` and then `Headers & Footers`. **Select** `Use header & footer paragraphs` and press the space bar. The `X` disappears. Select `O K`. The header and footer lines are removed from the file.

Adding Headers and Footers

1. From within a document, select `Print`.

   The Print commands appear.

2. Select `Headers & Footers`.

   The Headers & Footers box appears.

3. Press U to place an X before `Use header & footer paragraphs`.

   The `X` appears.

4. If desired, place an X to omit the header or footer on the first page.

   `X`s appear in either or both options if selected.

5. Select `O K`.

   The `H` and `F` appear in the far left column of the window.

6. Type the header and footer information after the `H` or `F`. Use Shift+Enter at the end of a line for multiple lines. Select `Edit` and then `Insert Special` to add page numbers or other special notations. Select `Print` and then `Page Setup & Margins` to enter a new first page number.

   The header and footer information appears.

7. Use the arrow keys to return to your document.

   You go back to the body of your text. The header and footer will appear in the proper positions when printed.   □

Deleting Headers and Footers

1. Select `Print` and then `Headers & Footers`.

   The Headers & Footers box appears.

2. Select `Use header & footer paragraphs` and press the space bar.

   The `X` disappears.

3. Select `OK`.   The header and footer lines
                                   are deleted.   ☐

Formats

As you learned earlier in this chapter, indents are considered a type of special formatting. There are a variety of other special formatting characteristics which you can select. Some may be dependent on your printer's ability to handle them. But most can be handled by standard printers.

To get to these special formats, use the Format menu. This menu is divided into three boxed areas. The commands in the first box govern characters. To use them, first select the text to be affected. Then select `Format` and the command from the Format menu. The selected text appears in the character format you identify. Following are the potential format options for characters:

`Plain Text`: returns any special character formatting you've entered to the plain, ordinary text.

`Bold`: makes the text stand out with thicker and darker characters.

`Underline`: places a single underline below each character or space.

`Italic`: makes the text appear in italics (not handled by all printers).

`Font & Style`: enables you to select different *fonts* (type styles such as Courier or Roman), *type sizes* (such as 10 characters per inch or 12 characters per inch), or *line position* (such as superscript or subscript).

Experiment with your printer to see the types of special character formats you can produce.

 Tip: You can enter more than one character format style. For example, text can be bold and underlined.

The next boxed area in the Format menu controls formatting for a paragraph. When you select an option, the paragraph in which your cursor resides is affected. If you want to affect more than one paragraph, select the text to be affected and then complete the command selection.

The Normal Paragraph command restores Works default paragraph options to a paragraph. This includes left justification, single-spaced lines, and no special indenting. The following four commands control how the paragraph is aligned between margins. Figure 10.6 illustrates each option:

Left: the text in the paragraph is lined up on the left margin leaving a ragged right margin.

Center: each line of the text in the paragraph is centered leaving a ragged left and right margin.

Right: the text in the paragraph is aligned on the right margin, which leaves a ragged left margin.

Justified: the text is spread between the right and left margins to achieve a straight right and left edge with extra spacing between words and letters.

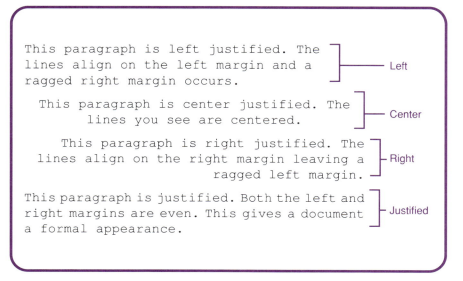

Figure 10.6   Paragraph alignment between margins

Chapter 10

Also in the center boxed area of the Format menu are the Single Space and Double Space commands. Select either of these and the spacing of the highlighted paragraph(s) is affected. See "Indents and Line Spacing" in this chapter for information about the Indents & Spacing command in the center boxed area of the Format menu. It is your option if you want spacing options other than single- or double-spacing.

The final format options are Tabs and Borders. Borders enables you to control the appearance of the window borders such as changing the style of the lines. Most users of Works leave the borders as they are.

Tabs is a more useful function that many Works users like to be able to control. Works comes with the tab settings visible. They appear in the top of the window as follows:

```
[.........1.........2..........3.........4.........5.........]..
```

This line is called the *ruler*. If your ruler does not appear, turn it on by selecting Options and then Show Ruler.

The left margin is shown as a left bracket ([). The right margin is shown as a right bracket (]). And each inch is represented by a number (1, 2, etc.). The tabs are set by Works at every half inch. That way, when you press the Tab key, your cursor goes quickly to the next tab setting.

> ▶ **Tip**: If the Show All Characters option on the Options menu is turned on, the tab stops appear on your screen as small arrows.

Works gives you several tab options. They are

Left: text aligns on the left.

Center: text aligns on the center.

Right: text aligns on the right.

Decimal: text aligns by the decimal point.

These options are illustrated here:

Left	Center	Right	Decimal
Part A	Winnabi	In stock	$49.65
Part B	Eli	Out of stock	$109.98
Part C	Biggerday	Not stocked	$1,009.90

You also can add a *leader* before the tab. A leader is a character that will repeat from when you first pressed the Tab key up to the text you enter. The options are none, dots, dashes, underlines, or equal signs. For example, dots are often used when creating a table of contents:

```
Chapter          1.............................................3
Chapter          2............................................14
```

To set new tabs, select `Format` and then `Tabs`. A box appears with the options. To enter the position you want to affect, press Ctrl+Left Arrow or Ctrl+Right Arrow. You can watch the position change on the ruler line, and the corresponding value appears in the field. Stop the cursor at the position you want. To leave the Position field, press Tab. Select `Alignment`. Then set the `Leader` as desired. Finally, select whether you want to `Insert`, `Delete`, or `Delete All`; return to the Works original default tab settings, or select `Done` to exit the box.

> ▶ **Tip**: If you intend to change several tabs in an existing document, you may want to save a version of the original file. That way, if you don't like your changes, you can always go back to the original file.

> ▶ **Tip**: If you commonly use tab settings other than Works defaults, you can create a document with those tab settings and save it as a boilerplate document. That way, you can open that existing file, save it under another name (keeping the original boilerplate document), and avoid having to consume unnecessary time setting the same tab stops over and over.

Search and Replace

The search and replace feature of Works can make your work go faster. If you make a common mistake throughout the document, such as a misspelled name, you can search for and replace each occurrence of the text. You also can find your place quickly in a long document by searching for key words in that part of the document.

To search, put your cursor where you want the search to begin. Go to the Select menu. Pick Search. Enter the text, symbols, and spaces to search for. Type in a question mark (?) to match any single character—instead of a specific character you enter. Mark Match whole word with an X if you want an exact match of the characters entered. For example, if you enter **cat** and select Match whole word, you only find cat—not catatonic or scat. Mark Match upper/lower case with an X if you want an exact match per the capital and small letters you entered. Otherwise, Works ignores the case. Select OK when you are ready to search. Works finds the first match. Press F7 to find the next match. To stop searching, press Esc.

To replace text, start with your cursor at the beginning of the text to search and replace. Use the Select menu and pick Replace. Enter the text to search for and the text to replace with. Enter the **?** for single, unknown characters. Put an X before the Match whole words message to match exact words—not identify parts of words. Put an X before the Match upper/lower case to only search out text matching the small and capital letters indicated. Select Replace if you want Works to stop before each replacement and ask you to select Yes or No to the suggested replacement. Select Replace All if you want Works to replace the text without asking your permission each time.

> ▶ **Tip**: You can enter special characters to search for particular characters or spaces. Some of these include:
> ^t   Tab mark
> ^p   Paragraph mark
> ^n   End of line mark
> ^?   Question mark
> ^w   White space (any amount)

Spell Checking

You don't have to be the winner of your high school spelling bee to turn out superior documents with Works. Works has a spell checker that identifies misspelled words along with words Works can't identify when it (very quickly) checks its dictionary.

To check the spelling in a document, place your cursor where you want to begin spell checking. Usually, this is at the top of the document; press Ctrl+Home to get there fast. Go to the Options menu and select Check Spelling. Works goes to the first word that is not in the Works dictionary. It may be a misspelling, typographical error, or a proper name (that may be correctly spelled). A box appears like that shown in Figure 10.7.

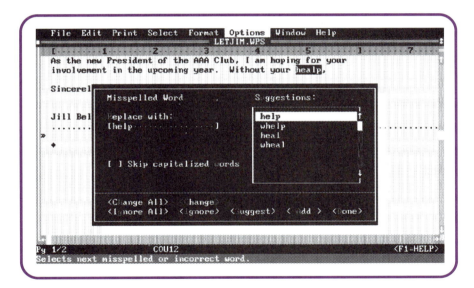

Figure 10.7   Spell box with suggestions

Your options are shown in the bottom area of the box. Just press Alt plus the highlighted letter to perform one of these options:

Change the word: type in the correct spelling in the Replace With field, and press Alt+C to change this single occurrence or Alt+H to change all occurrences.

Ignore the word and go on: press Alt+I to ignore this single occurrence of the word or Alt+G to ignore all occurrences of the word.

See other suggested spellings: press Alt+S to see the list, select the spelling, and press Enter or Alt+C to change the word.

Add the word to your personal dictionary: press Alt+A. Your name is a good word to add to your personal dictionary.

Done: Press Alt+D if you are done spell checking.

If you started the spell check in the body of the document (not at the beginning), the following message appears at the end of the document:

```
End of document: continue to check spelling from start?
```

Select OK if you want to pick up the portion of the document you missed at the beginning. Select Cancel to stop spell checking.

What You Have Learned

In this chapter you've learned to

- Change margins with the Page Setup & Margins option on the Print menu.
- Control indents and line spacing with the Indents & Spacing option on the Format menu.
- See formatting characters on your screen by selecting Show All Characters on the Options menu.
- Create headers, footers, and page numbers with the Headers & Footers option on the Print menu; use Ctrl+Enter at the end of header and footer lines.
- Use other menu and command options: Edit, Insert Special to add page numbers, etc; Format for special formats; Select to search or replace.
- Spell check with the Check Spelling option on the Options menu.

Chapter 11

MS Works—Spreadsheet and Charting

In This Chapter

- *Creating a spreadsheet including labels, numbers, and formulas*
- *Changing the appearance of the spreadsheet*
- *Controlling the cells and sorting data*
- *Printing and saving a spreadsheet*
- *Creating charts*

Spreadsheets

Need to work with numbers? A *lot* of numbers? Use Works spreadsheet tool. The spreadsheet is the ticket for activities such as performing calculations for budgets and what if scenarios for financial forecasts. Any time you need numbers and math, turn to Works' spreadsheet.

There are some general spreadsheet concepts for you to know before going further. A spreadsheet is organized in *rows* and *columns*. A row runs horizontally across the screen and a column runs vertically. Each row/column box created is called a *cell*. In cells, you enter *labels* for titles and headings and *numbers* for calculations. You also can put formulas in cells for calculating.

Figure 11.1 illustrates the concept of rows and cells. In this personal investment spreadsheet, the title Personal Investments is entered as a label as are the other text titles. The amounts shown (24000, 9000, 4000) are entered as numbers. And the total (37000) is calculated as a *sum* of the numbers. The *cell pointer* marks your place in the spreadsheet; here it is on the total amount.

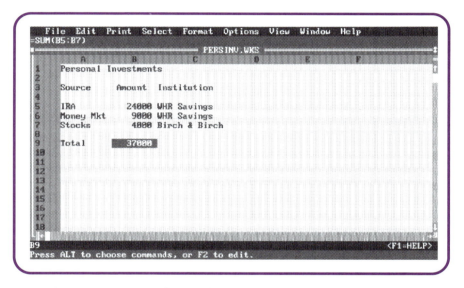

Figure 11.1 Sample Works spreadsheet

As you can see in the figure, the columns are assigned letters (A, B, etc.). The rows are assigned numbers (1, 2, etc.). A specific cell location is referred to by the column and row combined. For example, the sum in Figure 11.1 is located in cell B9. The formula to do the calculation is in the cell and is expressed as:

=SUM(B5:B7)

This formula means "Give me the sum of the cells from B5 through B7."

In this chapter, you will learn how to enter labels, numbers, formulas, and make the whole picture "prettier" with commas, different sized cells, and other format options. You can open a spreadsheet file in a manner similar to opening a word processing file. Select Microsoft Works from the System menu. Select File. Then select Create New File or Open Existing File. Continue to select the type or specific file to open.

Once inside the spreadsheet, you can move the cell pointer cell by cell with the arrow keys. On a small spreadsheet, this is the way to get around. But spreadsheets can be very large and moving cell by cell too cumbersome. To move quickly, press the Control key with an arrow key. To move to the upper left of your spreadsheet, press Ctrl+Home. To move to the lower right, press Ctrl+End. Press Home or End to go to the first or last cell in a row. Use Control with Page Up or Page Down to move right or left one window.

Entering and Deleting Labels and Numbers

A *label* generally is any cell that starts with a letter (rather than a number). Labels often include numbers. To enter a label or number, move the cell pointer with the arrow key to the cell you want. Type in the label or number. If you do need to enter a number as a label, enter a quotation mark (") before the number.

When you enter numbers, you can include minus signs and decimal points. Dollar signs you type in are ignored, commas are deleted, and the number before a percentage symbol (%) is turned into the percent (that is, 10% becomes .10).

As you enter a label or number, use the Backspace key to delete characters to the left of the cursor. After you press Enter or move the cell pointer, the value is entered and any calculations are recalculated.

To delete the contents of a single cell, put the cell pointer on the cell and press Delete and then Enter. Or you may type over the existing entry, but make sure you get it all.

To delete the contents of multiple cells in one swoop, select the cells with the Shift+Arrow key, or click and drag the mouse. Press Alt and go to the Edit menu. Select Clear. The contents are deleted.

Entering a Series of Cells

Some information you want to enter in a Works spreadsheet may be repetitive in nature. Therefore, Works has created a way to automatically enter common series. For example, budgets typically have information by month, and investment analysis may have information by year. Works can save you time if you enter a common series of numbers, days, months, or years.

To enter a series of cells, type in the first cell and press Enter. Select this cell and the cells to the right or below which will contain the series. Select Edit and then Fill Series. A box appears; choose the unit (Number, Day, Weekday, Month, or Year). Then enter the Step By information in the box. This is the increment you want. Select OK and your values appear.

For example, to enter **Jan** for January, select 12 cells; the Edit option, Fill Series, Month; and then Step by 1. All the months from January to December appear.

Formatting

Formatting affects the appearance of your spreadsheet. You can change the way labels and numbers appear, such as add dollar signs or commas, or control the width of the column. You can format a single cell or a range of selected cells. The Format menu is your key to the options.

For example, to add the dollar sign and commas to the numbers in Figure 11.1, select the numbers with Shift+Arrow Key. Then select Format and Currency. A box appears asking for the amount of decimal numbers. Leave the suggested value 2 in place and select OK to get the result shown in Figure 11.2—which needs some work!

The hashes appear in the first number and total cell in Figure 11.2 because the space required to add the comma and dollar sign is more than is available in the cell width. Cell widths can be changed through the Format menu. Select Format and then Column Width. By entering **12** as the new width and pressing Enter, the spreadsheet in Figure 11.3 appears.

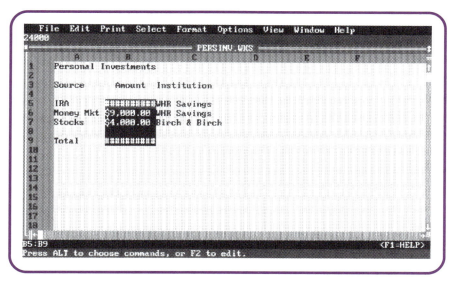

Figure 11.2 Result of selecting Format and Currency

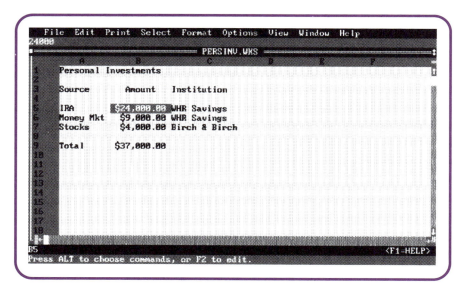

Figure 11.3 Result of widening the column

> **Tip**: When you enter a label in a cell, the text may still appear on the screen even though it is outside the cell. The complete label may not appear if text already appears in the next cell. Widen the column to include all the label. Otherwise, when you later go to move, copy, or delete the cell, you will not be able to see the text outside the column.

When you use any option on the Format menu, select the cells to be affected and then select the Format command. Complete any additional information required.

Following are the Format menu options:

General: displays your number as exactly as possible—even if it includes exponential notation.

Fixed: includes the number of decimal places you indicate in the result.

Currency: adds a dollar sign, commas, and the number of decimal places you indicate.

Comma: inserts commas every three places.

Percent: expresses numbers with the percent symbol (.10 becomes 10%).

Exponential: shows the result in exponential (scientific) notation.

True/False: displays a zero value as FALSE, and nonzero values show up as TRUE.

Time/Date: changes the way a time or date is displayed.

Font: selects a style of type, such as Courier or Roman, or a different size of type, such as 10 characters per inch or 12 characters per inch. You can use only one, nonproportional font per spreadsheet; the Fonts option works only if your printer handles different type styles.

Style: selects the alignment in a cell or a group of cells (General, Left, Right, Center) along with the style (Bold, Underline, or Italic).

> **Tip**: To enter the system date, press Ctrl+; (Control with the semicolon key). To enter the current system time, press Ctrl+: (Control with the colon key). If you want the cell to recalculate automatically to the date or time, enter this format in the cell:
>
> =now( )
>
> The date or time according to the current format appears. To change the date or time format, select Format, Time/Date, and then proceed.

Headers, Footers, and Margins

You can control page size and margins in spreadsheets just like in a word processing document. Select Print, Page Setup & Margins, and then complete the selections in the box. See the "Page Setup and Margins" section in Chapter 10, "MS Works—Advanced Word Processing," for more detailed information on using margins.

The process to set up headers, footers, and page numbering is much like that with a word processing document. Select Print, Headers & Footers, and then complete the box information. Type the header and footer information in the Header and Footer fields in the box—not on the spreadsheet itself. For more information, such as how to use the &p symbol to designate a page number, see the "Headers, Footers, and Page Numbers" section in Chapter 10, "MS Works—Advanced Word Processing."

Copying and Moving

You can copy and move cells, columns, and rows. To copy or move, select the cell(s) to copy or move. Select Edit and then Copy or Move. A message like this appears:

    Select new location and press Enter. Press ESC to cancel.

Place the cell pointer in the new location and press Enter. Or press Esc to stop the process. Then check your work to make any corrections or edits necessary.

For example, the Institution column in Figure 11.4 was moved one column to the right. The column was widened to accommodate the complete text.

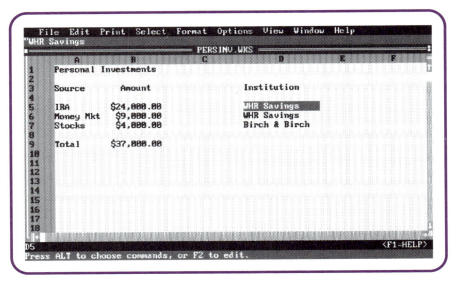

Figure 11.4 Column moved

> ⊘ **Caution**: When you copy or move cell contents, there can be some surprising outcomes. Always save your document before a copy or move so, if the results are unexpected, you can always go back to your original document. For example, if you move the contents of one column "over" the contents of another column, the existing column will be wiped out—not moved over. If you move a cell used in a formula, Works attempts to rewrite the formula to include the value you've moved. Sometimes this gives the right result. And sometimes the change made by Works adds other, unwanted values into your formula. Save a "pre-move or copy" version and check the result of your move or copy carefully.

Inserting and Deleting Rows and Columns

You also can insert and delete any existing row or column. When you delete a row or column, the remaining rows and columns adjust accordingly. Simply place your cell pointer on the row or column to delete. Select Edit and then Delete Row/Column. A box appears which enables you to identify whether you want to delete a row or column. Press R for Row or C for Column, or use your mouse. Select OK to complete the operation or Cancel to stop the operation. The row or column is immediately deleted.

> **Tip**: When you delete a row or column, check out the complete effect the deletion may have before you delete. Look at the entire row or column—not just what is on your screen. Use Page Up or Page Down to move around the spreadsheet just as you would a word processing document. Many users have deleted a row or column and then realized the complete effect too late.

Inserting a row or column is as easy as deleting. Place the cell pointer on the row to move down or on the column to move right. Select Edit. The box appears for you to select Row or Column. Then select OK. The row or column is inserted.

> **Tip**: If you are moving a row or column among rows and columns with labels and numbers, insert a row or column first to create space for the row or column you are moving.

Absolute Cell References

When you move or copy spreadsheet rows or columns, Works attempts to rewrite formulas to meet your intent. Sometimes you may want a formula to include the cell location—not the value. To identify a specific location, use an *absolute cell reference* by placing dollar signs around the reference. For example, to always go to cell A7, instead of using just A7 (which could be changed later by Works if you change the rows or columns), enter **A7**. You also can fix only the column or row such as **$A7** to fix column A or **A$7** to fix row 7.

Using Formulas

Master formulas and you master the most powerful part of spreadsheets, actually their "reason for being." There are a few simple conventions to follow. Every Works spreadsheet formula begins with an equal sign (=) or plus sign (+). The equal sign or plus sign is followed by any combination of a function name (such as SUM), cell addresses (such as B4), and operators (such as * for multiplication).

When you enter a formula in a cell, the result appears in the cell, and the formula bar appears just under the menu bar. To edit a cell, move the cell pointer to the cell and press F2 to enter the formula area.

Formulas can be long, so some quick editing keys help. In addition to typical editing keys, use Home or End to go to the beginning or end of the formula. Use Backspace or Delete to delete. You also can select characters in the formula bar.

Formulas may contain these operators and are evaluated in the order shown here.

Evaluated first	^ exponential
Evaluated second	– negative, + positive
Evaluated third	* multiply, / divide
Evaluated fourth	+ add, – subtract
Evaluated fifth	= equal to, <> not equal to, < less than, > greater than, <= less than or equal to, >= greater than or equal to
Evaluated sixth	~ NOT
Evaluated seventh	| OR, & AND

Use parentheses to group actions for processing. Consider this formula:

```
=(B1+C1)/D1
```

For example, suppose B1 is 10, C1 is 20, and D1 is 30. The result of the formula is 1 because the addition is handled first (10+20 =30). Then the division is handled (30/30=1).

Now consider this formula:

```
=B1+C1/D1
```

The result of the formula is rounded up to 11. The division is handled first (20/30=.67). Then the addition is handled (10+.67 rounds up to 11).

Formulas can have positive and negative numbers with or without decimals. Cells and ranges of cells may be included. For example, A6 indicates a single cell. Whereas, A6:B19 indicates all cells in the rectangular area with A6 as the upper left corner and B19 as the lower right corner.

Works' equations (called *functions*) can be used in formulas as well. Appendix B of your Microsoft Works Reference manual contains a list of the over 50 functions and information on how to use them. Most have to do with calculations related to math or business. Following are a few examples:

AVG	Calculates the average of the values in a range.
CTERM	Identifies the number of compounding periods for an investment given the rate, present value, and future value.
MAX	Identifies the largest number in a range.
SUM	Totals the amounts in a range.
TAN	Provides the tangent.

Hiding Cells

Some of the information in a spreadsheet may be confidential. Or you might find that the spreadsheet reads better without certain information appearing. Instead of deleting confidential or extraneous information, you can hide by columns. After one or more columns are hidden, you cannot scroll the column or enter information into the column.

Select a cell in each column to hide. Select Format and then Column Width. Enter zero (**0**) and choose OK. To later display a hidden column, pick Select, Go To (F5), and then type in the cell reference for the column. Pick OK. Select Format and then Column Width. Enter a value other than zero and select OK. The column displays.

Printing the Spreadsheet

To print your entire spreadsheet, simply pick Print and continue to identify the number of pages, page numbers to print, etc., just as you would any Works document. For more details on print options, see the "Printing" section in Chapter 9, "MS Works—Beginning Word Processing."

Works automatically determines where to break pages. Alternatively, you can identify where to place page breaks yourself. Place the cell pointer on the row or column for the page break. Select Print and then Insert Page Break. You can identify whether you want the page to break at a row or column. Once set, a *chevron* (double arrow) appears in the A, B, C or 1, 2, 3 area depending on whether you selected a row or column. To get rid of a page break you set, select Print and then Delete Page Break.

Because spreadsheets can be very large, you may want to print only a portion of a spreadsheet but not mess with setting page breaks and printing only certain pages. Instead, you can select the area to print. Then select Print and Set Print Area. To reset the entire area, select Print and then Set Print Area, or press Ctrl+Shift+F8.

Sorting

You can sort rows alphabetically or numerically. Simply select the rows to sort. You can include one or more columns in your selection.

Pick Select and then Sort Rows. A box appears with the first column to sort the rows by. Identify it by letter name and check whether you want to sort in ascending (A-Z, 1-9) order or descending (Z-A, 9-1) order. Within that sort, you can pick a second column to sort the data that is identical in the first column. And you may pick a third column to sort the information that matches in the second column.

In the following example, the "donations" rows were sorted first in descending order. Then when identical donations were encountered, the last name in ascending order was used for the sort. When both the donations and last name were a match, the first name in ascending order was used for the sort.

Donations:	**Last Names:**	**First Names:**
$5,000.00	Kelly	Barbara
$3,000.00	Jones	David
$3,000.00	Lincoln	Alice
$1,000.00	Jones	Alan
$1,000.00	Jones	Brice

Protecting Cells

Locking anything protects it. The same is true with cells. You may lock a cell so that the value or formula can't be changed. Initially, you can change any spreadsheet cells. The spreadsheet is unlocked, and the cells are unprotected. To use protection to lock cells: 1) select the cells to remain unlocked, and 2) protect the spreadsheet. When you protect the spreadsheet, the selected cells remain unlocked. The cells not selected are locked.

To select cells individually to remain unlocked, select `Format` and then `Style`. Select or unselect `Locked` depending on what you want. Select `OK`. To protect the cells not selected as unlocked, select `Options` and then `Protect Data`. You can turn the Protect Data option on or off as desired.

Saving and Closing the Spreadsheet

As you work on your spreadsheet, save it often. That way, you are protected from a power loss. To save the spreadsheet, select `File` and then `Save` to save under the current name or `Save As...` to save under a name you choose.

After you are done working on the spreadsheet, select `File` and then `Close` to close the spreadsheet. If you have changed the spreadsheet since the last save, a message appears asking whether you want to save the changes before the spreadsheet is closed. Respond by selecting `Yes` or `No`. The spreadsheet is closed.

Charts

Charts express information dramatically and quickly. With Works, you can create these types of charts automatically: bar, stacked bar, 100% bar, line, area line, hi-lo-close, pie, or X-Y. Figure 11.5 shows an example of a bar chart. Figure 11.6 shows an example of a line chart, and Figure 11.7 illustrates a pie chart.

To create a chart, you select the data to include on the chart, select `View`, and then `New Chart` to view the chart. After this is done, you are placed in CHART mode. Manipulate and print the chart as desired; then return to SPREADSHEET mode by selecting `View`. The specific steps follow.

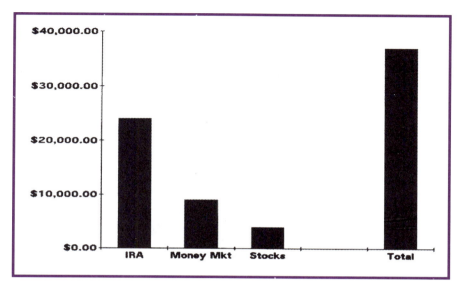

Figure 11.5   Bar chart

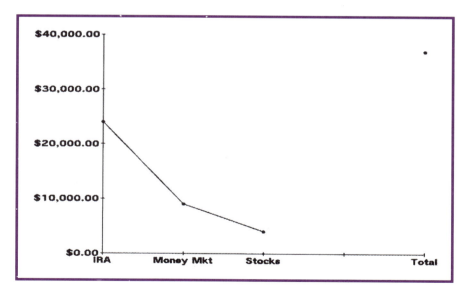

Figure 11.6   Line chart

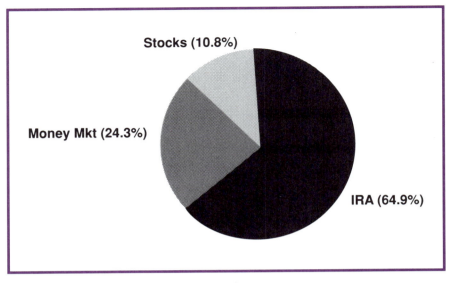

Figure 11.7   Pie chart

Creating a Chart

1. Select up to six rows or columns in your spreadsheet.	The adjacent rows and columns are highlighted.
2. Select View and then New Chart.	The chart appears on the screen.
3. Press Esc.	You return to the spreadsheet in CHART mode. CHART appears in the middle on the bottom of your screen.
4. Use the menu options to edit and print your chart.	You develop the chart further as necessary.
5. When done with the chart, select View and then Spreadsheet.	You return to the spreadsheet in SPREADSHEET mode; SPREADSHEET appears on the bottom of your screen.

▶ **Tip:** If you change the selected spreadsheet area for the chart, you must go back and select View and then New Chart to register the change in the selection. In addition, you must reset any format or other changes you have made.

There are many options to edit and print your chart. Following are some of the most used commands.

To identify the type of chart to develop, select `Format` and then the chart option (including `Bar`, `Stacked Bar`, etc.).

To change the appearance of the chart, select `Format` and then `Data Formats`. The Series box enables you to select the Y series or, if a pie chart, the pie slices for the selections. Make a selection and press Enter to lock in your selection.

To change the font style of the captions, select `Format` and then `Title Font` or `Other Font` and proceed.

If you want to add captions to the chart, select `Data` and then `Titles`, `Legends`, or `Data Labels`.

Ranges for X-Y axis charts are assigned positions in the Y series. To see—and potentially add, change, or delete—the Y series assignments for ranges, select `Data` and then `Series`.

To print a chart, select `Print` from the Print menu.

Experiment with charts. With just a little practice, you can enhance presentations and documents. For more details on using charts in word processing documents, see Chapter 13, "MS Works—Communications and Integrating Your Tools."

What You Have Learned

In this chapter you've learned

- ▶ To manipulate multiple cells, select them and then select `Edit`. Select `Clear` (to delete), `Copy`, or `Move`.
- ▶ To identify a row or column, select `Edit`, `Delete`, or `Insert Row/Column`.
- ▶ To enter a series of values, select `Edit` and then `Fill Series`.
- ▶ To change the appearance or width of cells, use the Format menu option.
- ▶ You can set up headers, footers, page numbers, and printing like a word processing document.
- ▶ To hide cells, select `Format` and set the Column Width option to zero.

- Protect cells with a combination of Format or Options menu selections.
- To sort rows that are selected, choose Select and then Sort Rows.
- You can develop charts from any spreadsheet value.

Chapter 12

MS Works—Database and Reporting

In This Chapter — 191

- *Entering database information*
- *Editing and formatting the database*
- *Setting up common report formats and printing*
- *Querying a database to select only specific information*

Databases

If your life involves lists of data, Works database tool can make life easier. You may need to use customer lists for a small business, lists of members for clubs, lists of students in classes, addresses, phone numbers, lists for holiday and birthday cards, lists of high scores in video games, and lists of vacation options. This list can go on and on.

With Works database, you can sort data, query for data meeting special conditions, and print reports formatted as you prefer.

To use the database, select `File`, `Create New File`, and then select `New Database`. Or if you want an existing database file, just select `File`, `Open Existing File`, and then enter the name of the file you want or choose a file from the list. Works database enables you to view your data in different forms (each called a *view*). Each view is useful for a different purpose described here.

Form View: for entering and editing data in an easy-to-read form.

List View: a spreadsheet-like format that enables you to see a great deal of data at once for comparisons and manipulation.

Report View: for entering headings and summaries, and for formatting the printed report.

Query View: for entering selection criteria to pick only the information you want from the database.

Use the View menu choice to flip between these views of your database. You cannot get to every view from every other view. Works lets you know what views are available from the view you are using.

The overall process of creating a database and generating reports can be broken down into the following major steps:

1. In Form View, you name general categories of individual pieces of data (called *field names*); enter field names and individual pieces of data. For example, "Last Name" may be a field name in an address list and "Jones" may be a piece of data for that field name.
2. In List View, you edit, change formats, and sort.
3. In Report View, you create report formats for your database and print reports.
4. In Query View, you gather specific data according to particular conditions you enter using Works operators.

That's the big picture. Now let's look at the details.

Entering Field Names and Data in Form View

As mentioned earlier, a field is a single piece of data, such as the last name "Jones." A field name is the name of the type of field, such as "Last Name." A *record* is all the information relating to a single entity. For example, there may be a record for John C. Jones that includes all the following individual fields (shown here by field name):

Field Name	*Field*
First Name	John
Middle Initial	C.
Last Name	Jones
Birth Date	9/30/53
Street Address	4500 Window Way
City	Phoenix
State	Arizona
Zip Code	85258
Phone Number	602-555-8907

After you select File, Create New File, and then select Database, you go to a database screen. You are in Form View (evidenced by FORM at the bottom of your screen). Form View enables you to create a form to enter data easily and to work on one record at a time.

Give your database a name by entering it in the upper left corner. The database name should be descriptive. It is not the same as the file name for the database.

Field Name

Use the arrow key to move down and type in the first field name. The field name must be followed with a colon. Editing text in the database is much like using a spreadsheet. Place your pointer on the text to be changed and press F2. Press Home to go to the beginning of the data or End to go to the end. Use the Delete or Backspace key to delete characters.

When you enter field names, be descriptive. Enter fields in a logical order for ease in adding the actual data later. Plan ahead so that you enter all the fields you will need to collect all the data at once. When you press Enter after typing in a field name, a box appears like that shown in Figure 12.1.

In the Field box, enter the Width (in characters) and Height (in lines). Select OK.

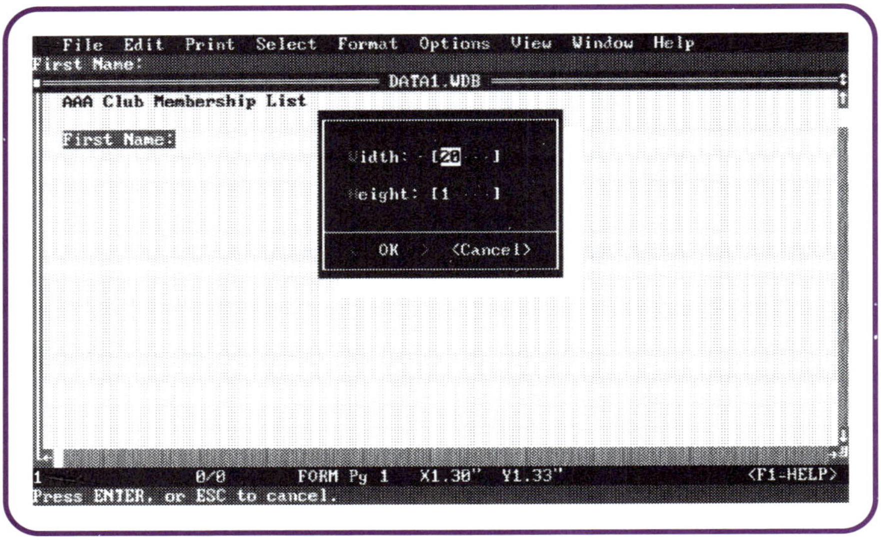

Figure 12.1   Field box

> ▶ **Tip**: Always enter a width greater than the current longest number of characters you will enter for this field. For example, if you were entering addresses, the longest address may be 37 characters long:
>
> **8433 North Weathersmith Way, Apt. 321**
>
> You should make the field larger than 37 characters because you will be adding to the database later and "longest field" lengths were made to be broken.

Continue entering each field name in this fashion until you have entered all of them.

> ▶ **Tip**: Take some time to save your work by selecting Save as... from the File option. Give the file a descriptive name.

Data

After you enter the field names, begin entering the data records field by field. Place the pointer after the first field name, enter the data, press Tab, and continue to enter each field in the record. Figure 12.2 shows the first record entered. Notice that the number 1 appears in the lower left corner. This indicates you are entering the fields for record number 1.

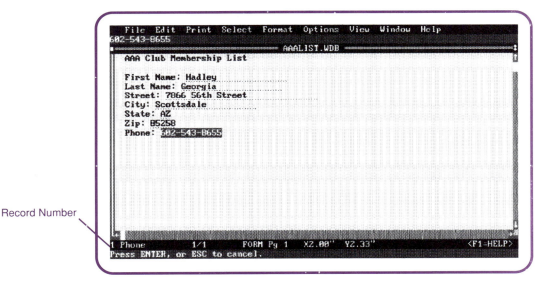

Figure 12.2   A record entered

After you complete all the fields in a record, press Ctrl+Page Down. The fields are saved in memory, and the field names appear with blanks after them so that you can enter another record. Continue entering all the records.

Editing Form View

You may edit the Form View of the database. Use the following keys and commands:

To change an existing field (with the pointer on the field)	Press F2 and edit.

To go to the next record	Press Ctrl+Page Down.
To change the size of a field (with data in the field and the pointer on the field)	Select Format, Field Size, and then enter the new size.
To affect the position or existence of records (pointer in the record)	Select Edit and then Move Record, Copy Record, Delete Record, or Insert Record; follow the prompts, if any.
To affect the position or existence of field names (pointer on the field name)	Select Edit and then Move, Clear, Delete, or Insert Line; follow the prompts, if any.

 Tip: The Clear command keeps the formatting in place but clears the data. Delete gets rid of the data and formatting.

Using Form View

1. Go to Form View by selecting File and then Create New File; File and then Open Existing File; or View and then Form.	FORM appears on the bottom of the screen.
2. Enter a database name in the upper left corner.	The database name appears.
3. Enter a field name followed by a colon.	The box for the field appears.
4. Identify the width and height of the field.	The field appears with dots for the data entry area.
5. Repeat steps 3 and 4 until you have entered all field names.	All field names for the records appear.
6. Place your pointer in the first field's data entry area and enter the data; press Tab and continue the process until one record is complete.	The data for the record appears.
7. Press Ctrl+Page Down to save the record in memory and start a new record.	The field data entry areas are cleared.

8. Continue to enter all records. Press Ctrl+Page Up or Ctrl+Page Down and edit record information if you make a mistake.

    Records appear in the form created.

9. Select `Edit` to move, copy, delete, or insert fields or records.

    Records and fields appear per your edits.

10. Save the database information you've entered by selecting `File` and then `Save As` to change the name or `File` and then `Save` to keep the current name.

    The data you've entered is saved to disk or diskette.

    ☐

As you work, you should save your work often. You do not want to lose any of the data you have tediously entered. To save the database from any View, use `File` and then `Save` to save the file under the current name or `File` and then `Save As` to enter a new name.

List View

The List View shows you more than one record at a time to allow comparison and manipulation. Figure 12.3 illustrates the membership list in List View. While the Form View is good for entering data, the List View is superior when you want to compare records. The List View resembles a spreadsheet with each field in a cell.

> ⊘ **Caution**: Although you may have set field lengths in Form View, the default width in List View is 10 characters. You may need to do some adjusting by selecting `Field Width` under the Format menu to expand or reduce some columns to display your information properly. Don't panic the first time you see the effect; your data is there, but it won't appear until you set the width properly. The width is also too small if you see ######### symbols in a cell.

Chapter 12

```
 File  Edit  Print  Select  Format  Options  View  Window  Help
"Hadley
                       AAALIST.WDB
  Hadley    Georgia   7866 56th Street      Scottsdale      AZ 85258
  Henry     Willows   897 El Camino         Phoenix         AZ 85221
  Jim       Leonard   3988 Oak Street       Random          AZ 84300
  Betty     Zallow    675 East Jefferson    Tucson          AZ 85321
  Kitty     Ruth      4498 San Miguel #1092 Albuquerque     NM 87109
  Bev       Shy       342 College           Lychfield Park  AZ 85340




1 First Name    7/7       LIST                              <F1-HELP>
Press ALT to choose commands, or F2 to edit.
```

Figure 12.3   List View

To go to the List View, select View and then List. As in a spreadsheet, you can select fields by pressing Shift and an arrow key. Also like a spreadsheet, you can select any of the following menu options:

Edit: to move, copy, clear, delete, insert, or change the field name.

Print: to print the database with what can be controlled from this screen. See the "Report View" section for information on setting up standard report formats including headers, footers, rearranged fields, etc.

Select: for activities such as hiding records and sorting records.

Format: to change formatting, control field width, and font style for printing from List View; Report View fonts are controlled through that view.

Options: to protect data.

These functions work very much like the spreadsheet activities. See Chapter 11, "MS Works-Spreadsheet and Charting", for information on using many of the commands also available to you through List View.

▶ **Tip**: Sorting and printing records through List View is a "quick and dirty" way to print the data. For more legible print—in formats you can save even when you leave your PS/1—use Report View. To select certain records of your choice—and omit others—use Query View.

Report View

Entering a lot of data is fine, but the data is of limited value unless you master the skill of creating and using different, useful reports from your data. To see a report, select `View` and then `New Report`. The information appears in *report form*. Figure 12.4 illustrates an example. Press Enter to continue looking at the data in this form until you come to the Report Definition screen shown in Figure 12.5. Notice that `REPORT` appears at the bottom of the page.

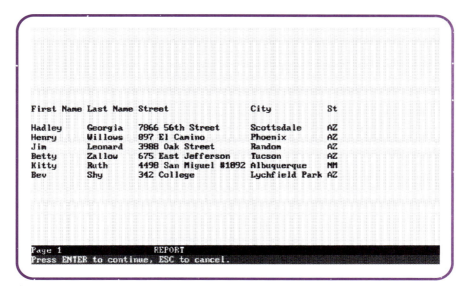

Figure 12.4   New Report screen

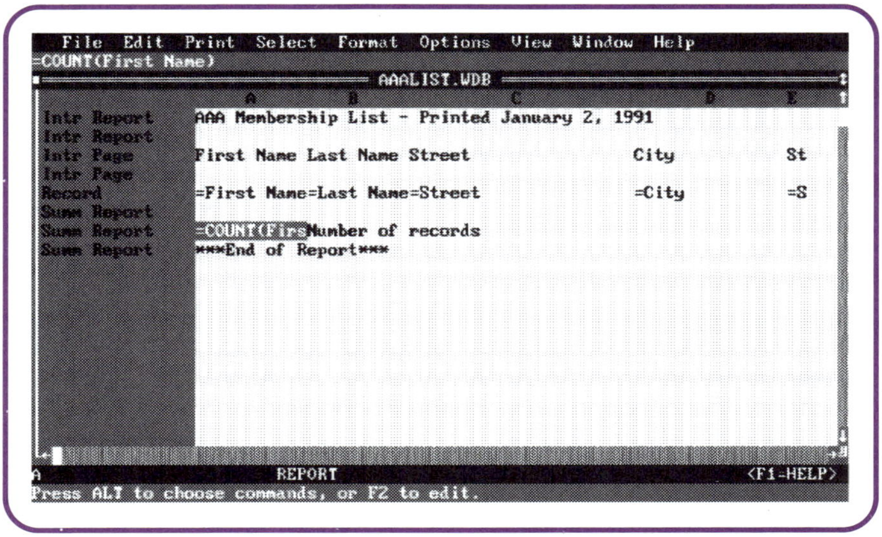

Figure 12.5   Report Definition screen

The Report Definition screen enables you to enter report titles, column labels, and summary formulas. The top of the screen shows the column headings. The left side of the screen shows the following row names where you may identify Introductory, Record, and Summary Report information.

`Intr Report`: Two Introductory Report rows are printed at the start of each report. Enter text for the report titles and any other information to be printed at the beginning of the report.

`Intr Page`: Two Introductory Page rows are printed at the top of each page in a report. Enter information you would like; the field names appear because they are typically the most important information to include on a report page. You can edit this information as you like, including copying or moving the information through the Edit option.

`Record`: The Record row holds the record data. To change the layout of the record, use the Edit options. For example, you can insert more record lines and move or copy fields to those lines.

`Summ Report`: The Summary Report row will appear at the end of your report. You can enter summaries, statistical data, or notes. You can use Works functions, which may be used with spreadsheets, in the summary. For example, you can use SUM or COUNT to add columns of numbers or count the number of records respectively. In Figure 12.5, this function appears to count the number of first name records:

```
=COUNT(First Name)
```

`Number of records` is a label which will print in the same line to indicate what the count means. You also can use spreadsheet-like formulas in a database report.

Now is a good time to set up the formatting information for the Report View. Use the Format option to set up the font, style, column width, etc. If you set up formatting through the List View, that formatting is not carried over to the Report View. However, any formatting you set up here is saved with the specific Report View you are creating.

After you complete the Report View, Works saves your report format as Report1, Report2, etc. You may later call up this report format by selecting `View` and the report format desired.

To get rid of report formats you no longer want, give the report format a more descriptive name; or copy a report format, select `View`, and then select `Reports`. Then proceed to change the report format information to your liking.

Printing the Report

You can print the report using the Print menu option (select `Print` and then `Print`). If you have a very large database, you may want to make a few test prints on only a portion of the database to make sure the report is set up properly. You can do a test by using the Query View to select only a few representative records. See the "Query View" section in this chapter for more information. Note: You cannot select or set page breaks through List View and then only print the selection or page through Report View.

Sorting the Report

The order of your report is maintained according to the last sort. For example, you may have sorted the data in List View. You can sort a

Chapter 12

report as often as you like. However, sorting in Report View provides more flexibility. In addition to sorting by up to three fields, you can create breaks (one or more blank lines) after field groups sorted.

To sort, choose `Select` and then `Sort Records`. A box appears. Complete the fields as you would with any sort. The records are sorted by the first field. Records selected by matching first fields are sorted by the second field identified. Records which match on the first and second field are sorted by the third field. Ascending order is A-Z, 1-9 and descending order is Z-A, 9-1. To set a break, place an X in the appropriate brackets. If you have a large database, you may want to break after every letter change for every sort. For smaller databases, you may want to reduce the number of breaks. Figure 12.6 shows the expanded and edited database report sorted by last name, and then first name and printed with no breaks.

```
AAA Membership List - Printed January 2, 1991

First Name  Last Name  Street                 City            State  Zip    Phone
Beth        Abernathy  PO Box 67430           Phoenix         AZ     85322  602-995-4493
Randy       Barrows    5300 Lincoln Way       Phoenix         AZ     85600  602-495-6677
Hadley      Georgia    7866 56th Street       Scottsdale      AZ     85258  602-543-8655
Jim         Leonard    3988 Oak Street        Random          AZ     84300  602-943-9542
Sharon      Leonard    943 Youngtown #209     Phoenix         AZ     85730  602-954-9899
Kitty       Ruth       4498 San Miguel #1092  Albuquerque     NM     87109  505-888-4234
Bev         Shy        342 College            Lychfield Park  AZ     85340  602-925-4322
Henry       Willows    897 El Camino          Phoenix         AZ     85221  602-231-9976
Ian         Willows    85222 75th             Phoenix         AZ     85730  602-443-9666
Betty       Zallow     675 East Jefferson     Tucson          AZ     85321  602-954-7234
10                     Number of records

***End of Report***
```

Figure 12.6 Sorted and printed database

> **Tip**: Notice that sorting by a field name does not cause that field name to appear first on the report. Only moving and copying determines position.

Using Report View

1. Go to List View by selecting `View` and then `New Report` to create a new Report View; or select `View` and then the existing Report View.

   `REPORT` appears on the bottom of the screen; selected data appears on-screen.

2. Press Enter to continue to the Report Definition screen.

   The labels on the right of the screen prompt you to enter Introductory and Summary Report information.

3. Enter the information for the introduction of the report and of each page, layout records as desired, and add Summary Report information.

   The areas include labels, formulas, and functions as needed.

4. Select `Format` and continue to set up formatting information such as font, style, and column width.

   Format information is complete.

5. Sort the report by choosing `Select` and then `Sort Records`; complete the box information and select `OK`.

   The report is sorted.

6. Print the report by choosing `Print` from the Print option.

   ☐

Query View

One of the beautiful elements of a database is the ability to select only certain records based on given criteria. You can't do this with a spreadsheet. But with a database, you can develop subsets of the data for given circumstances. For example, you may want to send a mailing to people who live in a specific city. Or you may want to identify customers who have spent over a certain limit with your small business. Pulling out records with certain criteria in common is called *querying*.

> **Tip**: When you build a query, all records are searched through—even if they are hidden or protected.

To build a query, go to Query View by selecting View and then Query; go to Report View or List View first if necessary. A screen that looks very much like the Form View appears (see Figure 12.7). However, notice that the word QUERY appears on the bottom of the screen.

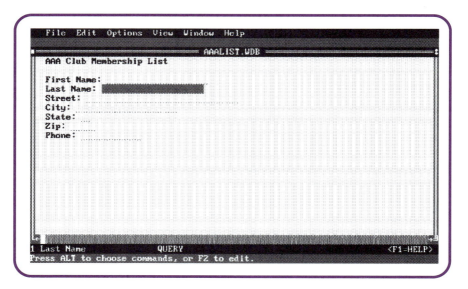

Figure 12.7 Query View

To enter the query, move to the field you want to select and enter the selection criteria. Selection criteria may include the following operators:

=   Equal to
<> Not equal to

<   Less than
\>   Greater than
\>=   Greater than or equal to
<=   Less than or equal to
&   AND
| OR
~   NOT

When you enter letters or names, place them in quotation marks.

You can also use the asterisk as a wild card in a query. For example, entering **B*** will select all the values for the fields that start with B.

> **Tip**: If you enter the selection criteria incorrectly, Works lets you know with the following message. Carefully review what you have entered, edit as necessary, and try again.
>
> ```
> Reference not valid or wrong operand type
> ```

Figure 12.8 shows a query set up. This instruction appears in the Last Name field:

```
<>"Leonard"&<>"Ruth"
```

The last name selected will not equal "Leonard" and will not equal "Ruth." Everyone with those last names will be omitted.

After you query, your query affects other views. To see the result of the query, select `View` and then `List`. The selections appear. Go to Report View to select a report format for printing. The last query is still in place. If no records meet your selection criteria, the message `No match found` appears when you try to go to List View or Report View.

Figure 12.9 shows the data printed in the report format used earlier. Notice that there are seven records selected; no one with the last name of "Leonard" or "Ruth" appears.

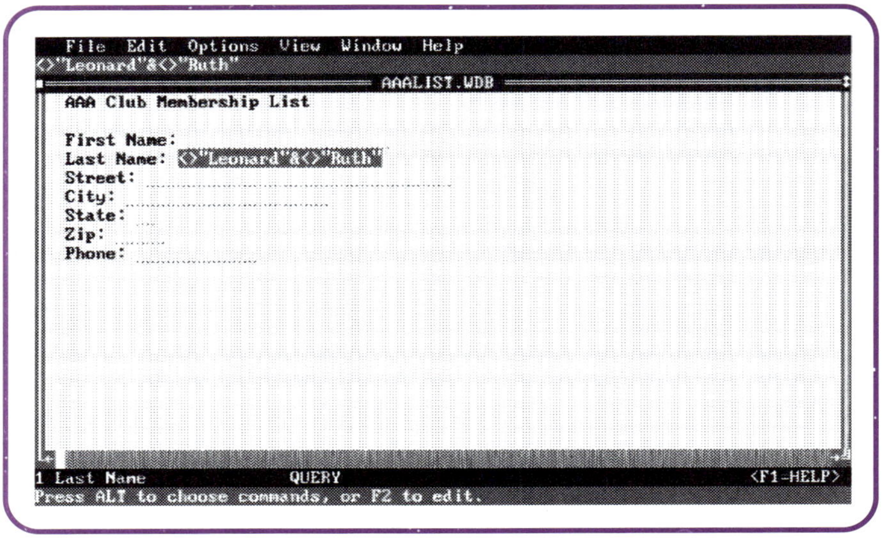

Chapter 12

```
    File Edit Options View Window Help
 <>"Leonard"&<>"Ruth"
══════════════════════════ AAALIST.WDB ══════════════════════
 AAA Club Membership List

 First Name:
 Last Name: <>"Leonard"&<>"Ruth"
 Street:
 City:
 State:
 Zip:
 Phone:




 1 Last Name              QUERY                        <F1-HELP>
 Press ALT to choose commands, or F2 to edit.
```

Figure 12.8   Query set up

> ▶ **Tip**: You can look at query records that were omitted from the query. Simply pick Select and then Switch Hidden Records. To go back to the selected records, use Select and Switch Hidden Records again.

> ▶ **Tip**: The result of a query is in place for all views. While in Query View, you can delete a query or clear the field contents. Select Edit; then select Clear Field Contents or Delete Query. Once you delete the query and return to List View, the complete database is displayed. If you have queries you use often, use the Print Screen key to keep the query information so that you can refer to it again.

Using Query View

1. Go to Query View by selecting View and then Query.
2. Enter the selection criteria in each field as appropriate.
3. To see the result of the query, select View and then List, or select View and then Report.
4. The query is in place for all views until you delete it through the Edit option on the Query View or change the query.

QUERY appears on the bottom of your screen.
Selection criteria appear.

The view you chose shows the records selected.

All views display only the selected records.

□

```
AAA Membership List - Printed January 2, 1991

First Name  Last Name  Street              City            State  Zip    Phone
Beth        Abernathy  PO Box 67430        Phoenix         AZ     85322  602-995-4493
Randy       Barrows    5300 Lincoln Way    Phoenix         AZ     85600  602-495-6677
Hadley      Georgia    7866 56th Street    Scottsdale      AZ     85258  602-543-8655
Bev         Shy        342 College         Lychfield Park  AZ     85340  602-925-4322
Henry       Willows    897 El Camino       Phoenix         AZ     85221  602-231-9976
Ian         Willows    85222 75th          Phoenix         AZ     85730  602-443-9666
Betty       Zallow     675 East Jefferson  Tucson          AZ     85321  602-954-7234
7                      Number of records

***End of Report***
```

Figure 12.9   Printed result of query

Views and Printing

You can print a database from Form, List, or Report View, but not Query View. For a particular report format, select the appropriate report you have developed in Report View.

To print the database, go to the view you want by selecting `View`. Select `Print` on the Print menu, and complete the print options as desired. If the print does not turn out as you expected, check how you sorted (by choosing `Select` and then `Sort Records`), the font size (by selecting `Format` and then `Font`), the column widths (by selecting `Format` and then `Column Width`), or other options from the view from which you are printing.

What You Have Learned

In this chapter you've learned

- ▶ To choose among different Works database views, select `View`.
- ▶ Many menu choices operate similarly in Works database as they do in Works spreadsheet.
- ▶ To edit data fields, point to the field and press F2; then complete the editing.
- ▶ The Edit menu enables you to insert, delete, copy, and move.
- ▶ The Select menu enables you to sort.
- ▶ The Format menu enables you to control fonts, column widths, and other format issues.
- ▶ Settings such as column widths or fonts from one view are not necessarily set in other views.
- ▶ When you develop a query, it is in place for all views until you change or delete the query.

Chapter 13

Communications and Integrating Your Tools

In This Chapter

▶ *Communicating with other computers (friends, colleagues, bulletin boards, and services)*
▶ *Putting a chart into a word processing document*
▶ *Creating form letters and mailing labels*
▶ *Copying and moving text between Works tools*

Communications

Earlier chapters covered how to use on-line services with your PS/1. You also can use the communications feature of Works along with your modem to link your PS/1 to any computer. Yes, that's *any* computer and not just IBM-based. You can exchange information with a friend, a colleague, or another service outside Prodigy, such as MCI mailboxes, CompuServe, The Source, or public domain software bulletin boards.

 To start, make sure your modem is hooked into the phone line. See Chapter 2, "Get Set" for information about the physical connections and Chapter 6, "Using Information (Especially Prodigy)" for general information about making the connection.

Chapter 13

Complete the following main steps to use Works communications:

1. Create a communications file for the correct settings to enable you to communicate with the other computers; the settings are saved in the file.
2. Connect with the other computer.
3. Transfer information.
4. Disconnect.

Creating a Communications File

Select `Microsoft Works` from the PS/1 System menu. Select `File`, `Create New File`, and then select `New Communications`. The Communications screen appears.

To see the current communications settings, select `Options` and then `Communications`. The box in Figure 13.1 appears.

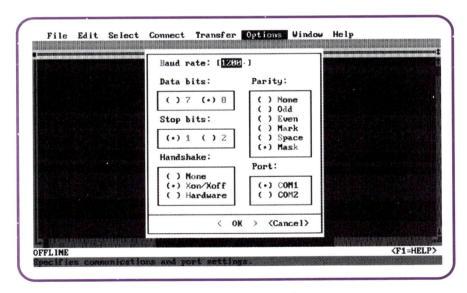

Figure 13.1   Communications Setting box

Following is a description of each option. Remember that the goal of setting communications values is to match the settings with your modem and the computer with which you are communicating. If you are communicating with a service or an existing bulletin board, the people handling the service or bulletin board can advise you about the settings necessary to make the communications link.

Baud rate: this option is where you set the speed at which the modem will communicate. Your PS/1 built-in modem can communicate at speeds of 300, 1200, or 2400 bits per second (bps). Check out the receiving modem and make the setting as fast as possible to save time.

Data bits: data is transferred over lines in units of 7 or 8 bits at a time. the PS/1 supports up to 8 data bits.

Stop bits: the stop bits separate the data as it is transmitted. Usually 1 stop bit is appropriate.

Handshake: the connection computers make during communication is referred to as a *handshake*. Xon/Xoff is a common standard. If you are linking directly to a computer through a cable, use Hardware.

Parity: this setting is the auditor of the transmission. If an error is sensed, an asterisk is placed. The Mask option restricts the auditor so that you can work with any computer.

Port: the PS/1 standard *port* (connection for your modem) is COM1.

Another box in which you can change settings is the Terminal box under the Options menu. The most important settings are covered here. You can select the terminal type—VT52. You also can determine the size of the buffer. The *buffer* is an area of memory to capture your incoming information; the approximate lines of text are: small, 100; medium, 300; and large, 750. If you have lines printing over one another, add LF (line feed) at the end of each line or, if the lines aren't flush left, add a CR (carriage return).

Connecting with Another Computer

After all your settings are in place, you can enter the instructions for dialing another computer. Select Options and then Phone. The box shown in Figure 13.2 appears.

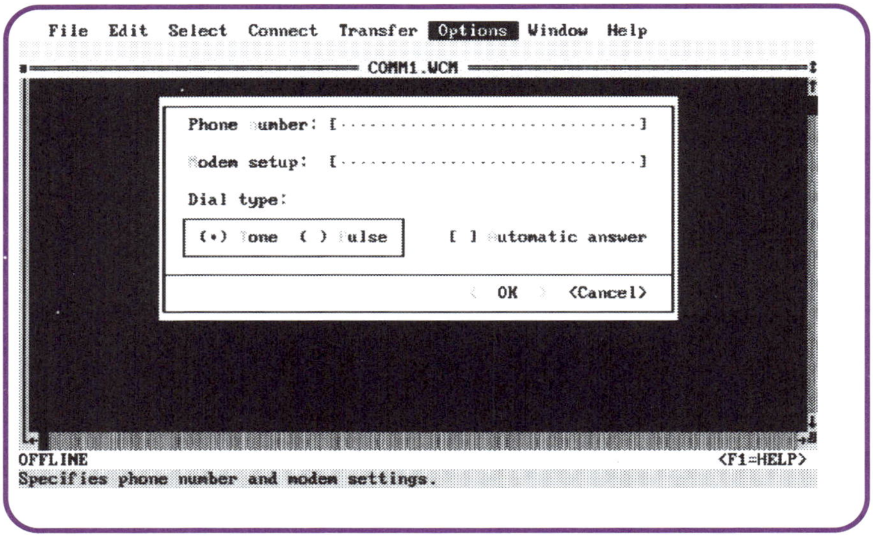

Figure 13.2   Phone Box

Enter the phone number (add any numbers for outside lines or long distance, 70* or 70# to disable call waiting—check the information in your phone book), and commas to separate the entities. For example, the following phone number dials 9 for the outside line, 70* to disable call waiting, and the phone number. Notice the placement of commas.

9,70*,5431234

You can use the modem setup to enter technical information to make modem adjustments although this is usually not necessary. The dial type should be Tone for a touch tone phone or Pulse for a dial phone. Only use Automatic Answer to have your computer automatically answer other people's calls through a special setup process.

To make the connection, select Connect on the Connect menu. If you hear a busy signal or have line problems, select Connect Dial Again. If you continue having problems making the connection, check your settings and continue trying.

> **Tip**: As you enter settings, save the communications file first by selecting `File` and then `Save As` to give the file a name. This name should remind you which service or destination the file is set to call. Later, just select `File` and then `Save`.

Transferring Information

After you have made the connection, there are two methods to transfer information: 1) sending a file, or 2) receiving a file.

To send a file, select `Transfer` and then `Send File`. (For the technically curious, the protocol is XODEM.) A box appears and enables you to select the format and any file to send. Use the Binary format if you are sending a Works file or a file from another software package. Use the Text format if you are sending an ASCII file. You also can control the line ending (`CR` to align text on the left and `LF` to prevent lines from printing over each other). Select `OK` when you are ready to transmit. The transfer takes some time, and Works keeps you posted on the progress. To stop at any time, press the Escape key. Otherwise, select `OK` when the transfer is complete.

To receive a file, make sure you have first established the handshake with the other computer; you either see the menu of a service, or you can type in text to talk to the other computer user. Receiving is easier because you simply get ready to receive and wait for the other computer to transmit. To receive, select `Transfer` and then `Receive File`. A box appears for you to enter the drive and file name that will be the location of the received information. Select the type of file (binary or text) and `OK`. Works lets you know what is happening. After you are done, select `OK`.

Disconnecting

To disconnect your modem, leave the service if necessary. Then select `Save` from the File menu; next, select `File` and then `Exit Works`.

You also can disconnect by selecting `Connect` on the Connect option. The following message appears:

```
Do you wish to disconnect?
```

Press Y for Yes to disconnect.

> ▶ **Tip:** If you select `Record Sign-On` on the Connect menu before you sign on, you save the sign-on process to get the service with the communications file by selecting `File` and then `Save` before you leave Works. When you open the communications file the next time, you are asked whether you want to sign on automatically.

Communicating with a Modem

1. Make sure the modem is hooked up, and select `Microsoft Works` from the System menu.

    The Works File menu appears.

2. Select `File` and then `Create New File`.

    The box appears with tool file options.

3. Select `New Communications`.

    A Communications file is created.

4. To complete settings, select `Options` and each of these three commands: `Communications`, `Terminal`, and `Phone`. Complete the box information for each option.

    The settings are complete.

5. To make the connection, select `Connect` on the Connect menu.

    An indication of a connection will be made.

6. To send or receive a file, select `Transfer` and then `Send File` or `Receive File`. Complete the box information.

    The file is sent or received.

7. To disconnect, leave the service if necessary. Select `File` and then `Save`; then select File and `Exit Works`. Or select `Connect` on the Connect option and then `Yes` to disconnect.

You are disconnected.

☐

Putting a Chart into Word Processing

You can insert a Works chart into a Works word processing document. When you do this, your word processing document is always updated every time you update the spreadsheet chart.

You must develop a chart from a spreadsheet (see Chapter 11, "MS Works—Spreadsheet and Charting"). Open the spreadsheet associated with the chart to insert. Then, without closing the spreadsheet file, open the word processing document into which you want to insert the chart. Place the cursor in the word processing document in the location where you want the chart. Select `Edit` and then `Insert Chart`. The Spreadsheet box shown in Figure 13.3 appears.

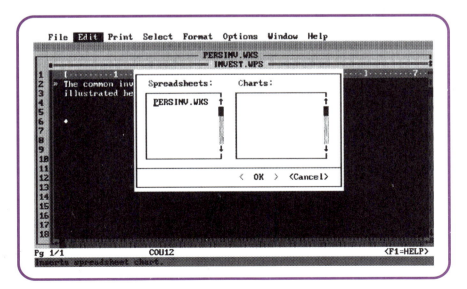

Figure 13.3 **Spreadsheet box**

Select the spreadsheet file with the chart. After you select the spreadsheet, the charts associated with the spreadsheet appear. Select a chart and then select OK. A placeholder with the name of the spreadsheet and chart appears in your word processing document. For example, the following placeholder is shown in Figure 13.4. Notice that the PERSINV.WKS spreadsheet is open as well as the INVEST.WPS word processing file.

```
*chart PERSINV.WKS:Chart3*
```

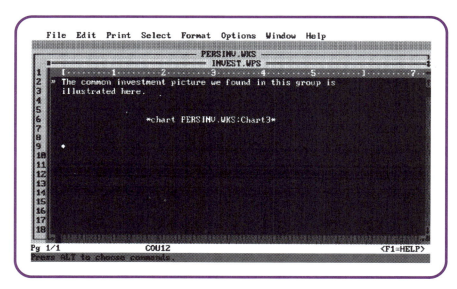

Figure 13.4   *Chart placeholder in a word processing file*

The chart prints when you print the document. You can copy, move, or delete the chart.

To change the size of the chart, put the cursor on the chart placeholder. Select Format and then Indents & Spacing. Enter the left and right indent, the chart height, and portrait (straight) or landscape (sideways). Select OK.

Form Letters and Mailing Labels

You can use an existing database and word processing together to create form letters. Simply create or open an existing database (see Chapter 12, "MS Works—Database and Reporting). Then create a word processing document. Enter boilerplate text to appear in the form letter. When you want to insert a field from the database, position your cursor in the spot and select Edit and then Insert Field. A Database box appears. Select the file to use. The field names in the file appear in the box (see Figure 13.5 for an example).

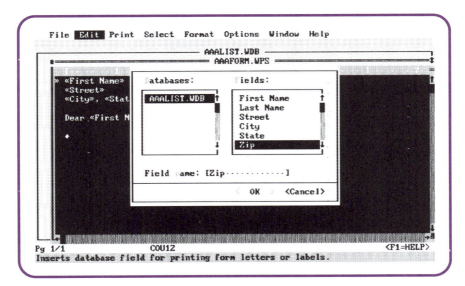

Figure 13.5 File and field names in a Database box

Select the field name to insert in the word processing document. The field name appears bracketed in chevrons in your word processing document. Continue until you develop the form letter. You can edit the word processing document the same as you would any word processing file. When you are done, save the word processing file by selecting File and then Save As.

A completed form letter is shown in Figure 13.6. Notice that the first name is used three times.

```
           File  Edit  Print  Select  Format  Options  Window  Help
                              AAALIST.WDB
                              AAAFORM.WPS

    «First Name» «Last Name»
    «Street»
    «City», «State» «Zip»

    Dear «First Name»,

    A special invitation is extended to join the AAA Club at a
    special event in the valley.  Your ticket is reserved for an
    evening with Janice Methan, a leading environmentalist.  The
    cost is just $35 with a complete dinner at La Norte
    included.  «First Name», I hope you'll join us January 12 at
    7 pm.  Call 435-9855 to confirm your ticket.

    Sincerely,

    Jill Bellows, President

    Pg 1/1              COU12                              <F1=HELP>
    Press ALT to choose commands.
```

Figure 13.6   Complete form letter

> ▶ **Tip**: Do not enter chevron symbols from the keyboard around file names you type. The form letter will only work if you select field names as prescribed.

To print the form letter, make sure the correct database records are selected (use Query View) and are in the correct order (use a sort command). When you print, a copy of the form letter for each record selected is printed in order.

With both the database file open and the form letter word processing file open, select Print and then Print Form Letters. In the Database box, select the file and then OK. Then, in the Print box, select the print options. The form letter prints. Check the result carefully to make sure it is what you expected.

An example of one letter printed from the form letter (shown in Figure 13.6) appears in Figure 13.7.

```
Beth Abernathy
PO Box 67430
Phoenix, AZ 85322

Dear Beth,

A special invitation is extended to
join the AAA Club at a special event
in the valley. Your ticket is re-
served for an evening with Janice
Methan, a leading environmentalist.
The cost is just $35 with a complete
dinner at La Norte included. Beth, I
hope you'll join us January 12 at
7 pm. Call 435-9855 to confirm your
ticket.

Sincerely,

Jill Bellows, President
```

Figure 13.7   Printed form letter

Mailing labels go hand in hand with form letters. Create mailing labels like you would a form letter. The important twist is entering print instructions to Works so that the addresses fit your labels. When you print, make sure the database and word processing file are both open. Select Print and then Print Labels. In the box, identify the database, the size of the labels, and the number of labels across the page. Select Test to test your label page. In the box that appears, enter the margin information and page size. Finally, complete the familiar Print box. The labels print.

> ▶ **Tip**: Always test a page of labels on plain paper first. Hold the print up to the actual labels to make sure they fit.

Copying and Moving Between Tools

You can copy and move between tools. First, open up to eight documents on the screen at once. Then select the text to copy or move. Select Edit and then the copy or move command. Before you complete the command, press Ctrl+F6 to go to the next window or Ctrl+Shift+F6 to go to the previous window. Then press Enter to complete the copy or move. You also can use the Menu window and choose the file that appears, or using the mouse, you can click on the window on-screen.

What You Have Learned

In this chapter you've learned to

- ▶ Create a communications file for each computer with which you communicate.
- ▶ Open a spreadsheet and word processing file at the same time, and select Edit and then Insert Chart to put a chart in a word processing file.
- ▶ Open a database and word processing file, and select Edit and then Insert Field to put database field names in a form letter; print by selecting Print and then Print Form Letters.
- ▶ Set up mailing labels like form letters; select Print and then Print Labels.
- ▶ Copy or move text between tools; switch files with Ctrl+F6 before pressing Enter to complete the copy or move.

Chapter 14
Promenade

In This Chapter

- Comparing Prodigy versus Promenade
- Signing on and off Promenade
- Using the Promenade screens
- Learning the services available
- Using Mail
- Getting member information

Promenade versus Prodigy

Promenade is an on-line service which comes with your PS/1. Promenade offers a variety of services from games to an encyclopedia. Why use Promenade when you have Prodigy?

The services with Promenade are different (see the "Promenade Services" section in this chapter). Also, with Promenade, you may *download* files from the Promenade library. This means you can copy files from Promenade to your PS/1. Downloading enables you to edit and save articles and text to your own diskette. Prodigy does not allow you to download files; all Prodigy information must be accessed while you are on-line.

In short, depending on what you want to do, you may want to use Promenade and Prodigy or one of the services, another brand of service, or none. The decision depends on you and your needs.

One of the big differences between Promenade and Prodigy is the contrasting billing approach. At the time of this writing, Prodigy bills members a flat fee of about $12 a month for the Prodigy services; some services on Prodigy cost extra, but most services fit in the blanket monthly fee. Promenade, on the other hand, charges per the minute (about 12.5 cents) with a higher rate (25 cents) for *prime time* which is defined as 6 a.m.–6 p.m. Monday through Friday. Promenade also has an offer of one free hour to allow a test run.

> **Tip**: Check out the billing of these and all on-line services carefully so that you avoid surprises. Read all terms and conditions carefully.

In and Out of Promenade

Getting into Promenade is easy. Make sure your modem is attached to a phone line, and have the Promenade diskette handy along with your Promenade Registration Certificate.

First, put the Promenade diskette in the diskette drive. Then pick Your Software from the system menu. Select drive A in the upper right corner of the screen. Next, select INSTALL, which appears in the open folder (along with PROMENADE). The Options screen appears. Then select Start, and Promenade will install. Finally, select C and then PROMENADE. **Note:** you cannot run Promenade from a diskette unless it is not write-protected. You must copy the original Promenade diskette to another diskette.

If this is your first time signing on, the sign-on process will take longer. You will go through a series of sign-on screens to identify your phone number, address, certificate number, and other information. Complete the screens until you are in Promenade. The Welcome to Promenade screen appears.

To get out of Promenade, select File and Exit. A window appears inquiring whether you are sure you want to sign off. Select Yes.

> ▶ **Tip**: After the initial sign-on process, simply select Sign On from the Welcome to Promenade window. Enter your password and you are done. The process is simple and quick.

> ▶ **Tip**: You can install Promenade on your fixed disk. That way, you don't have to insert the diskette in the drive each time you want to use Promenade. After you choose Your Software and select drive A, select INSTALL from the Promenade folder. Follow the instructions. A folder will be created for Promenade in Your Software menu. You can select Promenade from this folder in the future.

Q Getting On Promenade

1. Select Your Software from the System menu. — The options appear.
2. If Promenade is on the diskette in drive A, select drive A; if Promenade is on drive C, make sure you select that drive. — The folder with Promenade appears.
3. Select Promenade. — The Welcome To Promenade screen appears.
4. If you have signed on before, select Sign On and complete the information. — You enter Promenade. □

Q Leaving Promenade

1. Select File from the menu bar and then Exit. — A message appears checking whether you really want to sign off.
2. Select Yes. — You sign off Promenade. □

Promenade Screens

Promenade screens have *buttons* which are selections and basically look like a word in a box. You select buttons with bold lines. Press the Tab key to change the selection, and press the space bar to select a button. Or click the selection with the mouse. If a button is grey, it is inactive.

In addition to button selections, you can make selections from menu options. You will notice that the Promenade screens are set up like the Works and DOS screens with a menu bar. Use Alt and the arrow keys or the mouse to make a selection. You'll also notice that when the mouse pointer turns into a clock, Promenade is working. To scroll windows, use the mouse on a scroll bar on the right of the window areas.

To get out of a window, click outside the window area. Or click the upper left corner of the window and select `Close`.

Once you are in Promenade, the following options are available. The "Promenade Services" section of this chapter discusses individual types of services in more detail.

`Help`: the useful options are Getting Help (which leads to a menu of options), Setup (enter your phone and modem information), and Preferences (such as text size).

`File`: to create files from Promenade (perhaps to create a memo to mail or place Promenade information), save files, print files, handle logs of your activity, cancel an action (or use Ctrl+X), and exit Promenade.

`Edit`: to cut, copy, and paste which comes in handy when you want to save information from articles; cut and paste together are the same as move.

`Go To`: the options to go to a particular Promenade service appear.

`Mail`: the options to send or read mail appear along with using the FAX and paper mail services.

`Members`: includes the options for sending messages to members currently using the system and finding information about members.

`Window`: methods of handling windows show up here.

> ▶ **Tip**: The Browse the Service window appears when you pick an option from the Go To menu. This window enables you to see more detailed selections for the option.

Promenade Services

Promenade has a variety of services. Some will be of interest and some may not. Check out the full range to see where you want to spend your time.

You can use *Keywords* to get around Promenade fast. The Keyword is like JUMPword in Prodigy. Select a Keyword from the Go To menu; or press Ctrl+K, type in the word, and select OK. To see a list of current Keywords, choose Go To and then What's New & Member Services, Members' Guide Part 2—Using the Service.

Software & Computing

There is a variety of software available through the Software & Computing option on the Go To menu. You can see the software, talk to experts, load files to your own diskettes, and participate in forums.

Downloading Promenade library files is like checking out a book from a library that you never have to return. When you select the Software & Computing option from the Go To menu, you can see the list of software available along with a description including how long the file will take to download. Time in downloading wasn't billed to you when Promenade first came out for the PS/1; however, check the current billing terms and conditions. To download the file to your PS/1, select Download File. Then select the disk or diskette location for saving the file, and enter any additional information required.

> **Tip**: Have plenty of formatted diskettes available. The file may take up more space than you think!

Entertainment and Games

Choose `Entertainment & Games` from the Go To menu. This is your pathway into interesting games such as Casino and MasterWord. You also can get to the Entertainment Connection where you can converse with clubs and get entertainment-related software.

Go to Your Room

Promenade has *Interactive Communications Areas* which is a fancy term for a *room* where you can talk to other Promenade users. From the HQ Tools menu (which appears in the menu bar after you select `Entertainment & Games`, `Promenade Headquarters`, `Go To Room`). Once you select `Go To Room`, you can list the people in any public room, go to a private room, go to HQ community, or go to the Promenade Auditorium.

To get information about upcoming events in the Auditorium, see `What's New & Member Services (Don't Miss...)` or the `Box Office`. To get into the Auditorium, select `Entertainment & Games` from the Go To menu. Then select `Promenade Auditorium & Box Office`. Finally, select `Enter the Auditorium`.

> ▶ **Tip**: If you see shorthand expressions, you have discovered Promenade members' way of expressing emotions and body language. (How does that go ... one laugh is worth a thousand words.) To see all the shorthands available, select `What's New & Member Services` from the Go To menu.

Education and Reference

Promenade is a competent teacher. From the Education & Reference option on the Go To menu, you can access the Academic American Encyclopedia, Interactive Education Services, Computer Classes, Teacher's Information Network, College Board On-line, Career Center, and Entrepreneurial Information options. To find out about classes, check out each department, Auditorium and conference halls, What's Happening On-line (by selecting `New Members' Area` in the What's New & Member Services option), and the Box office options.

Clubs & Special Interest

On-line services are great for finding people who share your interests ... and Promenade is no exception. There are a host of clubs you can join including Asimov's Science Fiction Center, the Astronomy Club, the Grandstand Sports Forum, and more. From the Go To menu, select `Clubs & Special Interests`.

What's New & Member Services

The Go To menu selection `What's New & Member Services` has a variety of services including the Promenade Hotline where you can ask questions of Promenade—and get an answer in a day or two. You also can call Promenade at 1-703-448-8063 with questions; try the on-line message system first.

Use the What's New & Member Services option to check monthly bills through the Billing Information and Changes feature. Select `Check Your Current Bill` or `Check Your Previous Bill`.

Mail

On Promenade, you can write or read mail or send a FAX or paper mail. Just use the Mail menu from the menu bar.

Mail sent to you is deleted in seven days. You should check the Mail menu often to read your mail. If you are using Promenade, you can tell if you have mail because you hear a sound when it is received, or when you sign on and `You Have Mail` appears on the Promenade Welcome screen. To read mail, select `Read New Mail` from the Mail menu or press Ctrl+R. Select the `Mail` symbol on the Welcome screen. Then select `New Mail`. From there, simply select what you want to read. Options include

```
Reply to send a reply to a specific memo
See what file is attached to the memo (if any)
```

To look at mail you've read or sent, select `Check Mail You've Read` or `Check Mail You've Sent` from the Mail menu and proceed.

To send mail, select `Compose Mail`—or press Ctrl+M—and enter the name of the member to whom the mail is to be sent. You can "carbon copy" (cc:) other members. You also can attach files to the mail memo you send, and the file will be sent along with the memo. Simply select the `Attach File` symbol and enter the file information.

Members Menu

The Members menu selection from the menu bar is a way to get member information—select `Get Member Info`—assuming you know the member's name. To find a member, select `Find a Member On-line`. If you don't know the name of the member, you can search the Member Directory. You also can use the Members menu to send a quick message to someone who is currently on-line; select `Send Instant Message`.

What You Have Learned

In this chapter you've learned to

- ▶ Use the Promenade diskette in drive A to access Promenade, or install Promenade on your fixed disk.
- ▶ Exit Promenade by selecting `File` and then `Exit`.
- ▶ Use the mouse to make Promenade selections, or use the Alt and arrow keys to access and use the menu bar.
- ▶ Download files from Promenade if you want.
- ▶ Use the Go To menu selection to see the Promenade services.
- ▶ Use the Mail menu selection to read and send mail.

Chapter 15
Basics of BASIC

In This Chapter

- *What is BASIC*
- *Why you may want to learn BASIC*
- *Getting in and out of BASIC*
- *What are commands and syntax*

BASIC: Why Bother?

Through Microsoft Works, the PS/1 can handle a great deal of your computing needs. However, if you have a technical mind and want to create some of your own programs, you can use the computer language BASIC.

While many PS/1 users prefer to concentrate their effort on other aspects of the PS/1, some PS/1 users like to copy unique programs from BASIC books, alter programs given to them by friends or secured from public domain bulletin boards, or just work with the language for fun.

Chapter 15

This chapter won't teach you all you need to know about BASIC, but it will give you a taste of this simple but powerful computer language. To really learn BASIC, you should invest in one or more books devoted to the subject or take a class at a community college or other school. Get some experience writing a very simple program; then write one that is more complicated, and proceed in that manner. Before long, you'll be able to solve some pretty interesting BASIC program problems.

Getting In and Out of BASIC

Getting in and out of BASIC is uncomplicated. Select Your Software from the System menu and then select DOS. Select BASIC (or BASICA which is another similar version). The Options screen appears. Simply select Start. The BASIC screen appears (see Figure 15.1).

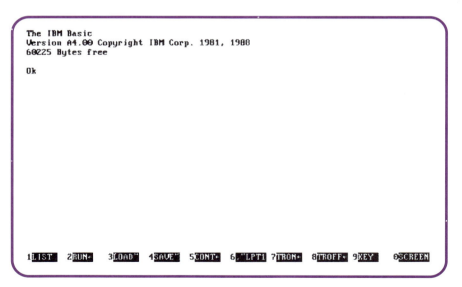

Figure 15.1   The BASIC screen

This screen identifies the version of BASIC you are using and says a friendly Ok which is BASIC for "your turn." Now you can enter commands or text, list a program to read its contents, or run a program to make it work.

After you are ready to get out of BASIC and return to other PS/1 functions, type in the following and press Enter:

system

This message appears:

```
Press Enter or mouse button to return.
```

Press Enter and you return to the Options screen.

 Getting Into BASIC

1. Select Your Software from the System menu.   Folder options appear.
2. Select BASIC.   The Options screen appears.
3. Select Start.   The BASIC screen appears along with Ok which means you can begin using BASIC.
4. Perform your work in BASIC.   Your program works, or BASIC lets you know there is a problem. ☐

 Getting Out of BASIC

1. Type **system** and press Enter.   The message Press Enter or mouse button to return appears.
2. Press Enter.   The Options screen appears. ☐

Getting Down to BASICs

A few of the common commands for BASIC are shown across the bottom of the screen. The number before the command tells you that you may press a function key rather than type in these particular commands. Several commands that are used over and over in BASIC are

LOAD   To place, or load, an existing program into memory from a disk or diskette; enter a quotation mark and then the name of the program.

SAVE   To save the program in memory to a disk or diskette for permanent storage; enter a quotation mark and then the name of the program.

LIST   To show you (list) the contents of the program in memory on your screen.

RUN   To start (run) the program in memory (sometimes called *executing* a program).

Try out this simple program. Beginning BASIC students start here, so you'll be ahead of the class. The command PRINT enables you to print a string of text on your screen. Type the following line with your name and press Enter (see Figure 15.2):

10 PRINT "(*your name*), you're super!"

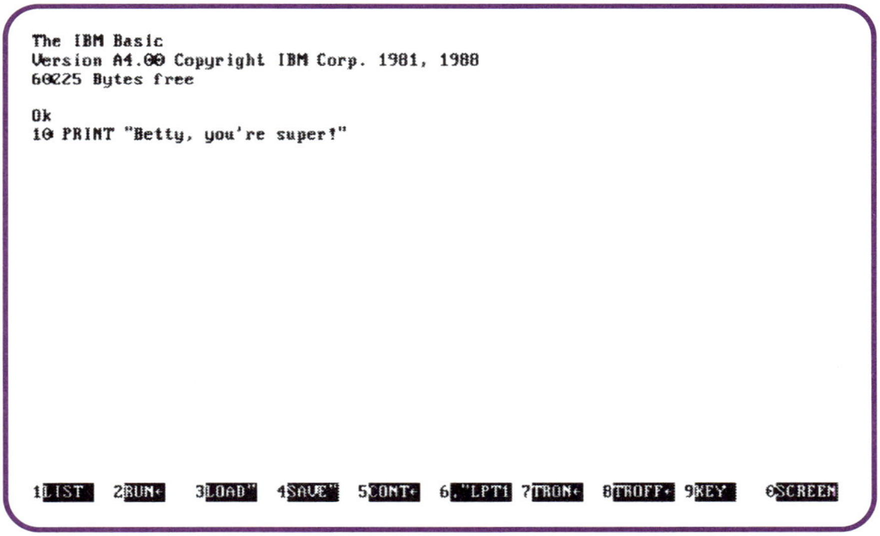

```
The IBM Basic
Version A4.00 Copyright IBM Corp. 1981, 1988
60225 Bytes free

Ok
10 PRINT "Betty, you're super!"
```

1LIST 2RUN◄ 3LOAD" 4SAVE" 5CONT◄ 6."LPT1 7TRON◄ 8TROFF◄ 9KEY 0SCREEN

Figure 15.2   A BASIC line

Then, after you type **RUN** and press Enter, this line prints on-screen with your name (see Figure 15.3):

(*your name*), you're super!

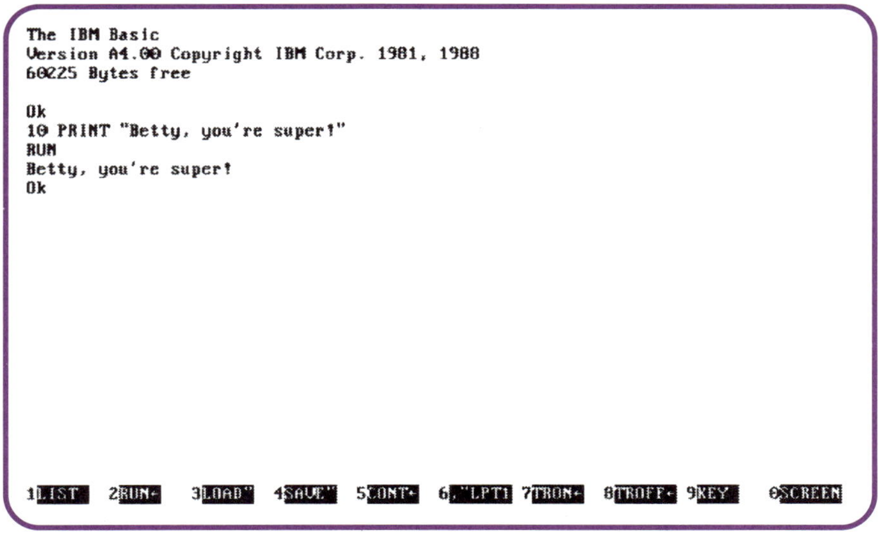

```
The IBM Basic
Version A4.00 Copyright IBM Corp. 1981, 1988
60225 Bytes free

Ok
10 PRINT "Betty, you're super!"
RUN
Betty, you're super!
Ok
```

```
1LIST  2RUN←  3LOAD"  4SAVE"  5CONT←  6,"LPT1  7TRON←  8TROFF←  9KEY   0SCREEN
```

Figure 15.3   The BASIC line RUN

Although this example is far from handling your inventory, it illustrates several points about BASIC. First, the 10 is the line number. Each line in BASIC begins with a line number which is a whole number. The line number you enter determines the order of each line in the program. BASIC always reads and executes Programs from top to bottom, and the order is important.

The word PRINT in this small program is a *command*. BASIC has many commands to choose from to accomplish the processing you want.

The (*your name*), you're super! part of the program is called a *text string*. The convention in BASIC to make text print on the screen is to type text within quotation marks after the PRINT command. Then, when you run the program, the quotation marks signify the beginning and end of the string to BASIC.

The types of "rules" described in this presentation of our program, such as the use of quotation marks and line numbers, are called *syntax rules*. Although BASIC is like English, you can't create free form commands for BASIC. It is very specific, and you must follow exact rules for punctuation and command entry. BASIC has a variety of common syntax rules, and if you violate any of them, your program won't run. Instead, the following message will show up on-screen:

    SYNTAX ERROR

This message means you must check your program carefully for violations of BASIC's "rules of the road."

The SAVE command is *very* important. Any program you enter is held in memory until you save it. If you lose power or mess up the program, you can't get it back unless it was saved. To save a program, enter **SAVE**, a quotation mark, and a program name like this:

SAVE"name

When you press Enter, the program is saved to the disk or diskette as NAME.BAS.

If you leave BASIC and reenter (or put another program in memory), you can get this program back by entering the following and pressing Enter:

LOAD"name

The LOAD command brings into memory the program you've named after the quotation mark.

Check out the LIST command. If you type **LIST**, the program is listed on-screen. In this case, our mini program appears.

    10 PRINT "(*your name*), you're super!"

As you learned earlier, all programs start at the top and move to the bottom. To add a line, put your cursor over the Ok at the bottom of your list, and press the Delete key to get rid of the Ok message. Then type the following, and press Enter:

5 PRINT "I said..."

Next type **RUN** and press Enter. The following message appears on your screen:

    I said (*your name*), you're super!

Type **LIST**, press Enter, and then you can see that the program is listed in the order of the line numbers.

    5 PRINT ""I said..."
    10 PRINT "(*your name*), you're super!"

The ability to insert lines by adding the appropriate line number is why it is a good idea to number lines 10, 20, 30, etc. rather than 1, 2, 3, etc. For example, you could easily add line 12 if you numbered lines 10, 20, 30, etc. But you couldn't insert a new line if you numbered 1, 2, 3, etc.

Not To Be BASIC

In addition to PRINT, BASIC has over 100 commands. You won't have to master all 100 to have a fairly good working knowledge of the language.

Some commands enable you to use sophisticated math functions. Simple math functions are easy to type in. For example, this program will print the result of 2+2:

10 PRINT "2+2="2+2

When you run this program, the result is:

2+2= 4

The first part of the line (through the second quotation mark) prints:

2+2=

Then the math 2+2 is calculated, and the result is displayed. You can perform more sophisticated math calculations.

Some commands enable you to send BASIC around your program to save time and accomplish more sophisticated logic. For example, you can add commands to *branch* which means the program executes to a certain point and then has a decision. This is handled by IF, THEN statements. IF a certain condition exists (such as the age is 65), THEN give a certain result (such as "hello golden ager"); otherwise, the program continues to process down the program line numbers.

Another movement option is to *loop*. This is often handled with a FOR statement. Usually, you want to do a certain operation FOR a given number of times. For example, you may want to print `Happy Birthday` ten times on-screen—without entering it ten times in your program.

Chapter 15

You also can put remarks in a BASIC program which are notes to you but don't affect processing; use logical operators, such as AND or OR; call for subroutines which are small programs you can use in multiple programs; and use a host of other options. Most books on BASIC have a complete listing and description of each BASIC command, along with the syntax rules for using the commands.

What You Have Learned

In this chapter you've learned to

- ▶ Get into BASIC through the Your Software and DOS options.
- ▶ Get out of BASIC by typing **system** and pressing Enter.
- ▶ Save your program by typing **SAVE"** followed by the program name.
- ▶ Use **LOAD"** and the program name to bring a program into memory.
- ▶ Type **LIST** to see the program and **RUN** to execute the program.

Index

Symbols

3.5 inch diskette, 16
5.25 inch diskette, 16
& (AND) formula operator, 182, 205
* (asterisk), 62, 205
» (chevron), 154, 218
/ (divide) formula operator, 182
$ (dollar sign) symbol, 181
= (equal to) formula operator, 182, 204
^ (exponential) formula operator, 182
> (greater than) formula operator, 182, 205
>= (greater than or equal to) formula operator, 182, 205
< (less than) formula operator, 182, 205
<= (less than or equal to) formula operator, 182, 205
* (multiply) formula operator, 182
– (negative) formula operator, 182
<> (not equal to) formula operator, 182, 204
~ (NOT) formula operator, 182, 205
| (OR) operator, 205
+ (positive) formula operator, 182

A

absolute cell reference, 181
ACTION (Prodigy) command, 102
action bar, File item, 59-60
adapter card unit, 7
add (+) formula operator, 182
Add (Program menu) option, 73
Add menu
    Command option, 74
    Title option, 74
Add Program, 78
add-ons, 5
adding
    footers, 165
    groups to programs, 79
    headers, 165
air travel, 124
Alarm Clock (Options menu) option, 145
Alt key, 17
Alt Select Print command, 155
ampersands, printing, 163
AND (&) operator, 205

Arrange (action bar) item, 64-65
arrow keys, 17
ASCII, switching to Hex, 61
Associate (File) option, 60
asterisk (*) symbol, 62, 205
attributes, changing, 61
AUTOEXEC.BAT file, 51
AVG function, 183

B

BACK (Prodigy) command, 102
backing up, 10, 22
   diskette-based system, 26
   fixed disks, 23-25, 27, 44-46
Backspace key, 17
Backup and Restore Your Fixed
    Disk... (IBM DOS menu)
    option, 45
bar charts, 186
BASIC, 229
   branches, 235
   commands
      LIST, 232, 234
      LOAD, 232, 234
      PRINT, 233
      RUN, 232
      SAVE, 232, 234
   exiting temporarily, 234
   getting in/out, 230-231
   logical operators, 236
   loops, 235
   math functions, 235
   strings, 233
   syntax rules, 233
batch files, 75
Baud rate (Communications
    menu) option, 211
blocks of text, 149
Bold format option, 166
branches, 235
Break key, 18
buffers, 211
Built-in DOS, 51
bulletin boards, 117

C

Calculator (Options menu)
    option, 144
CANCEL CHANGES Prodigy
    command, 106
Caps Lock key, 16
cell pointer, 174
cells, 174
   spreadsheets
      changing widths, 176
      copying, 179-180
      hiding, 184
      protecting, 185
   deleting contents, 175
   entering labels, 178
Center (Normal Paragraph menu)
    option, 167
Center tab option, 168
centering page numbers, 164
Change Attribute (File)
    option, 61
Change Colors (IBM DOS menu)
    option, 49
Change Hardware Configuration
    (Main Group menu) op, 52
changing
   cell widths in spread-
     sheets, 176
   colors, 49
   group program selections,
     81-82
   hardware configura-
     tion, 51, 53
   margins, 158
   program selections, 78
   sizes of charts, 216
characters, inserting into
    text, 148
charts, 186
   adding captions, 189
   axes, 189
   bar, 186
   changing
     appearances, 189

font styles, 189
  sizes, 216
choosing types, 189
creating, 186
entering into word processing, 215
line, 186
pie, 186
printing, 189
viewing, 186
Check Spelling (Options menu) option, 171-172
» (chevron) symbol, 154, 218
clicking, 18
close box, 141
closing
  files, 139
  spreadsheets, 186
colors, changing, 49
Column Width (Format menu) option, 176
columns alignment, 163, 173
Comma (Format menu) option, 178
Command (Add menu) option, 74
Command Prompt, 33
commands
  DOS, 82, 85
    DISKCOPY, 77
    PRINT, 60
    FORMAT, 35
  selecting, 134
Communications menu
  Baud rate option, 211
  Data bits option, 211
  Handshake option, 211
  Parity option, 211
  Port option, 211
  Stop bits option, 211
CONFIG.SYS file, 51
Copy (File) option, 61
COPY (status bar) option, 152
Copy a File (Main Group menu) option, 42

Copy Disk (File Management menu) option, 144
Copy File (File Management menu) option, 143
copying
  between tools, 220
  blocks of text, 149
  cells in spreadsheets, 179-180
  diskettes, 26, 38-41
  disks, 144
  files, 41-42, 59, 61, 143
  program selections, 79
  text, 151-152
Create Directory (File) option, 62
Create New File menu, New Database option, 191
CTERM function, 183
Ctrl key, 17
Currency (Format menu) option, 178
current directory, 58
cursor movement keys, 149
cursors, 17

D

Data bits (Communications menu) option, 211
databases, 133
  accessing, 191
  editing, 192
  entering
    data, 192, 195
    field names, 192
    headings, 192
    summaries, 192
  field names, 193-194, 196-197
  form letters, 217-218
  mailing labels, 217, 219
  naming, 193
  printing, 208
  queries, 203-205, 207
  reports, printing, 201
  saving, 197
  sorting
    as reports, 202

reports, 201
viewing, 208
   as reports, 199, 201
   as spreadsheets, 192, 197
   queries omitted, 206
views, 192
dates
  printing, 163-164
  setting, 34
Decimal tab option, 168
default values, 76
Delete (File) option, 61
Delete File (File Management menu) option, 144
Delete key, 17
deleting
  blocks of text, 149
  characters, 17
  columns, in spreadsheets, 181
  contents of multiple cells, 175
  directories, 61
  files, 61, 144
  footers, 165
  group program selections, 81-82
  headers, 165
  messages, 118
  program selections, 79
  restoring deleted text, 153
  rows in spreadsheets, 181
density, *See also* resolution, 155
Deselect All (File) option, 62
directories
  adding files, 68-69
  creating, 62, 68-69, 144
    on diskettes, 67-68
  deleting, 61
  naming, 62
  removing, 144
  renaming, 61
  selecting, 56
  subdirectories, 59
Directory Of (File menu) option, 138

directory tree, 56
  file list area, 57
  root, 57
Disk Copy (Main Group menu) option, 39
Disk Operating System, *See* DOS, 31
DISKCOPY DOS command, 77
diskette drives, 13, 15
diskettes
  3.5 inch, 16
  5.25 inch, 16
  copying, 26, 38-41
  creating directories, 67-68
  formatting, 36-38
  write-protecting, 16
disks
  copying, 144
  diskettes, 13
  fixed, 6, 13
    backing up, 23-25, 27, 44, 45
    backing up changes, 46
    restoring, 47
  formatting, 144
  hard, 6
display monitors, 13
Display Options (Options) option, 62
divide (/) formula operator, 182
documents
  boilerplate, 158
  creating, 147-148
  inserting text, 148
  printing, 155
  spell checking, 171
dollar sign ($) symbol, 181
DOS, 31
  AUTOEXEC.BAT file, 51
  Command Prompt, 33, 48
  commands, 82, 85
    DISKCOPY, 77
    FORMAT, 35
    PRINT, 60

CONFIG.SYS file, 51
error command, Insert diskette with batch file, 87
error messages
  Abort, Retry, or Fail?, 85
  Access denied, 85
  Bad command or file name, 86
  File not found, 86
  Insufficient disk space, 86
  Invalid, 86
  Not ready, 86
  Out of memory, 86
  Program too big to fit in memory, 87
  files, copying to diskette, 24
  Shell, 32
dot-matrix printers, 5 20
Double Space (Format menu) option, 168
double-clicking, 18
downloading, 221
dragging, 141
drives, 58
  current directory, 58
  diskette, 15
  identifiers, 58
  selecting, 56
  source, 26
  target, 26

E

Edit (List View menu) option, 198
Edit menu
  Insert Special option, 164
  Undo option, 153
Education & Reference (Go To Promenade menu) option, 226
ellipses (...), 32, 59
End key, 18
Enter key, 17

entering
  help text, 76
  in spreadsheets
    labels, 175
    numbers, 175
    series of cells, 176
  passwords, 77
  system dates, 179
Entertainment & Games (Go To Promenade menu) option, 226
entry fields, 75-76
equal (=) formula operator, 182
equal to (=) operator, 204
equations, *See* functions
Esc key, 18
existing files, opening, 138
Exit (action bar) item, 65
Exit (F3) function key, 65
Exit (Group menu) option, 82
Exit (Main Group menu) option, 72
EXIT (Prodigy) command, 102
exiting
  BASIC, 234
  Microsoft Works, 140
  Prodigy, 97
  Promenade, 222-223
Exponential (Format menu) option, 178
exponential (^) formula operator, 182

F

F1 (Help) function key, 33, 142
F2 (Save) function key, 78
F3 (Exit) function key, 65
F3 (VIEWPATH) Prodigy command, 105
F4 (PATH) Prodigy command, 105
F6 (JUMP) Prodigy command, 104

F10 (action area bar) function
   key, 59
field names, 193-197
fields, 75
File (action bar) item, 60
   Associate option, 60
   Change Attribute option, 61
   Copy option, 61
   Create Directory option, 62
   Delete option, 61
   Deselect All option, 62
   Move option, 61
   Open option, 60
   Print option, 60
   Rename option, 61
   Select All option, 62
   View, 61
file list area, 57
File Management menu,
   Copy File option, 143
   Create Directory option, 144
   Copy Disk option, 144
   Delete File option, 144
   Format Disk option, 144
   Remove Directory option, 144
   Rename File options, 144
   Set Date & Time option, 144
File menu
   Directory Of option, 138
   File Management option, 143
   Format option, 137
   Save option, 137
File Options (Options) option, 63
File System (Main Group menu)
   option, 56
Filename (Group menu)
   option, 80
files
   adding directories, 68-69
   batch, 75
   closing, 139
   communications, 210
   copying, 41-43, 59, 61, 143
      between diskettes, 42
      into diskette directories,
         67-68

text from one to an-
   other, 152
creating, 135
deleting, 61, 144
deselecting, 60
extensions, 42
Hidden, 61
linking, 60
moving from one file to another, 61, 153
names, 137
   printing, 163
opening existing, 138
printing to, 155
Read Only, 61
receiving, 213
renaming, 61, 144
saving, 136, 138
selecting
   from more than one direc-
      tory, 63
   with a mouse, 60
   with keyboard, 60
sending, 213
sorting, 63
FIND (Prodigy) command, 102
first line indents, 159-160
Fixed (Format menu) option, 178
fixed disks, 6, 13
   backing up, 23-25, 27, 44-46
   formatting, 15
   installing Promenade, 223
   restoring, 44, 47
Font & Style format option, 166
Font\ (Format menu) option, 178
fonts, 6
footers, 157, 161, 163
   adding, 165
   deleting, 165
   entering text, 163
   in spreadsheets, 179
   special characters, 163
forced page breaks, removing, 155
form letters, 217-218

Form View menu, 192
  editing, 195-196
  using, 196-197
Format (File menu) option, 137
    Format (List View menu)
    option, 198
Format Disk (File Management
    menu) option, 144
Format menu
  Column Width option, 176
  Comma option, 178
  Currency option, 178
  Double Space option, 168
  Exponential option, 178
  Fixed option, 178
  Font option, 178
  General option, 178
  Indents & Spacing option, 159
  Percent option, 178
  Single Space option, 168
  Style option, 178
  Tabs option, 169
  Time/Date option, 178
  True/False option, 178
formatting, 166
  Bold option, 166
  diskettes, 36-38
  disks, 16, 144
  down, 36
  fixed disk, 15
  Font & Style option, 166
  Italic option, 166
  Plain Text option, 166
  spreadsheets, 176
  Underline option, 166
formula operators
  & (AND), 182
  / (divide), 182
  = (equal to), 182
  ^ (exponential), 182
  > (greater than), 182
  >= (greater than or equal
    to), 182
  < (less than), 182

* (multiply), 182
- (negative), 182
~ (NOT), 182
<> (not equal to), 182
I (OR), 182
+ (positive), 182
formulas, *See also* equations, 182
  for grouping actions, 183
  moving within, 182
function keys, 18
  F1 (Help), 33
  F2 (Save), 78
  F3 (Exit), 65
  F10 (action area bar), 59
functions, 183
  AVG, 183
  CTERM, 183
  MAX, 183
  SUM, 183
  TAN, 183

G

General (Format menu)
    option, 178
Go To Promenade menu
  Software & Computing
    option, 225
greater than (>) formula opera-
    tor, 182
greater than (>) operator, 205
greater than or equal to (>=)
    formula operator, 182
greater than or equal to (>=)
    operator, 205
Group (Main Group menu)
    option, 72
Group menu
  Exit option, 82
  Filename option, 80
  Help text option, 80
  Password option, 81
  Title option, 80
group program selections
  adding, 79-80

changing, 81-82
deleting, 81-82
reordering, 81-82

H

Handshake (Communications menu) option, 211
hard disks. *See* fixed disks
formatting, 15
hardware configuration, changing, 51, 53
hardware requirements, 4, 7, 11, 12, 15, 23, 36
headers, 157, 161, 163
  adding, 165
  deleting, 165
  entering text, 163
  in spreadsheets, 179
  omitting, 164
  special characters, 163
Headers & Footers (Print menu) option, 162
HELP (Prodigy) command, 103
Help pop-up, 33
help reminder, 141
Help text, 76
Help text (Group menu) option, 80
hidden codes, 160-161
Hidden file, 61
hiding, cells in spreadsheets, 184
hobbies, 126-127
Home key, 17

I

I (OR) formula operator, 182
IBM DOS (System menu) option, 21, 32
IBM DOS menu
  Backup and Restore Your Fixed Disk...option, 45
  Change Colors option, 49
IBM PS/1 Users' Club, 116
  ABOUT THE CLUB option, 117
  ANSWER BANK option, 116
  INFO EXCHANGE option, 117
  NEWS TO USE option, 117
  WRITE TO US option, 117
icons, 58
impact printer, 5
indents,
  first line, 159-160
  margins
    left, 159
    right, 159
  setting, 159
Indents & Spacing (Format menu) option, 159
INDEX (Prodigy) command, 103
indexes, 104
information
  IBM PS/1 Users' Club, 116
  transferring, 213
Information (System menu) option, 21
Insert key, 17
Insert Page Break (Print menu) option, 154
Insert Special (Edit menu) option, 164
installing Promenade on fixed disk, 223
Intr Page (Report Definition menu) option, 200
Intr Report (Report Definition menu) option, 200
Italic format option, 166

J

J-Enter (JUMP) Prodigy command, 104
JUMP (F6) Prodigy command, 104
JUMPwindow, 107
JUMPwords, 104-109, *See also* Prodigy JUMPwords

Justified (Normal Paragraph menu) option, 167

K

keyboard, 16
  Alt key, 17
  arrow keys, 17
  Backspace key, 17
  Break key, 18
  Caps Lock key, 16
  Ctrl key, 17
  cursor, 17
  Delete key, 17
  End key, 18
  Enter key, 17
  Esc key, 18
  function keys, 18
  Home key, 17
  Insert key, 17
  Num Lock key, 18
  numeric keypad, 18
  options, 50
  Page down key, 18
  Page up key, 18
  Pause key, 18
  pointer, 17
  Print Screen key, 18
  selecting files, 60
  selecting menus, 22
  Shift key, 16
  shortcuts, 175
  templates, 113
keys, cursor movement, 149

L

labels, 174-178
laser printers, 5, 20
leaders, 169
leading, *See also* line spacing, 160
Left (Normal Paragraph menu) option, 167
left indents, 160

Left tab option, 168
less than (<) formula operator, 182
less than (<) operator, 205
less than or equal to (<=) formula operator, 182
less than or equal to (<=) operator, 205
line
  charts, 186
  positions, 166
  spacing, 160
linking files, 60
LIST (BASIC) command, 232, 234
List View menu, 192, 197
  Edit option, 198
  Format option, 198
  Options option, 198
  Print option, 198
  Select option, 198
LOAD (BASIC) command, 232-234
logical operators, 236
loops, 235

M

M-Enter (MENU) Prodigy command, 105
mail, 107
  checking, 120
  commercial, 119
  Promenade, 227
  sending, 119-122
  system, 118
  writing, 121
mailing labels, 217-219
Main Group menu
  adding options, 72
  Change Hardware Configuration option, 52
  Copy a File option, 42
  deleting options, 72

Disk Copy option, 39
Exit option, 72
File System option, 56
Group option, 72, 79
Program option, 72
Set Date and Time...
    option, 34
margins
  changing, 158
  footers, 157, 161, 163
    adding, 165
    deleting, 165
  headers, 157, 161, 163
    adding, 165
    deleting, 165
  in spreadsheets, 179
  indents, 159
    first line, 160
    left, 160
    setting, 159
  left, 159
  right, 159
  rulers, 168
  tabs, 169
MAX function, 183
maximize arrow, 141
Members (Promenade)
    menu, 228
memory expansion cards, 6
menu bar, 140
MENU (F9) Prodigy command, 105
menus, 13
  Form View, 192
  List View, 192, 197
  Main Group, 32
  Query View, 192, 203-204
  Report Definition, 200
  Report View, 192, 203
  selecting, 134
    with a mouse, 22, 33
    with the keyboard, 22, 33
  System, 13, 21
messages, 129
  deleting, 118
  lines, 141
  printing, 118
  replying, 118
  system, 118
Microsoft Works
  commands, 134
  communications, 133
  databases, 133
  exiting, 140
  menus, 134
  spreadsheets, 133
  starting from System
      menu, 134
  word processor, 133
Microsoft Works (System menu)
    option, 21
Microsoft Works menu, Works
    Tutorial option, 91
Microsoft Works Tutorial, 91
modems, 4, 19, 91, 209,
    211-212, 214
  commands, 19
  disconnecting, 213, 215
  instructions for use, 92
monitors
  display, 13
  PHOTOGRAPHIC display, 7
  VGA, 4
mouse, 4
  clicking, 18
  double-clicking, 18
  dragging, 141
  selecting
    files, 60
    menus, 22
Move (File) option, 61
moving
  between tools, 220
  blocks of text, 149
  in spreadsheets, 175, 179-180

text from one file to another, 152-153
multiply (*) formula operator, 182

N

N-Enter (NEXT) Prodigy command, 105
naming
  databases, 193
  directories, 62
  files, 137
New Database (Create New File menu) option, 191
Normal Paragraph menu
  Center option, 167
  Justified option, 167
  Left option, 167
  Right option, 167
not equal to (<>) formula operator, 182
not equal to (<>) operator, 204
NOT (~) operator, 205
Num Lock key, 18
numbers, 174-175
numeric keypad, 18

O

on-line services, 91, 92
  banking, 125
  Promenade, 227
  shopping, 123
Open (File) option, 60
operators
  & (AND), 205
  = (equal to), 204
  > (greater than), 205
  >= (greater than or equal to), 205
  < (less than), 205
  <= (less than or equal to), 205
  <> (not equal to), 204
  ~ (NOT), 205

| (OR), 205
Options (action bar) item
  Display Options option, 62
  File Options option, 63
  Show Information option, 64
Options (List View menu) option, 198
Options menu
  Alarm Clock option, 145
  Calculator option, 144
  Check Spelling option, 171-172
OR (|) operator, 205

P

P-Enter (PATH) Prodigy command, 105
page breaks, 154-155
Page Down (NEXT) Prodigy command, 105
Page down key, 18
page numbers, 162
  centering, 164
  designating, 164
  printing, 163
Page Setup & Margins (Print menu) option, 158
Page up key, 18
paragraphs, ending, 17
parameters, 75
Parity (Communications menu) option, 211
Password (Group menu) option, 81
passwords, 81
  changing in Prodigy, 100
  entering, 77
PATH (F4) Prodigy command, 105
Pause key, 18
Percent (Format menu) option, 178

Personal Control Financial Network, 125
PHOTOGRAPHIC display monitor, 7
pie charts, 186
pitches, 6
Plain Text format option, 166
pointer, 17
pop-up windows, 26, 33
Port (Communications menu) option, 211
positive (+) formula operator, 182
PRINT (BASIC) command, 233
Print (File) option, 60
Print (List View menu) option, 198
PRINT DOS command, 60
Print menu
　Headers & Footers option, 162
　Insert Page Break option, 154
　Page Setup & Margins option, 158
　Printer Setup option, 155
　Set Print Area option, 184
Print Screen key, 18
Printer Setup (Print menu) option, 155
printers, 20
　dot-matrix, 5, 20
　impact, 5
　laser, 5, 20
printing, 155
　ampersands, 163
　charts, 189
　databases, 208
　　as reports, 201
　dates, 163-164
　documents, 155
　draft quality, 155
　file names, 163
　form letters, 218
　page numbers, 163
　page ranges, 155
　spreadsheets, 184
　time, 163
　to file, 155
Prodigy
　adding Sign-On Shortcut, 100
　air travel, 124
　auto travel, 125
　changing
　　ID names, 100
　　passwords, 100
　　phone information, 101
　　Sign-On List, 101
　children's topics, 127
　commands, 102
　　CANCEL CHANGES, 106
　　F3 (VIEWPATH), 105
　　F4 (PATH), 105
　　F9 (MENU), 105
　　J-Enter (JUMP), 104
　　M-Enter (MENU), 105
　　N-Enter (NEXT), 105
　　P-Enter (PATH), 105
　　Page Down (NEXT), 105
　　R-Enter (REVIEW), 105
　　T-Enter (TOOLS), 105
　　U-Enter (UNDO), 107
　　UNDO, 107
　　V-Enter (VIEWPATH), 105
　credit card services, 124
　exiting, 97
　help lines
　　1-800-284-5933, 94, 129
　　1-914-962-0310, 129
　help service, 129-130
　hobbies, 126-127
　ID's, 96
　index, 104
　JUMPwords
　　about cr, 110
　　about prodigy, 110
　　accessworld, 124
　　ad info, 110

Index

ad review, 110
add member, 110
address book, 110, 120
advice, 127
arts club, 127
ask prodigy, 110, 128
bank online, 125
basics, 110
block, 126
business news, 125
business trav, 123
change pword, 110
changepath, 110
changingtimes, 126
city guide, 123
clubs, 110
coming soon, 110
commands, 110
communicating, 120
communication, 110
company news, 125
computer club, 110
cookbook, 127
cr travel, 123
eaasy message, 124
eaasy sabre, 124
email, 111
email, communication, 120
ev (city name), 123
ev (city), 111
fly aaway, 124
food and wine, 127
football, 126
football talk, 126
getting help, 111
help desk, 111
help hub, 111
highlights, 111
homelife, 127
ibm ps/1, 111
input fields, 111
jump, 111
jump tip, 111

jumpwindow, 111
jumpwords, 111
keyboard keys, 111
list, 120
mail, 111
mail, messagecenter, mailbox, 120
mailing list, 120
market update, 125
member list, 111, 120
membership, 111
message tips, 111
messagecenter, 111
money high, 125
money talk, 126
mousetool, 111
navigating, 112
new, 112
path, 112
pcfn, 125
prodigy help, 112
prodigy poll, 112
prodigy star, 112
questions, 112
quick start, 112
quote check, 125
schaap, 126
screens, 112
service hours, 112, 130
service sched, 112
shop online, 112
shopping, 122
short cuts, 112
ski forecasts, 127
sports, 126
sports extras, 126
sports games, 126
sports news, 126
sports survey, 126
target, 112
the club, 127
today, 112
trans world, 124

travel club, 123
travel high, 123
tutorials, 112
victorygarden, 127
w (city), 112
w (city name), 123
weather, 123
window tip, 112
write, 112, 120
keyboard templates, 113
mail, 107
  checking, 120
  sending, 119-120, 122
  systems, 118
  writing, 121
message system, 118
messages, sending, 129
on-line services
  banking, 125
  shopping, 123
passwords, 96
personal messages, 96
Phone Book, 95
removing
  Sign-On Selections, 99
  Sign-On Shortcuts, 101
Service PLUS, 124
signing on, 93-95, 98
sports, 126-127
stock trade, 125
traveling, 124
Prodigy commands
  ACTION, 102
  BACK, 102
  EXIT, 102
  FIND, 102
  HELP, 103
  INDEX, 103
Prodigy information service, 90
Prodigy keys
  arrows, 93
  Backspace, 93
  Delete, 93

End, 94
Enter, 94
Esc, 94
Home, 94
Insert, 94
Shift-Tab, 93
Tab, 93
Program (Main Group menu)
  option, 72
Program menu
  Add option, 73
programs
  adding, 73
  groups 79-80
  parameters, 75
  selecting, 56
  selections
    changing, 78
    copying, 79
    deleting, 79
  startup commands, 74
Promenade, 221
  billing services, 222
  buttons, 224
  clubs, 227
  downloading library files, 225
  Edit, 224
  exiting, 222, 223
  File, 224
  Getting Help, 224
  Go To menu, 224
    Education & Reference
      option, 226
    Entertainment & Games
      option, 226
    Software & Computing
      option, 225
    What's New & Member
      Services option, 227
  installing on fixed disk, 223
  Interactive Communications
    Areas, 226
  Keywords, 225

leaving windows, 224
mail, 224
    reading, 227
    writing, 227
Members menu, 224, 228
on-line services, 227
Preferences, 224
prime time, 222
screens, 224
Setup, 224
starting up, 222
PS/1
    booting, 51
    fonts, 6
    hardware, 5
    setting up, 9-10, 12
    software, 4
        Microsoft Works, 4
        Prodigy, 5
        Promenade, 5
    starting up, 49-50
    troubleshooting tips, 28-30
    turning off, 28
    Users' Club, 5
PS/1 User's Reference publication, 85

Q

Query View menu, 192, 203-204, 207
querying databases, 205

R

R-Enter (REVIEW) Prodigy command, 105
Read Only file, 61
Read Only Memory. *See* ROM (Read Only Memory)
receiving files, 213
Record (Report Definition menu) option, 200
records, 193
Remove Directory (File Management menu) option, 144
removing
    directories, 144
    forced page breaks, 155
Rename (File) option, 61
Rename File (File Management menu) option, 144
renaming files, 144
Report Definition menu, 200
    Intr Page option, 200
    Intr Report option, 200
    Record option, 200
    Summ Report option, 200
Report View menu, 192, 203
reports, viewing databases, 199
resolution, *See also* density, 155
restoring fixed disks, 47
Right (Normal Paragraph menu) option, 167
Right tab option, 168
ROM (Read Only Memory), 51
root, 57
rows, 173
    sorting, 185
rulers, 168
RUN (BASIC) command, 232

S

SAVE (BASIC) command, 232, 234
Save (File menu) option, 137
Save (F2) function key, 78
saving
    databases, 197
    field names, 195
    files, 136, 138
    spreadsheets, 186
scroll
    arrow, 141
    bar, 56, 141
search and replace, 170

Select (List View menu) option, 198
Select All (File) option, 62
Select menu, Sort Rows option, 185
selecting
  directories, 56
  drives, 56
  files
    with keyboard, 60
    with mouse, 60
  programs, 56
Service PLUS, 124
Set Date & Time (File Management menu) option, 144
Set Date and Time... (Main Group menu) option, 34
Set Print Area (Print menu) option, 184
setting
  dates, 34
  margin indents, 159
  tabs, 169
  time, 34-35
Shift key, 16
Show Information (Options) option, 64
Sign-On Shortcut List screen, 98
Single Space (Format menu) option, 168
size box, 141
Software & Computing (Go To Promenade menu) option, 225
Sort Rows (Select menu) option, 185
sorting
  databases, 201-202
  files, 63
  rows in spreadsheets, 185
source drive, 26
spell checking, 171
split bar, 141

sports, 126-127
spreadsheets, 133, 173-174
  () parentheses, 183
  absolute cell reference, 181
  cell pointer, 174
  cells, 174
    copying, 179-180
    hiding, 184
    moving, 179-180
    protecting, 185
  changing cell widths, 176
  charts, 186
  closing, 186
  columns, 173
  deleting
    cell contents, 175
    columns, 181
    multiple cell contents, 175
  entering
    labels into cells, 178
    numbers, 175
    series of cells, 176
    system dates, 179
  footers, 179
  formatting, 176
  formulas, 182
  grouping actions, 183
  headers, 179
  inserting
    columns, 181
    rows, 181
  labels, 174-175
  margins, 179
  moving in, 175
  numbers, 174
  printing, 184
  rows, 173
  saving, 186
  sorting rows, 185
starting up, 49-50
status line, 140
stock trade, 125

Stop bits (Communications menu) option, 211
strings, 233
Style (Format menu) option, 178
subdirectories, 59
SUM function, 183
Summ Report (Report Definition menu) option, 200
syntax rules, 233
system
  diskettes, 26
  units, 3, 13, 15
system dates, 179
System menu, 13, 21
  IBM DOS option, 21, 32
  Information option, 21
  Microsoft Works option, 21
  System Tutorial option, 90
  Your Software option, 21, 82
System Tutorial and Works Tutorial, 90

T

T-Enter (TOOLS) Prodigy command, 105
tabs
  Center option, 168
  Decimal option, 168
  default settings, 169
  leaders, 169
  left option, 168
  Right option, 168
  setting, 169
Tabs (Format menu) option, 169
TAN function, 183
target drive, 26
templates, 113
text
  automatic wrapping, 147
  blocks, 149
    copying, 149, 152
    deleting, 149
    moving, 149
    restoring, 153

entering
  into footers, 163
  into headers, 163
inserting characters, 148
moving from one file to another, 152-153
searching and replacing, 170
selecting, 149-150
  with the cursor, 150
  with the mouse, 151
time
  printing, 163
  setting, 34, 35
Time/Date (Format menu) option, 178
Title (Add menu) option, 74
Title (Group menu) option, 80
title bar, 140-141
tool keys
  Ctrl+:, 143
  Ctrl+;, 143
  Ctrl+End, 143
  Ctrl+F6, 143
  Ctrl+Home, 143
  Ctrl+Shift+F6, 143
  down arrow, 142
  End, 143
  F1 (Help), 142
  F3, 143
  F5, 143
  F6, 143
  F7, 143
  F8+arrow, 143
  Home, 143
  left arrow, 142
  Page Down, 143
  Page Up, 143
  right arrow, 142
  Shift+F1 (Tutorials), 142
  Shift+F3, 143
  Shift+F6, 143
  Shift+F7, 143
  up arrow, 142
tools
  copying between, 220

moving between, 220
traveling, 123-124
    by air, 124
    by car, 125
troubleshooting tips, 28-30
True/False (Format menu)
    option, 178
type sizes, *See also* fonts, 166

U

U-Enter (UNDO) Prodigy command, 107
Underline format option, 166
Undo (Edit menu) option, 153
Users' Club, 89

V

V-Enter (VIEWPATH) Prodigy command, 105
VGA display monitor, 4
View (File) option, 61
viewing
    charts, 186
    databases, 208
VIEWPATH (F3) Prodigy command, 105
volume labels, 37

W

What's New & Member Services (Go To Promenade menu) option, 227
windows, 140
    close box, 141
    help reminder, 141
    maximize arrow, 141
    menu bar, 140
    message line, 141
    panes, 143
    scroll arrow, 141
    scroll box, 141
    size box, 141
    split bar, 141
    status line, 140
    title bar, 140-141
word processors, 133
Works Tutorial (Microsoft Works menu) option, 91
wrapping text, 147
write-protecting diskettes, 16
WYSIWYG, 160

Y

Your Software (System menu) option, 21, 82

Sams—Covering The Latest In Computer And Technical Topics!

Audio

Audio Production Techniques for Video	$29.95
Audio Systems Design and Installation	$59.95
Audio Technology Fundamentals	$24.95
Compact Disc Troubleshooting and Repair	$24.95
Handbook for Sound Engineers: The New Audio Cyclopedia	$79.95
Introduction to Professional Recording Techniques	$29.95
Modern Recording Techniques, 3rd Ed.	$29.95
Principles of Digital Audio, 2nd Ed.	$29.95
Sound Recording Handbook	$49.95
Sound System Engineering, 2nd Ed.	$49.95

Electricity/Electronics

Basic AC Circuits	$29.95
Electricity 1, Revised 2nd Ed.	$14.95
Electricity 1-7, Revised 2nd Ed.	$49.95
Electricity 2, Revised 2nd Ed.	$14.95
Electricity 3, Revised 2nd Ed.	$14.95
Electricity 4, Revised 2nd Ed.	$14.95
Electricity 5, Revised 2nd Ed.	$14.95
Electricity 6, Revised 2nd Ed.	$14.95
Electricity 7, Revised 2nd Ed.	$14.95
Electronics 1-7, Revised 2nd Ed.	$49.95

Electronics Technical

Active-Filter Cookbook	$19.95
Camcorder Survival Guide	$ 9.95
CMOS Cookbook, 2nd Ed.	$24.95
Design of OP-AMP Circuits with Experiments	$19.95
Design of Phase-Locked Loop Circuits with Experiments	$19.95
Electrical Test Equipment	$19.95
Electrical Wiring	$19.95
How to Read Schematics, 4th Ed.	$19.95
IC Op-Amp Cookbook, 3rd Ed.	$24.95
IC Timer Cookbook, 2nd Ed.	$19.95
IC User's Casebook	$19.95
Radio Handbook, 23rd Ed.	$39.95
Radio Operator's License Q&A Manual, 11th Ed.	$24.95
RF Circuit Design	$24.95
Transformers and Motors	$24.95
TTL Cookbook	$19.95
Undergrounding Electric Lines	$14.95
Understanding Telephone Electronics, 2nd Ed.	$19.95
VCR Troubleshooting & Repair Guide	$19.95
Video Scrambling & Descrambling for Satellite & Cable TV	$19.95

Games

Beyond the Nintendo Masters	$ 9.95
Mastering Nintendo Video Games II	$ 9.95
Tricks of the Nintendo Masters	$ 9.95
VideoGames & Computer Entertainment Complete Guide to Nintendo Video Games	$ 9.50
Winner's Guide to Nintendo Game Boy	$ 9.95
Winner's Guide to Sega Genesis	$ 9.95

Hardware/Technical

Hard Disk Power with the Jamsa Disk Utilities	$39.95
IBM PC Advanced Troubleshooting & Repair	$24.95
IBM Personal Computer Troubleshooting & Repair	$24.95
IBM Personal Computer Upgrade Guide	$24.95
Microcomputer Troubleshooting & Repair	$24.95
Understanding Communications Systems, 2nd Ed.	$19.95
Understanding Data Communications, 2nd Ed.	$19.95
Understanding FAX and Electronic Mail	$19.95
Understanding Fiber Optics	$19.95

IBM: Business

Best Book of Microsoft Works for the PC, 2nd Ed.	$24.95
Best Book of PFS: First Choice	$24.95
Best Book of Professional Write and File	$22.95
First Book of Fastback Plus	$16.95
First Book of Norton Utilities	$16.95
First Book of Personal Computing	$16.95
First Book of PROCOMM PLUS	$16.95

IBM: Database

Best Book of Paradox 3	$27.95
dBASE III Plus Programmer's Reference Guide	$24.95
dBASE IV Programmer's Reference Guide	$24.95
First Book of Paradox 3	$16.95
Mastering ORACLE Featuring ORACLE's SQL Standard	$24.95

IBM: Graphics/Desktop Publishing

Best Book of Autodesk Animator	$29.95
Best Book of Harvard Graphics	$24.95
First Book of DrawPerfect	$16.95
First Book of Harvard Graphics	$16.95
First Book of PC Paintbrush	$16.95
First Book of PFS: First Publisher	$16.95

IBM: Spreadsheets/Financial

Best Book of Lotus 1-2-3 Release 3.1	$27.95
Best Book of Lotus 1-2-3, Release 2.2, 3rd Ed.	$26.95
Best Book of Peachtree Complete III	$24.95
First Book of Lotus 1-2-3, Release 2.2	$16.95
First Book of Lotus 1-2-3/G	$16.95
First Book of Microsoft Excel for the PC	$16.95
Lotus 1-2-3: Step-by-Step	$24.95

IBM: Word Processing

Best Book of Microsoft Word 5	$24.95
Best Book of Microsoft Word for Windows	$24.95
Best Book of WordPerfect 5.1	$26.95
Best Book of WordPerfect Version 5.0	$24.95
First Book of PC Write	$16.95
First Book of WordPerfect 5.1	$16.95
WordPerfect 5.1: Step-by-Step	$24.95

Macintosh/Apple

Best Book of AppleWorks	$24.95
Best Book of MacWrite II	$24.95
Best Book of Microsoft Word for the Macintosh	$24.95
Macintosh Printer Secrets	$34.95
Macintosh Repair & Upgrade Secrets	$34.95
Macintosh Revealed, Expanding the Toolbox, Vol. 4	$29.95
Macintosh Revealed, Mastering the Toolbox, Vol. 3	$29.95
Macintosh Revealed, Programming with the Toolbox, Vol. 2, 2nd Ed.	$29.95
Macintosh Revealed, Unlocking the Toolbox, Vol. 1, 2nd Ed.	$29.95
Using ORACLE with HyperCard	$24.95

Operating Systems/Networking

Best Book of DESQview	$24.95
Best Book of DOS	$24.95
Best Book of Microsoft Windows 3	$24.95
Business Guide to Local Area Networks	$24.95
Exploring the UNIX System, 2nd Ed.	$29.95
First Book of DeskMate	$16.95
First Book of Microsoft QuickPascal	$16.95
First Book of MS-DOS	$16.95
First Book of UNIX	$16.95
Interfacing to the IBM Personal Computer, 2nd Ed.	$24.95
Mastering NetWare	$29.95
The Waite Group's Discovering MS-DOS	$19.95
The Waite Group's Inside XENIX	$29.95
The Waite Group's MS-DOS Bible, 3rd Ed.	$24.95
The Waite Group's MS-DOS Developer's Guide, 2nd Ed.	$29.95
The Waite Group's Tricks of the MS-DOS Masters, 2nd Ed.	$29.95
The Waite Group's Tricks of the UNIX Masters	$29.95
The Waite Group's Understanding MS-DOS, 2nd Ed.	$19.95
The Waite Group's UNIX Primer Plus, 2nd Ed.	$29.95
The Waite Group's UNIX System V Bible	$29.95
The Waite Group's UNIX System V Primer, Revised Ed.	$29.95
Understanding Local Area Networks, 2nd Ed.	$24.95
Understanding NetWare	$24.95
UNIX Applications Programming: Mastering the Shell	$29.95
UNIX Networking	$29.95
UNIX Shell Programming, Revised Ed.	$29.95
UNIX System Administration	$29.95
UNIX System Security	$34.95
UNIX Text Processing	$29.95
UNIX: Step-by-Step	$29.95

Professional/Reference

Data Communications, Networks, and Systems	$39.95
Gallium Arsenide Technology, Volume II	$69.95
Handbook of Computer-Communications Standards, Vol. 1, 2nd Ed.	$39.95
Handbook of Computer-Communications Standards, Vol. 2, 2nd Ed.	$39.95
Handbook of Computer-Communications Standards, Vol. 3, 2nd Ed.	$39.95
Handbook of Electronics Tables and Formulas, 6th Ed.	$24.95
ISDN, DECnet, and SNA Communications	$44.95
Modern Dictionary of Electronics, 6th Ed.	$39.95
Programmable Logic Designer's Guide	$29.95
Reference Data for Engineers: Radio, Electronics, Computer, and Communications, 7th Ed.	$99.95
Surface-Mount Technology for PC Board Design	$49.95
World Satellite Almanac, 2nd Ed.	$39.95

Programming

Advanced C: Tips and Techniques	$29.95
C Programmer's Guide to NetBIOS	$29.95
C Programmer's Guide to Serial Communications	$29.95
Commodore 64 Programmer's Reference Guide	$19.95
DOS Batch File Power	$39.95
First Book of GW-BASIC	$16.95
How to Write Macintosh Software, 2nd Ed.	$29.95
Mastering Turbo Assembler	$29.95
Mastering Turbo Debugger	$29.95
Mastering Turbo Pascal 5.5, 3rd Ed.	$29.95
Microsoft QuickBASIC Programmer's Reference	$29.95
Programming in ANSI C	$29.95
Programming in C, Revised Ed.	$29.95
QuickC Programming	$29.95
The Waite Group's BASIC Programming Primer, 2nd Ed.	$24.95
The Waite Group's C Programming Using Turbo C++	$29.95
The Waite Group's C++ Programming	$24.95
The Waite Group's C: Step-by-Step	$29.95
The Waite Group's GW-BASIC Primer Plus	$24.95
The Waite Group's Microsoft C Bible, 2nd Ed.	$29.95
The Waite Group's Microsoft C Programming for the PC, 2nd Ed.	$29.95
The Waite Group's Microsoft Macro Assembler Bible	$29.95
The Waite Group's New C Primer Plus	$29.95
The Waite Group's QuickC Bible	$29.95
The Waite Group's Turbo Assembler Bible	$29.95
The Waite Group's Turbo C Bible	$29.95
The Waite Group's Turbo C Programming for the PC, Revised Ed.	$29.95
The Waite Group's TWG Turbo C++Bible	$29.95
X Window System Programming	$29.95

For More Information, Call Toll Free
1-800-257-5755

*All prices are subject to change without notice.
Non-U.S. prices may be higher. Printed in the U.S.A.*

Sams' First Books Get You Started Fast!

"The First Book Series ... is intended to get the novice off to a good start, whether with computers in general or with particular programs ...."

The New York Times

The First Book of WordPerfect 5.1
Kate Miller Barnes
275 pages, 7 3/8 x 9 1/4, $16.95 USA
0-672-27307-1

Look For These Books In Sams' First Book Series

The First Book of C
Charles Ackerman
300 pages, 7 3/8 x 9 1/4 $16.95 USA
0-672-27354-3

The First Book of dBASE IV 1.1
Steven Currie
300 pages, 7 3/8 x 9 1/4, $16.95 USA
0-672-27342-X

The First Book of DeskMate
Jack Nimersheim
315 pages, 7 3/8 x 9 1/4, $16.95 USA
0-672-27314-4

The First Book of DrawPerfect
Susan Baake Kelly & James Kevin Kelly
340 pages, 7 3/8 x 9 1/4, $16.95 USA
0-672-27315-2

The First Book of Fastback Plus
Jonathan Kamin
275 pages, 7 3/8 x 9 1/4, $16.95 USA
0-672-27323-3

The First Book of GW-BASIC
Saul Aguiar & The Coriolis Group
275 ppages, 7 3/8 x 9 1/4, $16.95 USA
0-672-27316-0

The First Book of Harvard Graphics
Jack Purdum
300 pages, 7 3/8 x 9 1/4, $16.95 USA
0-672-27310-1

The First Book of Lotus 1-2-3/G
Peter Aitken
350 pages, 7 3/8 x 9 1/4, $16.95 USA
0-672-27293-8

The First Book of Lotus 1-2-3 Release 2.2
Alan Simpson & Paul Lichtman
275 pages, 7 3/8 x 9 1/4, $16.95 USA
0-672-27301-2

The First Book of Microsoft Excel for the PC
Chris Van Buren
275 pages, 7 3/8 x 9 1/4, $16.95 USA
0-672-27322-5

TheFirst Book of Microsoft QuickPascal
Elna R. Tymes & Fred Waters
275 pages, 7 3/8 x 9 1/4, $16.95 USA
0-672-27294-6

The First Book of Microsoft Windows 3
Jack Nimersheim
275 pages, 7 3/8 x 9 1/4, $16.95 USA
0-672-27334-9

The First Book of Microsoft Word 5.5, Second Edition
Brent Heslop & David Angell
320 pages, 7 3/8 x 9 1/4, $16.95 USA
0-672-27333-0

The First Book of Microsoft Word for Windows
Brent Heslop & David Angell
304 pages, 7 3/8 x 9 1/4, $16.95 USA
0-672-27332-2

The First Book of MS-DOS
Jack Nimersheim
272 pages, 7 3/8 x 9 1/4, $16.95 USA
0-672-27312-8

The First Book of MS-DOS 5
Jack Nimersheim
275 pages, 7 3/8 x 9 1/4, $16.95 USA
0-672-27341-1

The First Book of Norton Utilities
Joseph Wikert
275 pages, 7 3/8 x 9 1/4, $16.95 USA
0-672-27308-X

The First Book of Paradox 3
Jonathan Kamin
275 pages, 7 3/8 x 9 1/4, $16.95 USA
0-672-27300-4

The First Book of PC-Write
Rebecca Kenyon, Ph.D.
350 pages, 7 3/8 x 9 1/4, $16.95 USA
0-672-27320-9

The First Book of PC Paintbrush
Deke McClelland
289 pages, 7 3/8 x 9 1/4, $16.95 USA
0-672-27324-1

The First Book of PFS: First Publisher
Karen Brown & Robert Bixby
308 pages, 7 3/8 x 9 1/4, $16.95 USA
0-672-27326-8

The First Book of PC Tools Deluxe, Second Edition
Gordon McComb
304 pages, 7 3/8 x 9 1/4, $16.95 USA
0-672-27329-2

The First Book of Personal Computing
W.E. Wang & Joe Kraynak
275 pages, 7 3/8 x 9 1/4, $16.95 USA
0-672-27313-6

The First Book of PROCOMM PLUS
Jack Nimersheim
250 pages, 7 3/8 x 9 1/4, $16.95 USA
0-672-27309-8

The First Book of PS/1
Kate Barnes
300 pages, 7 3/8 x 9 1/4, $16.95 USA
0-672-27346-2

The First Book of Q&A
Brent Heslop & David Angell
275 pages, 7 3/8 x 9 1/4, $16.95 USA
0-672-27311-X

The First Book of Quattro Pro
Patrick Burns
300 pages, 7 3/8 x 9 1/4, $16.95 USA
0-672-27345-4

The First Book of Quicken in Business
Gordon McComb
300 pages, 7 3/8 x 9 1/4, $16.95 USA
0-672-27331-4

The First Book of UNIX
Doglas Topham
300 pages, 7 3/8 x 9 1/4, $16.95 USA
0-672-27299-7

The First Book of WordPerfect Office
Sams
275 pages, 7 3/8 x 9 1/4, $16.95 USA
0-672-27317-9

To order books, call 1-800-257-5755.
For More Information, call 1-800-628-7360.

Sams Guarantees Your Success In 10 Minutes!

The *10 Minute Guides* provide a new approach to learning computer programs. Each book teaches you the most often used features of a particular program in 15 to 20 short lessons—all of which can be completed in 10 minutes or less. What's more, the *10 Minute Guides* are simple to use. You won't find any "computer-ese" or technical jargon— just plain English explanations. With straightforward instructions, easy-to-follow steps, and special margin icons to call attention to important tips and definitions, the *10 Minute Guides* make learning a new software program easy and fun!

10 Minute Guide to WordPerfect 5.1
Katherine Murray & Doug Sabotin
160 pages, 5 1/2 x 8 1/2, $9.95 USA
0-672-22808-4

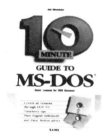

10 Minute Guide to MS-DOS 5
Jack Nimersheim
160 pages, 5 1/2 x 8 1/2, $9.95 USA
0-672-22807-6

10 Minute Guide to Windows 3
Katherine Murray & Doug Sabotin
160 pages, 5 1/2 x 8 1/2, $9.95 USA
0-672-22812-2

10 Minute Guide to Lotus 1-2-3
Katherine Murray & Doug Sabotin
160 pages, 5 1/2 x 8 1/2, $9.95 USA
0-672-22809-2

10 Minute Guide to Q&A
Sams
160 pages, 5 1/2 x 8 1/2, $9.95 USA
0-672-22832-7

**To order books, call 1-800-257-5755.
For More Information, call 1-800-628-7360.**

Sams Covers All Your Word Processing Needs

The First Book of WordPerfect 5.1
Kate Miller Barnes

This book offers an easy-to-read, concise introduction for first-time users, as well as a handy reference for experienced users. Quick Steps, key notes, reference tables, and reviews are included to help guide you quickly through the text.

275 pages, 7 3/8 x 9 1/4, $16.95 USA
0-672-27307-1

The Best Book of WordPerfect 5.1
Vincent Alfieri, revised by Ralph Blodgett

This essential guidebook present all the features of WordPerfect 5.1, including the pull-down menus, mouse support, easy labels, mail merge, font and character controls, and content-sensitive help.

800 pages, 7 3/8 x 9 1/4, $26.95 USA
0-672-48467-6

More Word Processing Titles From Sams

The Best Book of Microsoft Word for Windows
Richard Swadley
500 pages, 7 3/8 x 9 1/4, $24.95 USA
0-672-48468-4

The Best Book of Professional Write and File
Douglas Wolf & Joe Kraynak
475 pages, 7 3/8 x 9 1/4, $24.95 USA
0-672-22726-6

The Best Book of WordStar, Second Edition
Vincent Alfieri, revised by Robert Wolenik
850 pages, 7 3/8 x 9 1/4, $27.95 USA
0-672-48495-1

The First Book of Microsoft Word 5.5, Second Edition
Brent Heslop & David Angell
320 pages, 7 3/8 x 9 1/4, $16.95 USA
0-672-27333-0

The First Book of Microsoft Word for Windows
Brent Helsop & David Angell
304 pages, 7 3/8 x 9 1/4, $16.95 USA
0-672-27332-2

The First Book of PC-Write
Rebecca Kenyon, Ph.D.
350 pages, 7 3/8 x 9 1/4, $16.95 USA
0-672-27320-9

The First Book of Q&A
Brent Heslop & David Angeel
3275 pages, 7 3/8 x 9 1/4, $16.95 USA
0-672-27311-X

WordPerfect 5.1: Step-by-Step
Judd Robbins
575 pages, 7 3/8 x 9 1/4, $24.95 USA
0-672-22711-8

WordPerfect Bible
Susan Baake-Kelly
900 pages, 7 3/8 x 9 1/4, $29.95 USA
0-672-22746-0

To order books, call 1-800-257-5755.
For More Information, call 1-800-628-7360.

Reader Feedback Card

Thank you for purchasing this book from SAMS FIRST BOOK series. Our intent with this series is to bring you timely, authoritative information that you can reference quickly and easily. You can help us by taking a minute to complete and return this card. We appreciate your comments and will use the information to better serve your needs.

1. Where did you purchase this book?

☐ Chain bookstore (Walden, B. Dalton)   ☐ Direct mail
☐ Independent bookstore   ☐ Book club
☐ Computer/Software store   ☐ School bookstore
☐ Other _____

2. Why did you choose this book? (Check as many as apply.)

☐ Price   ☐ Appearance of book
☐ Author's reputation   ☐ SAMS' reputation
☐ Quick and easy treatment of subject   ☐ Only book available on subject

3. How do you use this book? (Check as many as apply.)

☐ As a supplement to the product manual   ☐ As a reference
☐ In place of the product manual   ☐ At home
☐ For self-instruction   ☐ At work

4. Please rate this book in the categories below. G = Good; N = Needs improvement; U = Category is unimportant.

☐ Price   ☐ Appearance
☐ Amount of information   ☐ Accuracy
☐ Examples   ☐ Quick Steps
☐ Inside cover reference   ☐ Second color
☐ Table of contents   ☐ Index
☐ Tips and cautions   ☐ Illustrations
☐ Length of book
☐ How can we improve this book? _____
☐ _____

5. How many computer books do you normally buy in a year?

☐ 1–5   ☐ 5–10   ☐ More than 10
☐ I rarely purchase more than one book on a subject.
☐ I may purchase a beginning and an advanced book on the same subject.
☐ I may purchase several books on particular subjects.
☐ (such as _____)

6. Have your purchased other SAMS or Hayden books in the past year? _____
If yes, how many _____

7. Would you purchase another book in the FIRST BOOK series? _____

8. What are your primary areas of interest in business software? _____

☐ Word processing (particularly _____)
☐ Spreadsheet (particularly _____)
☐ Database (particularly _____)
☐ Graphics (particularly _____)
☐ Personal finance/accounting (particularly _____)
☐ Other (please specify _____)

Other comments on this book or the SAMS' book line: _____
_____

Name _____
Company _____
Address _____
City _____ State _____ Zip _____
Daytime telephone number _____
Title of this book _____

Fold here

NO POSTAGE
NECESSARY
IF MAILED
IN THE
UNITED STATES

BUSINESS REPLY MAIL
FIRST CLASS   PERMIT NO. 336   CARMEL, IN

POSTAGE WILL BE PAID BY ADDRESSEE

SAMS

11711 N. College Ave.
Suite 141
Carmel, IN 46032–9839